教育部语信司—南京大学中国语言战略

● 主　编：徐大明　王铁琨
● 副主编：李现乐　齐汝莹

中国语言战略

2015.1

Volume 2
Number 1 (2015)

CHINA LANGUAGE STRATEGIES

南京大学"985工程"三期项目
江苏高校优势学科建设工程专项资金
南京大学"中国文学与东亚文明协同创新中心"
资助出版

南京大学出版社

教育部语信司—南京大学中国语言战略研究中心主办

中国语言战略

2015.1

Volume 2
Number 1 (2015)

CHINA
LANGUAGE
STRATEGIES

南京大学出版社

编 辑 委 员 会

出版说明

　　《中国语言战略》以语言规划为主题,由教育部语信司指导,教育部语信司-南京大学中国语言战略研究中心主办。

　　语言关乎个人的发展、文化的传承以及社会的稳定。语言规划有助于引导语言生活向健康、和谐的方向发展,有助于保障个人或群体语言使用权益的充分实现,有助于促进国家统一、民族团结、社会稳定、经济发展和文化进步,对于像我国这样的多民族、多语言国家来说,意义尤其重大。我国语言规划的实践可以追溯到秦始皇的"书同文"政策,其后各朝各代在社会语言文字使用方面也不断进行着引导或干预。现代科学意义上的语言规划研究始于二次世界大战以后,我国学者紧跟时代步伐、顺应社会需要,开展了一系列具有划时代意义的语言文字工作。老一辈语言学家罗常培、王力、吕叔湘、周有光等,肩负起知识分子的历史使命和社会责任,在推动、促进文字改革,推广普通话和现代汉语规范化方面发挥了重要的作用,为我们树立了优秀的榜样。

　　语言规划学是一门学术性和政策性、理论性和应用性兼重的学科,它的研究融语言本体研究成果与国家、民族和社会的发展需要于一体,不仅进行理论研究,而且力图影响国家和政府的语言政策和语言文字工作。目前,国际上语言规划的研究已有重要的发展,也创办了一些有影响的专业学术出版物,如:1977 年创办的《语言问题和语言规划》(*Language Problems and Language Planning*),2000 年创办的《语言规划的当前问题》(*Current Issues in Language Planning*)和 2002 年创办的《语言政策》(*Language Policy*)等。随着中国社会的发展,以中国语言规划为主要研究对象、以中文读者为主要读者群的专业学术出版物的出版也成为迫切的需求,《中国语言战略》就是对这一需求作出的反应。

　　《中国语言战略》着重关注中国社会所面临的种种具体的语言问题,以及这些语言问题与政治、经济、教育、文化等的相互影响,关注中国社会所发生的剧烈变化所引起的语言使用、语言认同、语言教育、语言保护、语言规范等方面的一系列变化。《中国语言战略》提倡实地考察和个案研究,强调运用科学的方法,对中国社会复杂而丰富的语言生活及相关问题进行描写、分析和解释,鼓励引进和借鉴国外的理论和经验,同时以中国语言规划的研究和实践丰富语言规划学的理论和方法。《中国语言战略》将遵循中国语言战略研究中心的宗旨,积极推动语言规划和语言政策的理论研究,促进适应中国国情的语言规划理论和语言规划学科的产生。

　　《中国语言战略》2012 年卷本由上海译文出版社出版,中国语言战略研究中心在此对上海译文出版社表示感谢。《中国语言战略》2015 年卷本出版工作由南京大学出版社承担,在组稿和审稿过程中得到了海内外学者的热情支持和帮助,在此表示诚挚的谢意。中国语言战略研究中心希望能够聚合国内外学者的智慧和力量,通过《中国语言战略》为语言规划、语言政策的理论和实践研究提供一个新的交流平台,我们热切地邀请海内外的学界同仁一起投身于这项事业,让我们一起为建设中国和世界的语言新环境努力!

目　录

1

Processability Theory, Question Constructions and Vocabulary Learning in
English L2 ………………………………………… Satomi Kawaguchi (170)

·翻译研究·

·简讯·

On the Nexus of Language and Economy

Florian Coulmas

Abstract: Although language has been of interest to economists for a long time, the application of economic theories and methods to the study of language must be seen as a result of the economization of life in our age. There exist differences between linguists and economists on the value variance of languages and on the advantages of language standardization. Combining the perspectives of linguistics and economics is a promising approach to comprehending the full significance of language for the human existence. Policy makers are well-advised to take cultural, emotional, and political dimensions of language valuation into account when designing language policies, rather than submitting all decisions to the imperative of economic gain.

Key words: economic dimension of language policy, the principle of least effort, human capital, internal economy of language, external economy of language

Introduction

A decline in the number of people worldwide who speak French could cost France 120,000 jobs by 2020 and half a million by 2050 due to missed economic opportunities, a report by Jacques Attali said in August 2014 (L'Express 2014). The report was commissioned by French President Francois Hollande in order to assess the extent to which French has lost ground to English in recent decades and what the economic repercussions of this development might be. While the relative decline of French is a matter of regret to the French, the report points out that the right policies in education and industry could increase the number of French speakers from an estimated 230 million in 2014 to as many as 770 million by the middle of the century. However, negligence on the part of policy makers could lead to further decline to less than 200 million speakers of French by 2050.

Two lessons can be drawn from this example. (1) Languages are evaluated in economic terms some of them having become substantial factors of their respective countries' economy. (2) It is considered a matter of course that policy interventions can influence the economic value of a language (in the event by deliberately increasing the number of speakers). Both of these notions are relatively new, testifying to the penetration of market mechanisms into ever more spheres of life. Although language has been of interest to economists for a long time, the application of economic theories and methods to the study of language must be seen as a result of the economization of life in our age. If we accept the common place that Adam Smith is the father of

1

economics as a scholarly discipline, it is worth noting that he himself had a profound interest in, and wrote about, language, although it was not the economic valuation of different languages which intrigued him. Rather, he directed his interest at the origin, make-up and functionality of language as such and its properties as an instrument of communication (Smith 1767). It is not too difficult to convince economists of the fact that language has characteristics that they can study, although economists who do research about language or languages are a marginal group in the field. Yet, linguists are much less inclined to accept that the economy is relevant for their proper field of inquiry, or that the tools of economics could be fruitfully applied to it.

Thus, not withstanding several monograph-length studies (e.g., Coulmas 1992; Rubinstein 2000), dozens of scholarly journal articles, and a recent review of the literature that looks back on 50 years of economics in language policy (Grin 2014), the nexus of language and economy is still a research domain that comprises many topics yet to be explored. This is mainly due to the traditional boundaries that separate scientific disciplines. The ever more sophisticated theories both economists and linguists have produced in the course of the past half a century have not made it easier to engage in interdisciplinary discussions.

Questions of common interest

However, it seems obvious that in regard to language, discussions across disciplinary boundaries are not just warranted,

but needed. Language is central to human existence. As a symbolic means of expression and exchange, it is unmatched and irreplaceable by any other system and, therefore, pervasive in almost all human activities. At the same time, most human activities have an economic dimension in the sense that they serve or are thought to serve, directly or indirectly, the survival of the individual, group, or species or the improvement of living conditions. Given these two most general conditions of the human existence, it stands to reason that there are many questions at the interface of language and economy that are unlikely to be answered exhaustively by linguists or economists alone, but which call for a collaborative approach.

There are also questions that both economists and linguists might ask, but answer differently. Consider for example that general question of goodness:

(1) Are there good languages? That is, are some languages better than others?

To an economist, who considers language as tool, this would seem to be an obvious and answerable question, for any two things of the same kind can be compared if a standard of goodness is defined. Linguists, by contrast, have a different notion of language not limited to its instrumental function. Hence their response to this question would be different. They would point out that any language is primarily a manifestation of *Language*, where Language (with a capital L) is part of the evolution of the species. Every language is built on the same foundation and has the same potential as any other, although at any historical moment different language may exhaust this potential not just differently, but to a greater or lesser extent. Because of this two-tier notion of language, the general question of goodness has a different character for linguists than for economists.

Or consider the question of a standard:

(2) Does language standardization have any advantages?

The economists' answer would be a clear "yes", for standards generate economic advantages by

—eliminating unwanted variability in process or product design (e.g., curricula, text books);

—facilitating the development of networks;

—improving the compatibility of products (e. g., reference works, style guides);

—enabling economies of scale (e. g., the markets of print products and software).

Linguists, by contrast, would point out that these and other advantages are external to language, which follows its own rules and is diverse and variable by nature. Its flexibility allows individual speakers and groups to express themselves for purposes of any conceivable kind, and to this end, they do not need an artificial standard. The essence of language is inexhaustible creativity. Without variability (which standards are intended to limit, if not eliminate), language could not evolve and adapt to changing circumstances. Thus, while economists would stress the advantage of

stability and homogeneity, linguists would emphasize the importance of flexibility and heterogeneity.

However, that economists and linguists would answer questions such as (1) and (2) among many others differently, does not mean that one is right and one is wrong. Language is a highly complex non-physical system as well as the most fundamental symbolic regularity in human interaction. As such, it is an object of scientific interest in various disciplines, but one—the system—does not exist in the absence of the other—the interaction. Combining the perspectives of linguistics and economics is a promising approach to comprehending the full significance of language for the human existence.

Internal and external economy of language

In the study of language, a distinction is commonly made between structure and function, or system and use. It corresponds, respectively, to the internal and external economy of language. The former has to do with code, the latter with practice.

1 The principle of least effort

As early as 1947, Zipf published a lengthy study relating certain characteristics of natural languages to an underlying economic principle at work in language evolution that he called "the principle of least effort". Its effects are summarily referred to as Zipf's Law, which states that in any text the highest-frequency expressions tend to be the lowest-complexity ones. Many studies about various languages have since corroborated this law. If language use is conceived as work and every speech act as contributing to the production and reproduction of the language system, Zipf's law means that in their speech work people, on the whole, tend to minimize energy expenditure. To name but a few examples, word length is inversely related to frequency. Complex phonemes as measured in terms of number of articulatory features rank lower on a frequency scale than simpler ones, even where the differences are minute. Number of strokes of Chinese characters and character frequency relate in the same manner, the characters consisting of the smallest number of strokes being the most frequent. These consistent findings testify to the instrumental nature of language and to the fact that on an unconscious level speakers follow optimization strategies that strike a balance between ease of production and ease of comprehension.

Optimization of ends-means relations is what economics is all about. Zipf's finding that this principle is driving the evolution of language on a subconscious level is the most important discovery of the internal economics of language so far. Many linguists assume a principle of thrift, efficiency, economy of effort, or parsimony as basic to the development of language (Coulmas 1992: 221 ff.). Eventually, and trivially, this reflects the finality of human life, that is, the fact that we do not have all the time in the world to say what needs to be said.

The drive to make language a more efficient instrument of communication has also been raised to the conscious level of deliberate intervention. For instance, spelling reform proposals regularly appeal to utility as the principal motivation of changing established practice. The Chinese character reform of the 1960s, for instance, was largely about limiting the number of characters in common use and reducing the number of composite strokes and thus improving the efficiency of the system. The German orthography reform of the 1990s likewise stressed simplification of rules and ease of learning (Coulmas 2013). The use of diacritics in preparing orthographies for hitherto unwritten or not alphabetically written languages is a related example (Wu 1987). Terminology formation, too, often aims at instrumental efficiency (Feng 1988). Although aesthetic and ideological (e.g., purism) considerations may come to bear here, utility is crucial. The ultimate rationale of all language planning can only be to raise aggregate welfare. Consciously and unconsciously speakers work to make their language optimally suitable to meet their needs. Catastrophic events in a speech community's environment, such as colonization or sudden contact with a language more suitable for modern pursuits may offset these efforts bringing about conditions where the internal and external economy of their language cannot be adjusted fast enough to stem its decline. The instrumental nature of language as tool of communication, information storage and cognition is at issue here. Today more than ever these functions concern utility and are intimately linked to the external economy of language.

2 Human capital

Viewed as a hereditary trait, language is adaptive and has survival value. No matter what the origin of language and how it evolved, it made human life possible. Its general features are species-specific, but at the same time, the universal faculty of language has been put to use in, and adapted to, particular conditions. Every language is the product of collective labour under particular circumstances and has been produced and reproduced by its speakers to suit their needs. Prior to the invention of writing, the variety of individual languages that evolved reflected the diverse functional requirements that were relevant to their speakers, but must otherwise be assumed to be on a par in regards to expressive power. With the advent of writing and the conscious attitude to language it brought in its train, this changed. Today, linguistic diversity correlates with inequality, that is, social inequality within countries, as well as inequality of development and wealth across countries. It is in this context that human capital theory and its application to language was developed (Becker 1975; Bourdieu 1982). The core argument of the theory says that language is a skill that contributes to increasing productivity and has a positive effect on labour income.

Since human beings are born to speak and all normal children grow up acquiring the language of their environment, the fact that by so doing they build up their human capital is not so obvious. Learning a foreign language, by contrast, very clearly means acquiring a marketable skill. Entire professions, such as editor, foreign language secretary, interpreter and translator, foreign language teacher, textbook writer, publisher, etc. depend on foreign language expertise. And many businesses engaging in cross border activities need foreign language skills. In this age of ever increasing global commerce, foreign language education has therefore become a veritable industry. The Internet has turned into a market place for foreign language training as well as the assessments of the economic value of language under titles such as "Languages your company should speak" (Kelly 2013), "Top business languages of the world" (Alexica 2013), "Economic powerhouse languages" (Schnoebelen 2013), etc. This literature is about the economic value of languages, but it is also about inequality. If there are any "economic powerhouse languages", there must also be economic basket case languages, and clearly this is so. The vast majority of all languages of the world are never systematically taught as foreign languages and, therefore, add little or nothing to anyone's human capital (except, perhaps, professional linguists').

In a comprehensive study, Davis (2003) correlated languages with gross domestic product (GDP) and found that English and Chinese had the most purchasing power of all languages, followed by other languages used by major economies, such as Japanese, Spanish, German, French, and Russian.

A 2008 study by the International Monetary Fund using the concept of percentage of

Gross World Product (GWP) ranks the economically most valuable languages as follows:

Table 1 Top languages by percentage of GWP

Rank	Language	GDP (in $ US Billions)	% of GWP	Cumulative % of GWP
1	English	$ 21,276	34.9%	34.9%
2	Japanese	$ 4,911	8.1%	43.0%
3	Simplified Chinese	$ 4,509	7.4%	50.4%
4	German	$ 4,393	7.2%	57.6%
5	Spanish	$ 4,170	6.8%	64.5%
6	French	$ 3,951	6.5%	71.0%
7	Italian	$ 2,481	4.1%	75.0%
8	Russian	$ 2,245	3.7%	78.7%
9	Portuguese	$ 1,915	3.1%	81.9%
10	Arabic	$ 1,903	3.1%	85.0%
11	Dutch	$ 1,386	2.3%	87.3%
12	Korean	$ 929	1.5%	88.8%
13	Turkish	$ 730	1.2%	90.0%
14	Traditional Chinese	$ 607	1.0%	91.0%
15	Polish	$ 528	0.9%	91.8%

(Source: IMF 2008)

These findings were not really surprising, but it is indicative of the economic importance of language that there is research of this kind, which gives rise to many further questions. Whether foreign language education should be reduced to follow the maxim of economic utility, is one.

The principal motivation for many national governments over the past several decades to expand English language education is economic. Similarly, it is economic rather than cultural motives, which fuel discussions about granting English official status in non-English speaking countries such as Japan, of using it as the principal language in international organizations, and about introducing English as an additional medium of instruction at university level in the Netherlands, Germany, and the Scandinavian countries, among others.

In the case of English, economic wealth combines with military and political power of major English speaking countries, USA, Great Britain, Canada, and Australia, to determine the preeminent position of English in the world today. The size of the speech community is an additional factor, which, however, is not decisive. Spanish outranks English in terms of native speakers, but carries less weight economically (as measured in terms of GDP per-capita, purchasing power of speakers, and size of language industry). An important difference that comes into play here is that between native (L1) speakers and second or foreign language (L2) speakers. According to estimates of the 2007 edition of *Nationalencyklopedin*, native speakers of Mandarin account for 14.4% of the world population, as compared to 5.43% of native English speakers. Yet, many more students learn English as a foreign language than Chinese. In terms of foreign learners, many languages with speech communities of tens of millions of speakers, such as Bengali, Tagalog, and Vietnamese, account for nothing. Outside their proper territory, they do not serve any important functions. Foreign language education hence has a bearing on the de-territorialization of languages, which is an asset in the globalizing economy.

In sum, the ranking of languages for economic potential needs to take into account a variety of factors, such as the size of the L1 and L2 speech communities, GDP and/or per capita income of L1 communities, political and military power, transnational functionality (e.g., presence in international organizations), and size of foreign language industry. To these may be added extent of literature—especially in science and technology—available in a language, degree of its development in terms of information storage and retrieval technologies, and its use in business and trade, domestically and internationally.

Other indices will likely be added, as economists have of late taken more interest in language than used to be the case formerly. This trend reflects the fact that in this age and day economic activity is more language-based than in the past. It should also be noted, however, that the commodification of language and the submission of foreign language education to market forces has sharpened the awareness that languages cannot be reduced to instruments of economic activity alone.

The Economics of Language needs to be supplemented by the Sociology of Language. One of the key questions investigated by the latter is how and driven by what forces the linguistic map of individual countries and that of the world at large changes. For change it does, and research in this field has shown repeatedly that, while economic forces are part of the equation, other forces, subsumed under such labels as "community", "identity", "emotional attachment", "sentimental value", are also at work. The multilingual regime of the European Union (Extra and Yağmur 2012) is a good example. Economic integration favours linguistic homogenization, but language policy at the union level and educational policies in the member states have been designed to counter this trend and strengthen the EU's national and, to some extent, minority languages in the face of the advance of English. All of these languages have quite a long literary tradition and have long enjoyed national recognition of one kind or another. These traditions are the most obvious, but not the only characteristics to demonstrate that, in addition to being a human capital component that can be evaluated, languages are associated with non-tangible values that cannot be expressed in monetary terms. In the European context, it is therefore relatively easy to implement policies that seem to contravene economic rationality. Whether in other parts of the world similar policies can be designed and implemented is today's an important question at the interface of language and economy. In this connection, it is important to emphasize the need to further develop research tools such as and in particular, cost-benefit analysis to capture and assess intangible results of language policies, such as, promoting, discouraging, or proscribing a certain language. Intangibles may be of various kind, for example, educational progress or regression, satisfaction or dissatisfaction with life, social peace or tension. It is highly desirable to develop methods for assessing intangible values of languages in this way by supporting international comparative research.

Conclusion

In this paper, I have stated some basic assumptions linguists and economists make about language and have then outlined a number of research domains where interdisciplinary exchange between them is possible and desirable. I have further argued that the Sociology of Language can serve as arbitrator between them, for while language is, on the one hand, a general human capacity and, on the other hand, a marketable component of human capital, it is also the foundation of society, the arena

in which the intangible value of all things is negotiated. Market forces have entered many domains of life, but they have not eliminated the appreciation of intangible goods without any commercial value. Policy makers are, therefore, well-advised to take cultural, emotional, and political dimensions of language valuation into account when designing language policies, rather than submitting all decisions to the imperative of economic gain.

References

Alexica. 2013. Top Business Languages of the World. http://alexika. com/why-alexika/world-business-languages/.

Becker, Gary S. 1975. *Human Capital*. New York: Columbia University Press.

Bourdieu, Pierre. 1982. *Ce que parler veut dire: l'economie des echanges linguistiques*. Paris: Edition de Minuit.

Coulmas, Florian.1992. *Language and Economy*. Oxford: Blackwell.

Coulmas, Florian. 2013.*Writing and Society*. Cambridge: Cambridge University Press.

Davis, Mark. 2003. GDP by Language. http://macchiato. com/economy/GDP_PPP_by_language. html.

Extra, Guus, Yağmur & Kutlay. 2012. *Language Rich Europe*. British Council, Cambridge University Press.

Feng, Zhiwei. 1988. The "FEL" Formula: An Economical Law for the Formation of Terms. In: *Social Sciences in China* (pp.171 – 180), Winter 1988.

Grin,François. 2014. 50 Years of Economics in Language Policy. Critical Assessment and Priorities. *ELF Working Papers* 13. http://www.unige.ch/traduction-interpretation/recherches/groupes/elf/documents/elfwp13. pdf.

Heller, Monica. 2005. Language, Authenticity and Commodification in the Globalized New Economy. http:// repositories.cdlib.org/wlicmc/2005 – 2006/1/.

Kelly, Nataly. 2013. Languages Your Company Should Speak (but Has Never Heard). http://blogs. hbr. org/ 2013/04/languages-your-company-should/.

L'Express. 2014. Un rapport d'Attali pour sauver la fran-
cophonie et notre économie En savoir plus sur. http://
lexpansion. lexpress. fr/actualite-economique/commen-
taire.asp? id＝1570378 (published 26/08/2014).

Rubinstein, Ariel. 2000. *Economics and Language*. Cambridge: Cambridge University Press.

Schnoebelen, Tyler. 2013. Economic Powerhouse Languages. http://idibon. com/economic-powerhouse-langua-
ges/.

Smith. Adam. 1767. Considerations Concerning the First
Formation of Languages. In: *The Early Writings of
Adam Smith* (pp.225 – 254), J. R. Lindgren ed. New
York: Augustus M. Kelley, 1967.

Wu, Apollo. 1987. The Economic Aspects of Diacritics.

In: *The Economics of Language Use* (pp.109 – 117),
H. Tonkin & K. M. Johnson-Weiner eds. New York:
Center for Research and Documentation on World Lan-
guage Problems.

Zipf, George Kingsley. 1949. *Human Behavior and the
Principle of Least Effort: An Introduction to Human
Ecology*. Cambridge, Mass.: Addison-Wesley Press.

Notes on contributors

Florian Coulmas (Email: florian.coulmas@ uni-due.
de), professor at University of Duisburg, Germany. His
research interests include language planning and language
policy, sociolinguistics, and Japanese society and culture.

论语言与经济的关系

弗洛里安·库尔马斯
德国杜伊斯堡大学社会科学学院

提 要:语言活动有一个经济学的维度,因此可以使用经济学理论和方法去研究语言。语言学家和经济学家对语言的价值及语言标准化的看法具有分歧。把语言学和经济学的方法结合起来有助于人们全面理解语言的重要性。本文建议语言政策制定者综合考虑语言的文化、感情和政治维度,而非仅以经济利益考量而做决定。

关键词:语言政策的经济维度　省力原则　人力资源　语言的内部经济　语言的外部经济

The Economic Status of Chinese and Japanese: An International Survey, Internet Searches and the Linguistic Landscape

Fumio Inoue

Abstract: The theoretical relations between language and economy are discussed on the basis of data from Japanese, Chinese and other languages. Three sets of data are used: (1) the linguistic landscape of Chinese and Japanese, (2) a worldwide survey on language learning, and (3) Google Internet searches of Japanese loan words. The three data sets show remarkable similarities in the distribution of language use.

Key words: linguistic landscape, language census, economic status of languages

Introduction: three investigations

Japanese is widely used overseas. However, this kind of global expansion is also observed for other languages. Multilingual signs are increasingly used all over the world, also in Japan and China. These movements can be interpreted as a mutual expansion of languages all over the world. Consequently, the future of Japanese should be predicted from such a wider viewpoint of international communication (Inoue 2000[①]).

Recent changes in the status of Japanese and Chinese are notable (井上 2000, 2010, 2011). Several related phenomena can be observed in certain aspects of the linguistic landscape (Inoue 2005, 2012)

and through Internet search trends (井上 2012). The underlying mechanism of the rise and fall of the market value of languages is presumed to be economics (Inoue 1997, 1998, 2007). This discussion is related to status planning of language.

The maps below show that the Chinese language is special among world languages in not using so-called "loanwords", or "borrowings", for new words and concepts from abroad; Chinese utilizes translations like "电视" or loan-translations like "可口可乐". This is in contrast with the Japanese language that tends to adopt foreign forms as loanwords like "terebi" (tv) or "koka koora" (coca cola). This phenomenon is related to corpus planning of language (Inoue 2000).

[①] Most of the English papers by F. Inoue are accessible through the Internet.
http://dictionary.sanseido-publ.co.jp/affil/person/inoue_fumio/doc/.
http://www.urayasu.meikai.ac.jp/japanese/meikainihongo/18ex/achievements.xls.

1. Linguistic landscape

In Section 1 the linguistic landscape will be analyzed. While traveling abroad, I took photos whenever I noticed Japanese language signs. When examining the old photographs all together, a similarity between the linguistic landscape and the statistical data of an international survey shows up. In Europe, Japanese generally shows up when there are seven or eight languages in a sign, as exemplified by a photo taken in the Netherlands (see Figure 1). However, Chinese sometimes shows up instead of Japanese.

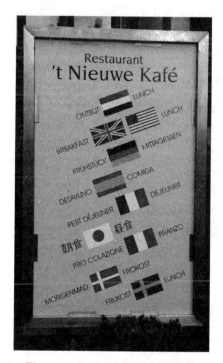

**Figure 1   Japanese language in the
Netherlands (2003)**

In contrast, in Asia Japanese shows up as the second or third language used in signs, as shown in Figure 2. Note the translation errors in this Chinese sign.

Figure 2   Japanese language in China (2013)

All over the world, the quality of the foreign languages is sometimes inferior, containing mistakes. E.g., Chinese characters get broken down into parts and are written incorrectly. In Figure 3, a picture taken in Greece, two of the elements of the Chinese character on the right are not arranged horizontally as they should be, but vertically, as if they were two different characters.

**Figure 3   Chinese characters misspelled
(Greece 2003)**

Thus, the significance of the linguistic landscape is undeniable, but even so we must pay attention to languages invisible in linguistic landscape. Sometimes a language may be forbidden and is not displayed in sight. In some parts of the Baltic states, Russian signboards have disappeared, although there were many of them in the past and there still live many Russian speaking people. English was forbidden in prewar Japan and is still forbidden in present-day Iran. "Text critique" or a critical eye is always necessary to determine history on the basis of documents.

2. International survey

The results of an international survey will be discussed in Section 2. The "international census on Japanese language" is a large-scale survey that NINJAL performed in the 1990s (NINJAL 2002). It was carried out in 28 nations, spreading over the world. It has not been fully analyzed yet, but the digital data for each country are released on the Internet.

Figure 4 gives an overview of the results. The distributions (percentages) per country were weighted by the population size to estimate the total number of people in the world. Based on the data of the 28 countries, numerical values for the countries that were not investigated can also be estimated, using the numerical values of the nearby countries. The graph in Figure 4 shows that English language is first, Chinese second, French third, German fourth, Spanish fifth and Japanese sixth. Chinese data, comprising a population of more than one billion, give the most conspicuous evidence concerning the popularity of world languages. Chinese people ranked Chinese as No. 1, English as No. 2, and Japanese as No. 3 in the order of languages in the world.

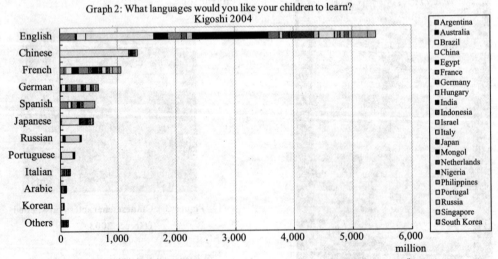

Graph 2: What languages would you like your children to learn?
Kigoshi 2004

Figure 4　What languages would you like your children to learn? *

People tend to think that languages in neighboring countries will become important in the future. The Chinese data strongly influence the overall high rank order of the Japanese language. However, its order is different in other countries in the world.

---

* Some figures in this paper are printed in color and presented in the end of this book, including Figures 4, 7, 11, 14, 15, 17 and 18.

Next, the survey data was entered in a world map in Figure 5. The countries nearest to Japan rank Japanese higher. In Europe and America, Japanese language is the 6th or 7th language. Thus it can be concluded that the "geographical proximity effect" works worldwide.

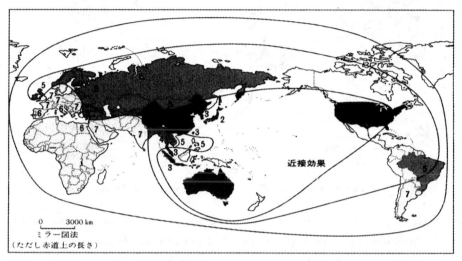

Figure 5　Rank order of Japanese language

Borrowings from the Japanese language were also investigated in the "international survey on Japanese language". Four words were collectively described in this global map in Figure 6. They are distinguished by the directions of the bars.

The vertical bars are *kimono*. The word is used in many areas of the world[①]. The bars facing the upper right are *shogun* 将军 (a general). Europe and the United States are the biggest centers using it. Its spread is caused by the popularity of a movie with this name. The horizontal bars are *sakura* (cherry tree). As for many plant names, the language of origin tends to be used in the world. *Sakura* is used more often in Asia. However, few realizations were attested in the USA, although there is a cherry tree festival in Washington.

The bar facing the lower right is *sukiyaki* (Japanese beef hot pot). For food names, the language of origin is used in the world. *Sukiyaki* is often used in Southeast Asia. It tends to spread to countries that use chopsticks or where people eat together taking food from the same tableware.

Africa and India show hardly any Japanese words in Figure 6. As Section 3 shows, when searched in Google the four words showed the same tendency collectively, used in Europe, the United States, and the Southeast Asia. Thus, all three kinds of data gave similar results, giving triangular support.

---

①　In China "和服" is used with the meaning of kimono.

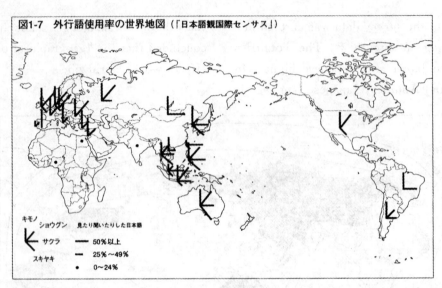

Figure 6   Usagemap of four words borrowed from Japanese

Although fragmentary and sporadic, the data of the linguistic landscape is in agreement with the extensive data of the international census, which has systematic high reliability.

The number of students learning Japanese can be another reliable index for the market value of languages. The data of Japanese and Chinese languages are most interesting these days. The economic relationships between the countries work as a basic factor and the geographical proximity effect can also be applied.

In Figure 7 data from the Japan Foundation or the Agency for Cultural Affairs shows the recent number of learners of Japanese. South Korea is first, China second, and then the Pacific Rim countries follow. "Neighboring-country" consciousness works strongly. In the background, the size of economic strength and the numerousness of economic exchanges are working.

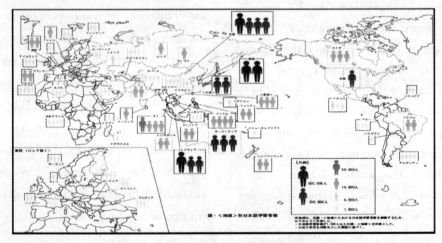

Figure 7   Number of Japanese language learners

3. Google search

In the third section, the above result concerning the linguistic landscape and the international survey is confirmed through the Internet search. Particularly effective is *Google* search, which can be divided into five techniques.

(1) Google picture search

(2) Bird's eye view: Google maps

(3) Fly's eye view: Google street view

(4) Witch's eye view: Google trends

(5) Historian's eye view: Google Ngram Viewer

In addition, the *field work*, taking photos, can be called "insect's eye view" because people must crawl (walk) on the ground like insects. Various examples are provided in the first section of this study. This is an orthodox technique utilized before the appearance of Google search.

(1) Google picture search

Google picture search can be used to find photos showing linguistic landscapes. In Figure 8 examples of "关东煮" (or *kan-to-daki* in western Japanese dialect for *Oden*) in China are amply shown. We can now detect that this representation is actually used in the Chinese language without actually visiting China.

(1)
Google picture
??煮

· 香港

Figure 8   Picture search of "关东煮" borrowed from Japanese

（2）Google maps

Google maps are often used to look for the position of a store or a building; however, the map is also expandable to the entire world. Since it looks down from above like a bird, it can be called a "bird's eye view". It is especially effective in order to investigate the words that entered from Japanese into other languages as borrowings. Borrowed or loan words from Japanese were generally found distributed over the United States, Europe, Southeast Asia, etc. and were in agreement with the signboards and advertisements which I have observed in many countries until now. Such investigation was almost impossible in the past.

As an example of borrowed words from Japanese, the map in Figure 9 shows the worldwide distribution of the Japanese word for Japanese martial arts, *budo* 武道. The Japanese language seems to be experiencing global expansion. The bird's eye view of *samurai* 侍 (warrior) shows a similar distribution, though maps are omitted here. Many other borrowed words from Japan were searched in Google maps. They are mostly distributed over the United States, Europe and Southeast Asia.

Figure 9　Google map of "budo", borrowed from Japanese

（3）Google street view

In some western areas of the world, continuous street scenes can be observed using *Google street view*. Google street view can be thought of as a "Fly's eye view" because of the compound eyes with 360 degree vision. When looking for language signs, we can cover wide expanses in just a few minutes.

We can jump to Google street view by moving the controls on the left-hand side of the screen. A typical example of a dialectal shop name is *Okini* (meaning "very much" in Western Japan), used worldwide. Many more examples are observable using Google maps or Google insights.

Figure 10 shows that this restaurant is a large building along a main street, with an Asian owner.

Figure 10   Google street view of "Okini"，a borrowed word from a Japanese dialect

（4）Google trends

Google trends can be called a "witch's eye view". It shows a world map and also a trend graph for the past eight years. As to the usage of words borrowed from Japanese，the United States is overwhelming and Europe and Oceania follow. This is a new technique that was unimaginable in the past. The Google trends totals a lot of language used for the Google search for every country. Both a map and the graph according to year are produced.

In Figure 11，sushi，a borrowed word from Japanese is shown. The lines in the graph on top show the trend for eight years. Sushi is used most frequently and the number is still increasing now.

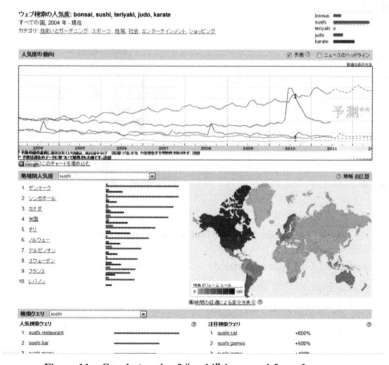

Figure 11   Google trends of "sushi" borrowed from Japanese

Karate is the second most frequently used. It is in decline, except for 2010. *Bonsai* and *judo* have also been in decline. *Teriyaki*, though unpopular, has been on the rise for a while. The Japanese boom is at an end and only food may maintain popularity in the end.

The world map on the bottom shows trends for *sushi*; the other four words, although investigated simultaneously, were omitted. The map shows differences even within nations. For example, though not shown here, one map shows elevated use of *sushi* by the West Coast of the USA.

The data of various techniques of Google search turned out to be reliable similar to the international survey. Four words *kimono*, *shogun*, *sakura* and *sukiyaki* had been studies in the international survey. When searched by Google trends in Figure 12, they showed the same tendency collectively, used in Europe, the United States, and the Southeast Asia. Thus, all three kinds of data gave similar results, giving triangular support.

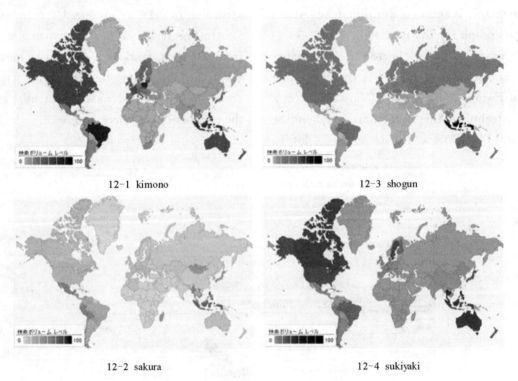

12-1 kimono

12-3 shogun

12-2 sakura

12-4 sukiyaki

Figure 12　Google trends of four words borrowed from Japanese

Differences between Chinese provinces can also be detected. Figure 13 shows the search results for "关东煮"(*Oden*). The difference between the ocean coast region and the inland is conspicuous.

Thus, language use of every country in the world can be observed in the study room without spending money for an actual survey. This may be the most economical technique for linguistic economics.

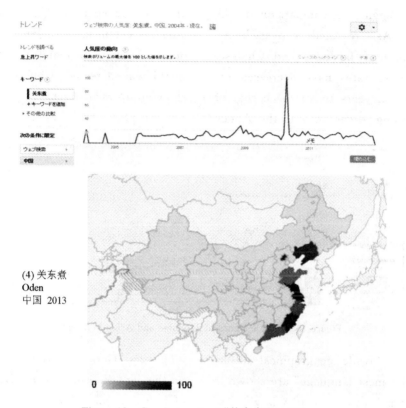

(4) 关东煮
Oden
中国 2013

0   100

Figure 13　Google trends of "关东煮" in China

(4') Google trends for names of languages

The present status of languages can be estimated by search trends extracted from Google Trends. As Figure 14 shows, English is overwhelming according to the trend graph. Then French, German, Spanish, and Japanese languages follow. Japanese is the lowest among these from 2010 onward.

In addition, searches for all the language names show a decline in recent years. It seems that serious topics such as language names are no longer searched in the whole Google search. Instead, the ratio of topics related to amusement shows a general upward trend.

As pictured in Figure 15, using the

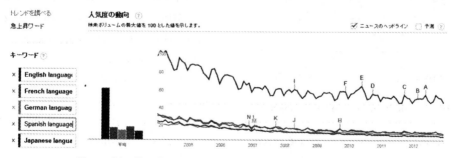

Figure 14　Google trends of Japanese and European languages

same search engine, a comparison of the languages of Asia revealed an overwhelming dominance of Japanese and Chinese. However, their rates have decreased for the past several years to approach that of Korea. A strong resemblance to the change of the prospective Japanese language students (applicants for Japanese language) of universities in many countries of the world was detected. Chinese and Korean show an upward trend.

Figure 15　Google trends of Japanese and Asian languages

The worldwide geographical differences for "Japanese language" are shown in Figure 16. Small countries in Asia give exceptionally high value.

Figure 16　Google trends of Japanese language

(5) Google Ngram viewer for language names

Google Ngram viewer can also be utilized to estimate the rank order of languages. Google Ngram viewer is based on the data of *Google books*. Large amounts of text data spanning 500 years (including English and Chinese) have been amassed and are now retrievable on the Internet. This time language names in English were searched. "Japanese language" ranked from 5th to 8th in the world.

The graph in Figure 17 shows that the ranking of English, French, German and Spanish has not changed much for 200 years, although war influenced for a short period. Use of the Japanese language was also influenced by war, and in 1990s it surpassed Spanish, perhaps because of Japan's economic prosperity.

When Spanish, Japanese, Chinese, and Russian languages were compared in Figure 18, an interesting phenomenon was discovered. "Chinese language" was the center of attention in the books in the past, showing a peak at the time of the Opium

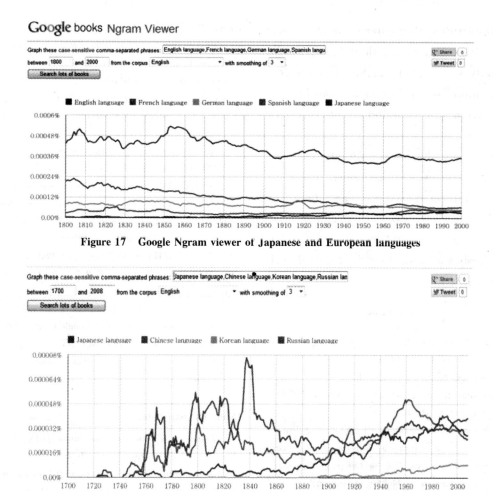

Figure 17   Google Ngram viewer of Japanese and European languages

Figure 18   Google Ngram viewer of Japanese and Asian languages

War. "Japanese language" showed rapid growth in two centuries. It was mentioned mostly at the time of World War Ⅱ. Fortunately, the peaks after 1990 for both Chinese and Japanese languages are not because of war, and can be interpreted as based on their rapid economic development.

Conclusions

Thus three kinds of data including the linguistic landscape, a worldwide survey, and Google internet searches, gave similar and mutually reinforcing results. The same tendencies appeared when various Google search techniques were applied to loanwords (or borrowings) from foreign languages, like *rodeo*, *malasada*, *kimchi*, *hula*, *halal*, *namaste*, *telecopier*, etc. Language choice in the field work, the international census and Google search show a lot of similarities. GDP, nightlight on the Earth and density of the linguistic landscape also show similarities. The amount of loanwords or mutual exchange of borrowings (or more correctly of new concepts) is highly correlated with the economical development of a society. The countries with a large amount of Japanese loan words are also countries with greater economic power and with close trade relations (井上 2012). Not only status planning but also the corpus planning side of languages can be analyzed from the standpoint of linguistic economics.

Probably the latest mutual expansion of languages owes to economy. Economy can be interpreted as serving as a backdrop to language. A research field called "language economics" or "econolinguistics" is now firmly established on the basis of various concrete data.

References

Inoue, Fumio. 1997. Market Value of Languages in Japan. *Japanese Linguistics* 2, 40 – 61.

Inoue, Fumio. 1998. Language Market and Its Basic Mechanisms. In: *Area and Culture Studies* (東京外国語大学論集) 57, 83 – 103.

Inoue, Fumio. 2000. English as a Language of Science in Japan. In: *The Dominance of English as a Language of Science on the Non-English Language Communities*, Ulrich Ammon ed. Mouton de Gruyter.

Inoue, Fumio. 2005. Econolinguistic Aspects of Multilingual Signs in Japan. *IJSL* 6, 157 – 177.

Inoue, Fumio. 2007. Changing Economic Values of German and Japanese. In: *Language Regimes in Transformation Contributions to the Sociology of Language*, Florian Coulmas ed., 93, 95 – 113.

Inoue, Fumio. 2012. Improvements in the Sociolinguistic Status of Dialects as Observed Through Linguistic Landscapes. *Dialectologia* 8, 5 – 132. www.publications.ub.edu/revistes/ejecuta_descarga.asp? codigo=725.

NINJAL(国立国語研究所). 2002.「東アジアにおける日本語観国際センサス」*International Census on Attitudes Toward Japanese Language in East Asia*. http://www.ninjal.ac.jp/archives/n_census/result/list01/.

井上史雄.2000.「日本語の値段」.大修館.

井上史雄.2010.「日语的价格」.延辺大学出版社(李斗石訳).

井上史雄.2011.「経済言語学論考」(*Keizaigengogaku Ronko*).明治書院(Meiji Shoin).

井上史雄.2012.「日本語世界進出のグーグル言語地理学」(Nihongo sekai shinshutsu no Google gengo chirigaku). 明海日本語(*Meikai Nihongo*) 17, 29 – 42. http://www.urayasu.meikai.ac.jp/japanese/meikainihongo/17/inoue.pdf.

Notes on contributors

Fumio Inoue (Email address: innowayf @ nifty.com; Personal website: http://www.tufs.ac.jp/ts/personal/inouef/index-e.html), visiting professor of National Institute for Japanese Language and Linguistics. His research interests are sociolinguistics and dialectology.

汉语和日语的经济地位
——网络搜索、语言景观和国际调查

井上史雄

日本国立国语研究所

提　要:本文在日语、汉语和其他语言的数据基础上,研究了语言和经济的理论关系。本文讨论了三种类型的数据:(1) 语言景观;(2) 一个世界范围的语言使用情况调查;(3) 谷歌网络搜索。语言使用的分布在三类数据中具有高度的一致性。

关键词:语言景观　语言普查　语言的经济地位

Why Speaking Two Languages Is Advantageous for the Speaker

Bruno Di Biase and Qi Ruying

Abstract: This article is addressed to parents, teachers and other carers in a migration situation, such as Chinese parents in Australia, facing the dilemma of whether it would be best for their children to learn only English so as to optimize their future academic and professional development. Apart from the well-known socio-cultural and economic advantages brought about by bilingualism, much recent research into bilingualism has uncovered specific lifelong cognitive advantages for those who regularly use two languages since childhood. This finding also extends to those bilinguals who learned their second language later in life.

Key words: bilingual children, family, cognition, health

This article was conceived at the Bilingualism Research Lab at UWS aiming to inform particularly concerned parents and teachers about current research on the cognitive and health benefits of bilingualism.

In the situation of migration many parents may reduce the use of their home language with their children or stop altogether in favour of the language which is dominant in their adopted country. They may reach this state of affairs under the assumption that it may help the children to learn the mainstream language better and hence do better in their study, achieve good academic qualifications and eventually be successful in their chosen profession. Sometimes this language shift is simply due to the fact that parents may be at a loss as to what may be best for them to do with their children's languages.

Even when they try to maintain their home language, they may not succeed as children grow up and their English becomes stronger at child care centre and later at school, and the parents simply give up or reduce the quantity and quality of the home language used with the child whereby only the most basic everyday communication is carried in the parents' and grandparents' language. Naturally enough the child's mother tongue may stop developing altogether both in terms of receptive and productive knowledge and skills in that language. Does this language situation result in gains to the child? Or will it result in disadvantage? These dilemmas concern and sometimes worry many Chinese immigrant families in Australia and in other countries.

On the other hand those parents and children may be quite unaware of the lifelong rewards that may accrue to them from the efforts exerted in bringing up their children bilingually and cherishing the development and the continued use of two languages. This is not only for their children's educational and professional opportunities and life chances but also for the family's long term health and wellbeing(De Houwer 2009; Xu 2013). In this brief article we wish to summarise first some of the better known social and cultural advantages and then point out some of the newly discovered and less obvious, but certainly not less important, benefits of bilingualism, that is, the lifelong advantages of regularly speaking more than one language.

Undoubtedly, being able to speak to your grandmother in a language she understands allows the child to "inherit" her cultural practices and knowledge and, by communicating in her language, benefit directly from her life experiences and wisdom. Where two or more languages are present in a social environment, few would doubt that the professional who is able to speak the language of their client, the teacher who is able to speak their pupil's language, the student who is able to speak the language of their school, the shopkeeper who can sell their goods in the customer's language, the tourist, the business person, the politician who may be able to communicate to people in their particular language can successfully access hearts and minds with greater chance than those who can not.

Unfortunately for many parents, including those who are themselves

bilinguals, even such clear social, cultural and economic benefits may become obscured, or hopelessly underestimated, perhaps because of the lack of prestige of their language in a migration situation or their own non-standard Mandarin variety, or dialect. Chinese parents in situations of migration, in Australia and elsewhere, may experience difficulties when they are trying to learn to communicate in the dominant language, English, well enough to participate effectively in the society. These difficulties are due in part to their trying to learn the second language rather later in life. They also realize that their own home language is not used nor required in educational or other institutional contexts. From their own hardship they often, unfortunately, conclude that if they themselves find it so difficult to learn English "properly" then it may be best for their own children to learn, and focus ONLY on, English. Some parents even come to believe that their home language is more a hindrance than a help for their children, and so stop using it with their children at home, favouring the dominant language for communication with them. This effectively turns their children into monolinguals.

As we will show, the exclusion of the home language from communication with their children is unnecessary and deprives both parents and children of important benefits accruing from the habit of communicating daily in two or more languages. In fact, depriving children of the heritage language input at home will ensure they won't even acquire the so-called "passive" (or rather "receptive") knowledge of the home language. Such choice would be not only unfortunate but well and truly shortsighted. Parents should lose no sleep at all over their children's opportunity to learn English in Australia or other migration contexts. The peer group in the child care centre and the school will make sure that they learn English, as confirmed by in-depth research at our own and other universities(e.g., Clyne 2003; Di Biase & Dyson 1988; Qi, Di Biase & Campbell 2006 among others). For instance Qi's (2011) study of an Australian-Chinese child who learned English mainly through his child care centre, found that his English development closely resembles that of monolingual English peers while his Chinese also developed in similar ways to monolingual Chinese peers in China. Another recent study (Medojević 2014)in a different immigrant community specifically focusing on the effect of schooling on bilingual children found that the second and third generation Serbian-Australian children, within the first year of school, learned English as well as their monolingual peers.

On the other hand, the danger of complete language shift or even language death (e. g., Clyne 1995; Evans 2010) is well documented whereby immigrant or indigenous children within the school and the peer group context might turn into monolingual English speakers, with only tacit knowledge of the home language. Indeed in most cases in some communities the home language disappears altogether within the third generation and is unlikely to develop any further.

On the other hand, bringing up children bilingually can count on many success stories (The Australian article— Higher Education 2014; The North Shore Time article—HSC Success 2015). For instance, it appears that students born in Australia to foreign-born parents score much higher on an international reading test than other Australian-born students (Ferrari 2011). For an example from the USA, a large study from Johns Hopkins University that tracked nearly 11, 000 young immigrants all the way to adulthood found that children who immigrate to the United States with their families are likely to outperform kids with a similar background who were born in the USA. Their own children are also likely to do better than their peers when they grow up. The study also found that by the third generation, that advantage will be gone(Dye Lee 2012).

So, depriving the children of their home language will serve, then, no purpose at all except depriving the children(and the parents by the way) of the advantages reserved by nature for those who have the good fortune of using more than one language in everyday communication. Most of these parents may be, probably, unaware of the scientific evidence which has been mounting over the last few years from research on bilingualism by linguists, psycholinguists and neurolinguists(Kharkhurin & Li Wei 2015; Bialystok & Barac 2013; Li-Hai Tan et al. 2011; Li 2013; Yip &

Matthews 2007) quite apart from all the other socio-cultural, educational and economic benefits and advantages already mentioned above. So, what are those other advantages?

Curiously enough, the benefits of bilingualism appear to relate more to areas such as human cognitive functioning and health in old age rather than within language competence and use. Early research concentrated on the latter and looked at areas such as metalinguistic awareness, which is "the explicit knowledge of linguistic structure and the ability to access it intentionally" (Bialystok and Craik 2010). These abilities are crucial for the development of the more complex uses of language in children and, critically, also for the acquisition of literacy. According to these authors, in their 2010 review of the evidence thus far, the important differences picked up by the earlier research was that bilingual children seemed to be similar to monolingual children in detecting grammatical violations in meaningful sentences (e.g., "Apples growed on trees"). However, with semantically anomalous prompts(e.g., "Apples grow on noses") bilingual children were more accurate than monolinguals. In such cases (prompts with anomalous meaning) successful performance relies on "the ability to ignore the misleading meaning and focus only on the grammar". So, the bilingual's advantage in accurately judging such sentences does not have that much to do with metalinguistic awareness but rather with "an attentional advantage in selectivity and inhibition". These are key processes of the brain's executive functioning.

According then to Bialystok and Craik (2010), the development of the executive-function system is the most important cognitive achievement in early childhood because through it "children gradually master the ability to control attention, inhibit distraction, monitor sets of stimuli, expand working memory, and shift between tasks". Those who have had professional experience with older people find that exactly these same cognitive processes are the first to go, so to speak, in aging individuals. Then, these authors argue, "if bilingualism affects executive functioning, the impact should be found across the entire cognitive system and throughout the entire life span".

And yes, this kind of "reserve" power for bilinguals is what later research eloquently supports. For instance, looking at cognitive performance of 110 older bilinguals and monolingual peers, Gold, Kim, Johnson, Kryscio & Smith (2013) in a specialised neuroscientific journal maintain, already from the title of their article, that "Lifelong Bilingualism Maintains Neural Efficiency for Cognitive Control". The results obtained by these researchers "suggest that lifelong bilingualism offsets age-related declines in the neural efficiency for cognitive control processes". But why should that be? What arcane powers might confer such advantages? In fact the reasons seem to be relatively straightforward. Remember that when the bilingual speaks, he/she activates two different linguistic systems, each with its own set of sounds, words, and rules for their combination. But quite clearly only one of these systems can be used at the one time, the other language system has to be kept under control. When this is not possible, as may happen with aphasics, the linguistic result is uninterpretable. As these neuroscientists explain: "It appears that the lifelong bilingual experience of continuously switching between two languages strengthens general-purpose executive control systems, maintaining their neural efficiency in aging. Lifelong bilingualism thus confers not only social and economic advantages, but benefits the functioning of the aging brain." This is excellent news for bilinguals.

The next issue was to sort out whether these advantages belong only to those who have acquired their two languages from birth either simultaneously or sequentially (one after the other) but still in early childhood. That is, could such neuropsychological advantages be found also in those bilinguals who learned their second language (L2) not in early childhood but maybe at school, at work and so on, later in life? Well, the good news is that yes, this also turns out to be the case as it appears from a current article in the prestigious American journal *PNAS* (*Proceedings of National Academy of Sciences*) which is freely accessible online. The results from the research presented in the latter article, by Pliatsikas, Moschopoulou & Saddy (2015) confirm earlier results on the

effects of bilingualism on cognitive functions suggesting that the experience of bilingualism results in a cognitive "reserve" in older age and that this reserve, according to these researchers, has a neurological basis (changes in the structure of certain areas of the brain) and that similar changes are evident not only in early bilinguals but also in older bilinguals who learned their second language later in life.

We can only conclude that it is important to encourage, and for governments and educational institutions to support, the continuous learning and use of languages both in children and adults, at home, at school and in other social contexts. If this is an effort, and it may also come at a cost in terms of resources, think of it as an important investment for the future health of individuals to keep them functioning as long as possible out of degenerative diseases of the brain. The cost of old age care needs also be factored in!

In this article, we have shown various advantages uncovered by recent research relating to raising children bilingually, particularly in the case of parents in immigrant setting where the dominant language is different from the home language. Parents' home language policy adopted in their children's early age has a life-time impact on the children but also has beneficial effects on the parents themselves in delaying degenerative effects of ageing on brain functions.

References

Bialystok, E., & Barac, R. 2013. Cognitive Effects. In:

The Psycholinguistics of Bilingualism(pp. 192 – 213), F. Grosjean & Ping Li eds. Malden, MA: Wiley-Blackwell.

Bialystok, E., & Craik, I. M. 2010. Cognitive and Linguistic Processing in the Bilingual Mind. *Current Directions in Psychological Science* 19(1), 19 – 23.

De Houwer, A. 2009. *Bilingual First Language Acquisition*. Clevendon/Buffalo: Multilingual Matters.

Di Prinzio, A. 2014. Language at Home. *NSW Federation of Community Language Schools Magazine*, April 2014, p.22.

Evans, N. 2010. *Dying Words: Endangered Languages and What They Have to Tell Us*. Malden, MA: Wiley-Blackwell.

Ferrari, J. 2011. Children of Migrants Outclassing the Locals at School. *The Australian*, September 14, 2011.

Gold, B. T., Kim, C., Johnson, N.F., Kryscio, R.J., & Smith, C. D. 2013. Lifelong Bilingualism Maintains Neural Efficiency for Cognitive Control. *The Journal of Neuroscience* 33(2), 387 – 396.

Kharkhurin, A. V., & Li, W. 2015. The Role of Code-switching in Bilingual Creativity. *Journal of Bilingualism and Bilingual Education* 18(2), 153 – 169.

Lane, B. 2014. Having Two Languages a Boost to Brain Power. *The Australian/ Higher Education Section*, Wednesday August 20, p. 29.

Lee, Dye. 2012. Why Immigrants' Children Do Better in School. *ABC News*, Sept. 21, 2012, via Good Moarning America.

Li, P. 2013. Neurolinguistic and Neurocomputational Models. In: *The Psycholinguistics of Bilingualism*(pp. 214 – 248), F. Grosjean & Ping Li eds. Malden, MA: Wiley-Blackwell.

Medojević, L. 2014. *The Effect of First Year of Schooling on Bilingual Language Acquisition: A study of Second and Third Generation Serbian-Australian 5-year-old Bilingual Children from a Processability Perspective*. Unpublished PhD thesis, University of Western Sydney.

Nicastri, D. 2015. Baccalaureate Star's Future Focus—Joy's Ambition to be Prime Minister. *The North Shore Times/HSC Congratulations Section*, January 23,

p. 31.

Pliatsikas, C., Moschopoulou, E., & Saddy, J. D. 2015. The Effects of Bilingualism on the White Matter Structure of the Brain. *PNAS* (*Proceedings of the National Academy of Science*) 112(5), 1334 – 1337.

Qi, R., Di Biase, B., & Campbell, S. 2006. The Transition from Nominal to Pronominal Person Reference in the Early Language of a Mandarin-English Bilingual Child. *International Journal of Bilingualism* 10(3), 301 – 329.

Qi, R. 2011. *The Bilingual Acquisition of English and Mandarin: Chinese Children in Australia*. New York: Cambria Press.

Tan, Li-Hai, Chen, L., Yip, V., et al. 2011. Activity Levels in the Left Hemisphere Caudate—Fusiform Circuit Predict How Well a Second Language Will Be Learned. *PNAS* (*Proceedings of the National Academy of Sciences*)108(6), 2540 – 2544.

Xu, D. 2013. The Political and Economic Benefits of the Policy of Equality of Native Languages. *Journal of Yunnan Normal University* 6, 1 – 6.

Yip, V. & Matthews, S. 2007. *The Bilingual Child: Early Development and Language Contact*. New York: Cambridge University Press.

Notes on contributors

Bruno Di Biase, PhD, Associate Professor in School of Humanities and Communication Arts, University of Western Sydney. His research interests are second language acquisition, bilingual first language acquisition, language learning & teaching and CALL.

Qi Ruying, PhD (Email: r.qi@uws.edu.au), Senior Lecturer and PhD supervisor in Bilingualism and Chinese, the School of Humanities and Communication Arts at the University of Western Sydney; the Director of Bilingualism Research Lab @ UWS-JNU and Leader of the China Liaison Unit (Language and Culture) and an adjunct member of ARC Centre of Excellence for the Dynamics of Language. Her research interests are Mandarin-English bilingual children's language acquisition, early bilingual education, bilingualism and biculturalism, language acquisition, Chinese language and cultural teaching and learning.

关于双语人的优势

Bruno Di Biase

School of Humanities and Communication Arts，University of Western Sydney

齐汝莹

Bilingualism Research Lab @ UWS-JNU

提　要：移民社会环境中家长，如澳大利亚的华人父母，和教育工作者所面对的一个困境是到底要不要让孩子只学英语，以便更有利于他们未来的学业和职业发展。本文针对此问题展开论述。首先，双语带来众所周知的社会文化和经济优势。其次，近期双语学研究发现那些自幼年开始经常使用双语的人群拥有某些伴随终身的认知优势。最新研究进一步证实这一优势不仅限于儿童早期双语学习者，那些童年之后才开始学习第二语言的人群在某种程度上同样具有这一优势。

关键词：双语儿童　家庭　认知　健康

动态普通话:规范与变异*

黄　行

提　要:标准普通话与普通话地方变体及其应对策略的研究既有学术层面的意义,也有政策规划层面的意义。地方普通话是普通话使用发展的正常状态,对其应当采取承认、包容和尊重事实的态度与政策应对。地方普通话要区分社区变体与个人变体,二者的区别在于变体的系统性和稳定性有所不同。由于语言认同差异影响普通话推广的效果,地方普通话可以起到中介或过渡的作用。

关键词:标准普通话　地方普通话　变体　规范　变异

各位代表:

受会议组织人委托,特向各位就参会的心得体会做一简单总结与汇报交流。

本次会议之主题是,标准普通话与普通话地方变体的关系及其应对策略。此议题之于当前国家语言社会生活既有学术研究层面的意义,也有政策规划层面的意义。

与会代表发表论文及学者讨论互动的内容可大致分为两类。

1. 理论概括类:如周明朗、刘乐宁、周庆生、徐杰、姚德怀、侍建国、赵丽明、武春野等教授的论文,集中探讨了(1)标准与变异,(2)变异与变体,(3)变异与偏误(或变异的可接受度),及(4)语言身份认同及其形成与建构等问题。

2. 实证分析类:这类论文是基于语言个案分析的理论探讨。如 Sali 教授关于加拿大英语的社会变异研究,刘俐李教授基于若干汉语方言案例提出的普通话—地方普通话—普通地方话—方言的语言变异连续统;此外还有张璟玮、张凌、蔡冰、付义荣、郭骏、方小兵、张妍、乔秋颖、张斌华、张媛媛、杨婕等关于无锡方言、香港普通话、农民工普通

话、唐山话、徐州话、山西太谷话等地域方言或社会方言的使用、变异及认同状况的实证性研究等。

会议通过广泛深入的学术讨论,就标准普通话与地方普通话的地位和关系问题达成以下共识。

1. 中国地方普通话或标准汉语的变体是普通话使用发展的正常状态,属于"求同存异"、"和而不同"的"和谐语言社会"范畴,对其应当采取承认、包容和尊重事实的态度与政策应对。

2. 与传统注重单纯普通话或某具体方言的调查研究不同,本会议题发表的成果注重二者之间的变体——地方普通话(含地方普通话、行业普通话、族群普通话等)的调研及理论思考,填补了中国语言政策规划和推广国家通用语言研究领域的空白。我们期待通过此次会议的推动,促进国家语言规划和国家通用语言事业的学术研究和问题对策研究。

3. 地方普通话要区分社区变体与个人变体,二者的区别在于变体的系统性和稳定性有所不同。而具有系统性和稳定性的社

---

* 首届"动态普通话:规范与变异"学术研讨会(2014 年 12 月 1 日—2 日,澳门大学)闭幕辞。

区语言变体既是动态的,也有可能形成自己的规范,正如各国的英语都有不同的规范,因此地方普通话或将与标准普通话长期共存,形成对应、互补甚至竞争的局面。

4. 普通话和地方普通话现象具有世界普遍性,同时也具有中国国情的特殊性。原因之一是(据认为)汉语标准语和方言变体之间不仅本体结构差异是世界上最复杂的,语言身份认同差异也是世界上最复杂的,因此严重影响了普通话推广的实际效果。在这个意义上,地方普通话可以起到积极的中介或过渡的作用。

会议的深入讨论,也带给我们一些深层次的理论和问题思考。

1. 目前政府和学界对地方普通话的认可度越来越高,这应该说是一种进步。但是地方普通话政策层面和技术层面可操作的标准都还很欠缺,需要开展地方普通话的深入研讨,因此召开本次以地方普通话规范与变异为议题学术会议非常必要,也非常及时。

2. 地方普通话变异的可接受度问题,或者是变异和偏误之间的临界点问题。对此徐杰先生认为,变体的偏误可以通过其与标准语沟通度的自然调整而解决,可参照标准英语和各种国际英语的处置方法。

但是标准语变体变异的容忍和迁就应该是有限度的,汉语诸方言的多样性已经十分复杂,如果再把非汉语母语人的普通话变量加入的话,情况会更加复杂。如蒙古语、维吾尔语母语人普通话不带声调,壮语母语人普通话无送气音,白语母语人普通话无阳声韵等变异似乎更接近偏误。

3. 语言身份、语言认同,乃至标准语和

变体本身的形成,是天然赋予还是主观建构问题(民族学界对此问题的关注度要超过语言学)。周明朗先生认为人的语言社会角色是开放和可选择的,徐大明先生认为人的语言身份认同主要是建构的而非规定的等观点极具启发性。例如对母语母言认同度低的社区,一般也会进一步影响到该社区带有母语母言特点的地方普通话的认同,这有利于标准普通话的推广,如杨婕同学列举的山西方言的情况(其实整个北方中原官话区的母语母言认同度都不高);反之,对母语母言认同度高的社区,则会干扰该社区标准普通话及地方普通话的认同,例如一些少数民族语言地区。因此当前在民族地区强力实施和"跨越式发展"的以推广国家通用语言为主要目的的"双语教学"规划,以及一些政府文件所提"在民族地区推广国家通用语言,有利于加强少数民族的祖国意识和中华民族认同感"的政策取向,是否适当和有效是可以商榷的。

4. 此次会议名曰"首届"学术研讨会意味着"动态普通话"问题之研讨应该成为系列或品牌,我们期待二届、三届的后续学术研讨得以可持续的发展。

最后请允许代表诸位受邀参会人员对澳门大学人文学院成功举办首届"动态普通话"研讨会,和对所有志愿参与会议服务的各位老师同学致以衷心感谢!

作者简介

黄行,中国社会科学院民族学与人类学研究所研究员,博士生导师,主要研究领域为汉藏语系语言、少数民族语言规划等。

Dynamic Putonghua: Standardization and Variation

Huang Xing
Chinese Academy of Social Sciences

Abstract: The study on standard and regional Putonghua is not only academically significant but also relevant for language planning. Regional Putonghua is a normal state of the spread of Putonghua and should be recognized and accepted in language planning. Individual and group variations should be distinguished and measured in stability and system consistency. Regional Putonghua plays an important role in mediating the popularization of Putonghua, overcoming the problems of language identities.

Key words: standard Putonghua, regional Putonghua, variety, standard, variation

关于在我国中西部地区首先开展多样化的第二语言教育的建议[*]

徐大明　张璟玮

提　要：本文以语言习得研究成果为基础，结合我国中西部地区语言教育的发展现状，针对我国中西部地区当前的语言问题，建议在我国中西部地区，缩减英语教育的规模，增加作为第二语言的民族语言以及周边国家语言的教学，增加普通教育和高考语言的语种，培养国家急需和特需的外语人才和民族语言人才。

关键词：第二语言教育　语言习得　少数民族语言

一　总述

《国家中长期语言文字事业改革和发展规划纲要（2012—2020 年）》指出："语言文字事业具有基础性、全局性、社会性和全民性特点，是国家文化建设和社会发展的重要组成部分，事关历史文化传承和经济社会发展，事关国家统一和民族团结，事关国民素质提高和人的全面发展，在国家发展战略中具有重要地位和作用。"鉴于国家语言文字事业的重要地位和作用，南京大学中国语言战略研究中心从国家语言战略的高度，以已有的语言习得研究成果为基础，结合我国中西部地区语言教育的发展现状，针对我国中西部地区当前的语言问题，提出如下政策建议：

在我国中西部地区，缩减英语教育的规模，增加作为第二语言的民族语言以及周边国家语言的教学，增加普通教育和高考语言的语种，培养国家急需和特需的外语人才和民族语言人才。

本文将论证"开展多样化的第二语言教育"建议的理论基础和现实基础，并讨论其预期的政策效果。

二　当前的形势和语言问题

我国的语言政策，包括通用语、民族语言和外语教育的政策，是在科学规划的基础上制定的，已取得了重要的成果。然而，有关政策和规划需要根据国内外形势的发展而不断调整、完善。目前，我国周边外交局势日益复杂；国内民族分裂主义势力不断抬头；东部劳动密集型产业正在向中西部有序转移，并成为中国经济增长的新的动力。面对国家政治、经济发展的形势和新需求，我国的语言教育政策也需要不断调整和优化，以达到提高国民语言能力且为国家输送和储备拥有合格语言能力的人才的基本目标。

本文讨论中西部的语言教育政策，按照国家经济区域的分类，中部地区包括：山西省、河南省、湖北省、安徽省、湖南省、江西省；西部地区包括：内蒙古自治区、新疆维吾尔自治区、宁夏回族自治区、陕西省、甘肃省、青海省、重庆市、四川省、西藏自治区、广

---

[*] 本文为 2014 年 6 月提交给南京大学和 2015 年 2 月提交给国家语委的报告的基础上的修改稿。

西壮族自治区、贵州省、云南省。在中西部首先开展多样化的第二语言教育的建议的内容主要是由当前国家政治、经济和外交形势所决定的。

国家当前的政治安全形势。近年来，对国家安全构成严重危害的是民族分裂势力、暴力恐怖势力和宗教极端势力"三股势力"。这些势力以企图实现分裂国家为目的，不断地挑起暴乱、骚乱，制造社会恐慌。这一问题在中西部地区尤为突出。面对当前的严峻形势，我们需要反思已有的民族语言政策，并做出调整和应对。不仅如此，还需要反思现行的语言教育政策。语言和文化的差异客观上影响了跨民族的沟通与交流。只有少数民族和汉族相互学习语言，才能更有效地、双向地消除交流和理解的障碍。

当前经济发展形势。近期，国务院出台一系列政策促进东部劳动密集型产业西移。同时，"一带一路"战略也将加快产业向中西部转移，助推中西部新型城镇化。李克强总理在2014年6月25日主持召开的国务院常务会议上指出：改革开放以来，西部地区向东部地区流动的农民工为我国的经济发展做出了巨大的贡献。然而，随着经济发展，东部沿海地区劳动力成本日益上升，产业竞争力开始有所削弱。东部沿海地区的部分产业必须转移出来，而转移的方向就是中西部地区。这将引导一亿人在中西部地区就近城镇化[①]，这一过程必将导致中西部地区人口构成和语言环境的变化。过去，中西部相当一部分青壮年劳动力以东南沿海地区作为就业目标社区；如今，就业目标社区的转变将对中西部劳动者已经习得并熟练掌握的语言能力提出新的挑战。应对这些挑战，需要出台相应的语言教育政策，未雨绸缪地支持和帮助中西部学生学习适应本地城镇化所需的语言能力。

当前中国与周边国家外交形势。巩固发展与周边国家的睦邻关系是我国周边外交的一贯方针。加强与邻国的跨境贸易、人文交流是贯彻这一方针的有效手段。这些都需要相应的语言人才。不论是从文化渊源，还是从人员交流等方面看，中西部都具有相对优越的培养跨境语言人才的条件，可以事半功倍地为国家培养大量掌握跨境语言的双语人才，以面对周边外交、贸易和民间交流中日益增加的需求。"跨境语言"是指同时分布在我国及其邻国的语言。我国的跨境语言有30余种，其中大部分是聚集在中西部地区的少数民族语言，包括蒙古、藏、维吾尔、苗、彝、壮、布依、瑶、哈尼、哈萨克、傣、傈僳、佤、拉祜、景颇、柯尔克孜、布朗、塔吉克、怒、乌兹别克、俄罗斯、鄂温克、德昂、京、塔塔尔、独龙、门巴、珞巴等[②]。而且，从地区发展的需求来看，开展这些语言的教育，将改善有关地区的就业条件，有利于特色性地区经济的发展。

面对由当前形势所带来的多重挑战，我国现行的语言教育并不能够行之有效地应对。我国语言教育方面存在的问题包括：

一、现行的语言教育忽略了语言学习的一些客观规律，没有根据不同地区的情况和条件来制定语言教育规划，导致一定程度的教育资源的浪费，加剧了教育不公平和社会不平等的现象，这些问题在中西部地区尤其严重。

二、当前的外语教育已不能完全适应新形势下国家经济社会发展的需要，不能及时提供急需和特需的外语人才，这种情况在中西部地区尤其显著。

面对上述问题，我们应该用科学的语言观去指导中西部地区的语言教育规划。针对中西部母语为汉语的学生，需要规划第二语言的选择，同时解决怎样提高第二语言学习效率的问题。

三 语言习得理论和科学的语言观

我国外语教育事业自改革开放以来蓬勃发展,为国家的经济建设和国际交流做出了重要贡献;但是,随着社会经济形势的发展,现有的外语教育政策已经不适应当前发展的需要,亟需改革。学界已有的呼声包括改变目前"以英语代外语"的倾向,增加多语种的外语教育等意见;但是目前尚未见新的支持多样化第二语言教育的政策出台。

开展有效的第二语言教育需要遵循两条语言习得的原则:社会环境支持的原则和与本族讲话人互动的原则。符合语言学习规律的原则是"学以致用",语言能力的获得来源于丰富的社会实践,任何脱离社会实践的语言教学都难以奏效。如果学生在课堂之外无法观察到实际的语言使用、无法接收到真实性语言输入,将导致事倍功半的学习效果。

在我国中西部的大部分地区,相较于经济较为发达的东部地区,广大英语学习者与英语母语人直接互动的机会十分有限,所以很难获得真正的语言交际能力。包括众多少数民族地区在内的中西部地区的传统文化也与英语母语国家的文化差距较大,缺乏文化认同成为进一步拖累外语学习的不利因素。

相反,中西部地区具有良好的学习我国多个少数民族语言的社会环境和文化环境,以及与这些语言的本族讲话人互动、方便学以致用的语言学习条件。不去学习和掌握这些语言,而学习那些没有直接应用价值、缺乏文化兼容性的而且难以成功掌握的语言,可谓"舍近求远"、"本末倒置"了。

基于语言习得的规律,我们认为,我国中西部的语言教育政策、双语教育、三语教育政策需要作出调整,应该大幅度减少英语的教学,增加、扩充作为第二语言的少数民族语言和周边国家语言的教学,增加普通教育和高考语言的语种。而且,从体现民族地区自治法的视角看,有必要进一步提高少数民族语言的社会地位。然而,少数民族语言地位的提高直接受制于其作为教学、考试科目和以此作为第二语言学习的学生人数的影响。

接受多样化的第二语言教育的政策建议,需要克服以下几个观念的影响:

一、文化相对论,认为少数民族语言是与落后的文化相连接,不适应现代化经济社会发展的需要。从语言科学的角度,文化相对论已受到足够的批判,学界目前认为语言与文化是动态互动的关系,各民族语言不仅承载了部分独特的传统文化,也具有无限的适应新经济文化模式的潜力。因此,各民族语言文化的发展是相辅相成的,脱离文化单纯地发展语言,脱离语言发展文化都将产生困难。作为第二语言学习者的大批汉族学生进入民族语言的交流社区,会带来促进文化交流、文化交融和文化发展的作用。对于文化创意、科技创新、转变经济发展方式将产生积极的推动作用。

二、语言学习无局限论。语言教育的成功依赖于一定的客观条件,是一种高成本的投入。目前的外语教育,缺乏实践的检验,在知识爆炸、专业技能日益深化的时代,把宝贵的教育资源和有限的学习时间浪费在无效率或低效率的外语教育上,是一个错误的选择。除了充分发展母语教育之外,儿童和成人最需要的就是对本社区流通的第二语言的应用能力。语言资源既是文化资源,也是社会资源和经济资源。从国家利益的视角,我们应该尽可能地继承和发展原有的言语社区,利用传统语言的认同和沟通作用,全面开发语言资源,使之产生政治经济的正效益。中西部地区丰富多样的语言资源,是我国人力资源的重要组成部分,有待于进一步开发利用。由于语言学习是一个实践过程,错误的目标语言的选择,会导致脱离实践的学习,是对教育资源和人力资源的浪费。脱离实际的多语言的学习目标不可能实现,是因为学习者的学习时间和实践机会有限,三语四语的同时学习会出现顾此失彼或一事无成的结果。世界上目前已经实现的三语或多语能力,都是不同程度的社区语言的反映,而非像大部分中西部地区现有的英语教育这样外语教育模式的成果。

三、语言屏障论。将语言隔阂作为切断信息传递的手段,自古有之并影响至今。但是,在全球化带来的便捷的交通条件和信息时代提供的发达的网络通讯条件下,语言隔阂阻碍信息传递的作用日益减弱并终将失效。目前,如果不发展多语言的信息传输通道,国内外多个言语社区的成员会进一步依赖英语作为信息手段、依赖英语国家的信息源,不利于构建和谐的信息化社会,实现社会的公正和公平。英语作为世界上最流通的语言,目前还远没有成为世界上大多数人口掌握的语言,目前改变英语独霸信息世界,就像改变美元统治国际金融界一样,还为时未晚。

四、语言削减论。该观点认为人类语言在趋向统一,未来的世界将是一个语言统一的世界。由于各国大力推广强势语言,也由于强势语言借力西方现代化的经济模式,当前的世界确实呈现少语化的发展趋势,但是这不是一个可持续发展的模式,该趋势也会尽快出现逆转。联合国教科文组织和各国的语言学者都指出,语言多样性与文化多样性是相辅相成的,人类的未来是一个文化多样化、多种文化相互促进的可持续发展的未来。至少,对于我国中西部地区的发展来说,地区语言、跨境语言、周边语言的多语言信息化发展还是很不够的。语言多样性与发展的关系是在保障语言人权,克服语言隔

阂的前提下,通过促进沟通和信息化的条件下实现的。促进不同母语群体间的沟通,不应该是仅仅依赖强制少数群体花费大量的时间和精力来学习语言,通过放弃自己的语言文化传统,这样一种方式来实现。还可以通过各民族之间相互学习彼此的语言,通过发展语言科技、语言产业、语言服务来实现。而且,语言科技、语言服务和语言产业带来语言经济,成为新的经济增长点,不但不会拉经济发展的后腿,还会成为经济发展的推动力。

四 预期效果

学界已经指出,中国作为世界上英语学习的第一大国,产生了维护英语的国际霸权的地位的间接作用,对于各国人民争取国际话语权,发展多极化的国际社会是一个不利因素。从我国中西部地区的那些英语学习效果欠佳,英语应用机会较少的地区开始减少英语教育的投入,转而把稀缺的教育资源投入到跨境语言和周边国家语言的教育中去,具有一举两得的效益。从国际范围,体现了中国作为支持联合国语言多样性主张的示范作用。从国家利益的角度,有利于地区安全、地区合作和全方位的国际贸易的发展。

发展国内少数民族语言的教育,特别是作为第二语言的教育,有力地体现了民族平等、民族团结的政策,将促进民族地区的和谐稳定,地区经济贸易的发展,以及作为中华民族文化的组成部分的地区文化的发展和繁荣。特别是,如果把国内民族语言提高到超越英语等外语的地位,对于增强包括我国各族人民的文化自信心会产生强有力的作用。

"在我国中西部地区首先开展多样化的第二语言教育"的建议,针对目前国际形势的变化,结合我国中西部地区语言教育的发

展现状,应对我国经济社会和谐稳定发展的迫切需求,提出缩减无效率和低效率的英语教育,增加我国少数民族语言作为第二语言的教育,同时增加我国周边国家的语言作为语言教学科目,并且在普通教育和高等教育中增加对这些语言的教学投入,逐步将这些学习难度小、实践机会多、应用机会多、更有利于社会和谐及经济发展的语言科目替代英语作为高考科目,将收到促进中西部地区大开发、教育平等、社会和谐及经济发展等多重效益。

附　注

① http://news.xinhuanet.com/house/bj/2014 – 06 – 26/c
_1111320369.htm

② http://yywz.snnu.edu.cn/show.aspx? id = 1148&cid
= 24

作者简介

　　徐大明,博士,澳门大学教授,博士生导师,主要研究方向为社会语言学、语言规划学等;张璟玮,博士,南京大学文学院助理研究员,主要研究方向为社会语言学、语音学等。

A Suggestion on Diversifying Second Language Education First in Central and Western China

Xu Daming,Zhang Jingwei

The China Centre for Linguistic and Strategic Studies

Abstract: Based on the research results on language acquisition, this study analyzes the problems existing in language education in central and western China. The problems are low-efficiency and ineffective English learnings in bilingual and trilingual educations. Accordingly, it suggests to downscale the teaching of English in general education and to upscale the education of minority languages and the languages spoken in the neighboring countries of China. It also suggests to increase the number of languages taught in schools and to include more of them as subjects in the National College Entrance Examination in order to foster language talents who meet the urgent needs of current development.

Key words: second language education, language acquisition, minority language

汉语战略和汉字改革刍论

史有为

提 要：从语言学习、使用角度看，语言可以按功能分为文化语言、实务语言、生活语言。汉语为达到世界性文化语言的战略目标，必须提高自身文化、科技、经济、军事的实际水平。汉语的国内战略目标则是统一语言与文字，服务于国家统一。为此必须反思汉字改革与汉字战略。目前阶段在面对某些重大语言问题上宜乎"以退为进，步步为营"。

关键词：汉语战略　文化语言　汉字战略　汉字改革　认同

一　引言

完整的战略设计应该由两部分构成：战略目标与战略路径。在推行战略的过程中还将对应不同需要或条件设计并区分若干战略分期，以利推进。战略目标决定战略路径；战略路径与战略分期保证战略目标的达成。某目标事物的战略可能还与上位事物或相关事物的战略有关，这就有了更宏观的大战略观念。战略又是与该战略适用事物的性质、状况、环境密切相关。为此，本文先从语言、文字本身作些必要交代，然后分别切入主题。

二　语言的应用性分类

（一）语言的分类

语言可以从语言自身角度分类，比如从形式特质分成屈折语、黏着语、孤立语，从结构特性分成话题凸显语言、主语凸显语言，或 SVO 语、SOV 语，等等。但对于语言战略来说，更重要的是从应用或社会角度的分类。因为语言的本质属性是社会应用。认清语言的应用或社会的类别，对认识并制定语言战略具有重要的意义。自觉认清本语言所处类别，也将使领导者获得自由与

目标。

（二）语言的用域分类

习惯上人们喜欢以语言的分布地域或应用地域来分类，这样的分类可以简称为"语言用域分类"。语言用域的大小是相对的。我们可以从国家角度看，也可以从世界角度看。从后者看，语言用域角度分类的语言（简称"用域语言"）可以分成四种，其上位语言的用域一般可以包容下位语言的用域，反之则一般不能。

1. 世界性语言。世界上所有人、所有国家使用并通行的语言即世界语言。世界语言是程度最高的世界性语言。到目前为止，人类尚未形成或出现世界语言。最接近的是英语，但也仅止于"准"世界语言。英语离为所有人都接受的世界语言还有很长的一段距离。

2. 国际性语言。一种语言为多个国家通行并承认为公用语言者即国际语言。英语、汉语、法语、阿拉伯语、西班牙语、俄语都是国际语言。但国际语言中仍有功能等级，现在英语已经无可争议地成为最具优势的国际语言。实际上，国际性也分大小，也可用"区域性语言"来表达。例如阿拉伯语仅限于阿拉伯诸国范围，只是该区域的国际

语言。

3. 全国性语言。在一个国家中全国通行、通用并作为官方语言的语言即为国家语言。国家语言在日本和中国通常也称之为"国语"。日本所称的"国语"即以东京语音为标准音的日本语。中国早年所称的"国语"已经缩窄使用，仅通行于台湾地区，大致相当于今日之汉语普通话。民国时制订的老"国语"较为含混，更重视与中古音对应；今日之普通话则定义明晰，更贴近实际北京口语。如"期"，台湾"国语"读第二声，大陆普通话则读第一声。

4. 地方性语言。在一个多民族国家中，限于某地方某民族的全民族语言，也只是地方语言，例如中国云南白族的白语、四川阿坝州羌族的羌语。如果把语言扩大到方言，那么绝大多数方言都是地方性语言。像上海话、广府话、闽南语虽然影响很大，但也只是地方语言。

在一个地域范围内人们普遍所使用的语言才能分类为不同用域语言。如果跳出此前提，还可以有 种"社会阶层"语言，仅在非常局限的某种社会圈子中使用，例如黑话，但它们只是某种语言或方言的有限变异，还谈不上独立的语言，甚至也谈不上地方语言。

（三）语言的社会功能分类

语言可以从语言社会功能角度分为三种类别：

1. 文化语言。用于高端文化活动的语言。如科学研究使用的语言，阐述科技与哲学使用的语言，高端文化交流时使用的语言，其中也包括宣讲宗教经典时使用的语言。在一定场合下，文化语言相当于有人所称的"上游语言"。

2. 实务语言。用于处理实际事务的语言，如商贸、军事、旅游中分别使用的语言。最典型的是上海开埠之时出现的"洋泾浜英语"，仅用于商业实务。两国民间贸易时也常常将对方的语言作为实务语言。它们常常是急就篇式学习的目标，语汇有限，语法也有限，很难用于更高的科学文化领域。"二战"前日本曾针对二语学习，广泛使用"实务语言"一词。笔者受此启发，应用于此。

3. 生活语言。用于处理日常生活的语言。家庭生活中使用的语言，乡亲间日常交谈所用的语言，都属于此类。它们是所有其他功能语言的基础。

实务语言的功能级别高于生活语言；而文化语言的功能级别又高于实务语言。一种语言只有居于文化语言才能保证被更多人使用，保证用于更长时期、更广地域。

语言社会功能的评价是相对的。从不同地域、不同时期观察同一种语言，甚至从不同主观态度去处理，常常会有不同的社会功能评价。因此，须要慎重，须要尽量保持客观。更合适的评价应该是功能结合用域的综合性类别。出于语言战略，则必须从世界角度去考虑这种评价。比如门巴语在本民族中会既是生活语言、实务语言，也是文化语言，但对西藏甚至中国而言，这种语言在现代甚至连实务语言也很难算上，更别说世界了。从世界角度看，最高等级的是世界性文化语言。这种文化语言需要有该语言所在国家或区域的文化实力支持。文化实力即在该时期占据相对高的自然科学技术水平、哲学和社会科学水平、相对高的文化生活水平，相对高的民众文化素质。另外还可以有军事力量与人口体量作为文化实力的另一种支持。没有国家的文化实力，该国的语言是不能为世界其他国家认可为文化语言的，即使可以，也无法长久维持。高端的文化语言需要获得更多话语权的支持。因为使用该语言的人有了创造或创新，该语言就成为该创造的权威阐释语言。创造创新越多,该语言被世人追求的程度才能更高。英语、德语、法语都曾占据世界性文化语言的地位,它们都是靠着英、美、德、法在科学、技术、文化等各方面创新与领先的支持得以维持的。失去文化领先就意味着失去文化语言的地位,也就会使国家地位掉落下去。

这些功能类别是语言在交际活动中表现出来的,是在实践中由世界各国民众认定的,而不是纯粹人为规定的。因此,只有从社会功能结合用域来观察的语言类别才最有意义。

当然,语言也有以某种权力机构作人为的功能规定,比如政府或学校可以做出某种决定,硬性指定某一语言具有某种功能。比较常用的有:通用语、官方语言、工作语言、教学语言(或教学媒介语)。为了政府或多国组织工作方便,有时还可以在多种官方语言或多国官方语言中再指定一种"行政语言"(如新加坡指定英语为行政语言①)。这些也都是应用范畴的类别。

除此之外,还可以有一种非功能性的素质教育标准,从现代公民应该具有某种文化教养的角度去确定"教养语言"。现代社会人,现代受教育者,应该接受一种或几种外语的教育,这些外语并不一定要求能说能写,具有该语言的基本训练与知识即可。这就是一种最低外语修养,以便为今后进一步提升打基础。这也如同人们在中学接受数学、物理学教育一样,作为人的应有素质而规定。教养语言中的外语未来可以是生活语言、实务语言,也可以是文化语言。

(四)文字跟随语言

没有完全独立于语言的文字。一般认为,文字是语言的书面承载形式。但一旦文字符号产生,便会因需要多样、因时间或地域的差别,而产生具有一定独立性的书面语言。尤其是汉字,可以产生在相当程度上远离当前口语的书面语言。几百年来通行的文言文,便是一个例子。一旦形成成熟的书面语,它就是口语之外的另一种需要另行学习的语言。以此看来,《淮南子·本经训》所言"昔者仓颉作书而天雨粟,鬼夜哭",也可以理解为对文字影响语言与生活的某种预言。生活语言和实务语言常常可以不需要文字。在现代社会条件下,文化语言一般来说必须有文字作为重要支撑。因此,文字是文化语言的必要条件。从用域角度看,国际语言,世界语言,也必须有文字作为重要的支撑。可见文字是重要级别的用域语言的必要条件。文字的优劣对语言的地位会产生一定影响,但并非决定性影响。决定某文字能否成为更大世界所接受的文字,其决定因素在于语言的地位,实际上是其背后的文化地位与国家实力。因此,结合用域的语言社会功能才是最重要的,是语言战略、文字战略的决定性因素。

由于汉字与当前口语的特殊关系,与厚重的历史文化的特殊关系,我们又不能仅仅根据口语这一个维度去决定汉字的走向,去决定汉字的战略。在一般性之外,我们还必须照顾特殊性,而不要照搬西方的经验。

三 汉语地位的简略回顾与反思

(一)所谓语言战略

战略是一项长期而全局性的策略。语言战略是一个民族对语言未来较长时期走向的自觉认识与自觉规划。语言是条不知疲倦的长河,在长河的任何一个重要区段,由于环境与条件在质方面的大不同,对语言的战略考虑可能会有所改变。语言战略又是国家地位、国家整体战略的一种平行反应。语言战略必须服从并服务于该国家的大战略。有无语言战略的自觉将会对语言战略的高下有着重要的甚至决定性的影响。

语言战略应有国内与国外两个方向。

处理好国内与国际的语言关系以及语言应用、语言教育，都应属战略视野之内。"打铁还需自身硬"，没有国内的强壮体质，没有对内的良好"语言养护"②是建构不起强壮而有效的对外政策的。本文侧重论述面向国际的战略。

文字从属于语言，又在更高的高度上体现并提升了语言。因此，文字战略实质上是语言战略的一部分，在一定情况下可以体现语言战略。文字战略从属于语言战略，但又可能区别于后者。文字的特殊性使我们仍须视不同文字状况而另行考察、制定文字战略。

(二)书同文：秦定大局

在秦始皇时代，秦并六国，天下统一。此时，维持并巩固统一，是最高的战略考虑。在这样的大战略考虑下，秦始皇用强力消弭六国文字，实现"书同文"，实际上是以文字的统一来逼迫语言统一。先秦当时的六国语言可能只是若干大方言，然而，方言若缺少一种高于其上力量的约束，可能就会最终分裂为各自独立的语言。秦始皇时代，义字可能就是超越六国语言之上的约束力量。消弭了异体以及方言用字，实际上就逼迫方言区使用小篆所表示的语素与用词，客观上相当于语素与用词的统一，从而势必导向共同语化。相对于语言统一，文字统一是最经济、最容易达成的战略目标。除了文字体系的更换，一般来说，语言的变异远比文字来得快、来得大。世界上任何民族都不可能为不同方言创建不同文字。因为人们在心理上都明白，不同的文字会分裂一个民族，也会分裂一种语言。欧洲语言的分裂、印度语言的分裂不就是最好的样本吗？方言的分歧在任何时代都是一种自然存在，无法消除。统一文字不但是为了民族统一，也是最可能实现的行为，是人们最能接受的行为。因此，"书同文"无疑是中国首次明确而又以

文字切入的语言战略。由此，秦始皇（也许还应算上李斯）应该是中国历史上第一个伟大的语言战略家。自秦始皇一朝以降，直到清亡，中国再也没有出现过第二个这样重大的语言战略。各个朝代基本上是继承前代、任其自然，啃着始皇帝带来的统一汉字，啃着汉唐的文化遗产，让四方朝贡。此后的隶代篆、楷代隶，都是在秦小篆基础上的隶变与楷化，基本的统一基础未变。在此期间中国广狭不同的地域也曾经让契丹、女真、蒙语、满语 时占领过官方语言的地位。但由于秦汉隋唐所奠下的由汉字所创所记文化之厚重与先进，让这些统治民族不得不采用汉语文作为另一官方语文，并最后都拱手让位于汉语文。对于这些民族，采用汉语文作为第二官方语文，是一种无奈，也是一种统治策略，但无形中又成为打倒本民族语文的语言战略。如今，这些民族语只是在汉语中留下多多少少的借词/外来词作为来客的见证，而且他们在这些场语言竞争中遭到大大缩小或甚至完全泯灭的结局。因此，汉语文在中国甚至在周边国家的地位是由超过三千年的文明实践、文化科技创造所铸成的，也是由许多融入族群在与主体族群共同生存、共同发展中共同浇灌而成的。这显示了汉语文无可比拟的特质。

这些历史告诉我们：一种语文要站住脚，要长久生存下去，必须以先进的文化、经济、科技作为基础、作为依靠，而不是武力。

(三)汉语曾有的地位与危机

1. 汉语战略地位的下降

从远古至近代 17 世纪，地球实际上是分割成多个"世界"的，各个国家并未接连成一个世界。东亚是一个世界，以印度为中心是一个传说世界，以罗马为中心是另一个传说世界，阿拉伯与非洲则是更遥远的传说世界。中国在两千年历史中始终是东方这个"世界"中的最高文化科技拥有者，汉语也始

终是这个"世界"中的世界语言,是一种上游语言,被周边民族与国家学习、移用、借用,营养着他们。而另一些"世界"则是遥远的,被大自然或自然力隔绝的。只是借着传说和传闻,若隐若现,朦朦胧胧。它们所用的语言和汉语在功能上有什么不同,中国从不了解也不关心。中国对未知的外域一般都是被动型的,很少主动对外开拓与联络。从上古至近代,出名的有两次主动出访或开通③,一次是汉代张骞受派出使西域,一次是明代郑和七下西洋(1405—1433)。这两次都是以互通交好为宗旨,是和平的使者。在汉民族传统的主张中,没有主动侵犯或侵略的习惯。至于成吉思汗与忽必烈的南下西向的武力扩展,那时他们还不属于中国,中国在当时也是被侵占的一方。而近代西方则完全不同,他们是以主动的武力侵略扩展为习惯为守则的。荷兰、葡萄牙、西班牙、法国、英国、美国等以及后来者日本,循着海盗的习惯,四处侵略。它们借助 15 世纪哥伦布发现新大陆的刺激,16 世纪开始西方列强分别入侵印度次大陆、马来亚半岛、印尼和菲律宾,侵占我国的澳门,并于 17 世纪侵占我国的台湾,18—19 世纪全面侵占并瓜分东南亚各国。直到 1840 年鸦片战争,彻底打开中国的大门,再次迫使清廷割让香港、九龙。从此,世界完全终止了被自然力的隔绝,而在武力下开始被迫联接成一片;从此,中国也翻开了屈辱的新一页。只有在此时,人们才开始有语言功能的世界性比较,才感觉到中国的衰落以及汉语所处的"世界性"地位的下降,几乎被降为一种下游语言,人们也才真切地感受到威胁和危机。

2. 汉语曾经的危机

中国在古代曾有过几次局域性或全国性的非汉族政权,并由此产生过对汉语的一定威胁。但古代少数民族语文化与汉语文化的高下差距,使少数民族统治者不得不仍

然维持汉语原有的地位。威胁并未真正成为实际危机。真正的危机开始于 1840 年鸦片战争的外国侵略。威胁首先是由传教士的"异教"、"异说"带来的,然后是西方语文书写的先进科技文化。这些威胁引起当时有识之士如李鸿章、张之洞、康有为、梁启超、谭嗣同等的反思,并做出不同的积极反应,包括派遣留学考察、维新政改、实业洋务、中西体用之辩,等等。然而这又引起对中国传统文化以及它的载体汉语文的怀疑和不自信,生出日后对西方的迷信或崇拜。

另一个真正的威胁来自日本。1895 年4 月 17 日甲午海战失败,签订屈辱的《马关条约》,从此中国的台湾落入日本侵略者之手,台湾同胞开始了被逐渐"皇民化"的过程,日语文在相当一部分台湾人(尤其是高山族)那里成为第一交际语言。而这个威胁随着日本侵略中国东北以及大陆其他地区,越来越加重加深。从 1932 年假惺惺成立伪满洲国④开始,短短的几年间,日语成为必学语言,许多汉族和朝鲜族几乎以日语当作工作语言和生活语言,并生出了洋泾浜式的"协和语"这样的怪胎。汉语空间的被挤压、被夺去是真真切切的。

这些威胁与危机让人们觉察到,如果没有军事、经济、科技实力,国家都保不住,更何况祖先赐予自己的语言文字。因此,保卫语言文字,首先就要强壮国家或民族的综合实力,然后才谈得上强壮语言文字。否则,汉语就可能永远落入仅限于中国范围的境地,至多具有小范围的国际性。

四 当前中国需要的汉语战略

(一)语言"软实力"与国家/民族的"硬实力"

一个国家的"国力"不但包含经济实力、军事实力和科技文化实力,而且应当包括语言实力。语言实力就是语言承载文化、承载应用后所具有的竞争力。相对于作为硬实

力的经济、军事实力,语言实力,包括文字,同科技文化实力相似,是一种软实力。一个国家或民族的语言实力越强,该国家或该民族就越会获得更多的尊重与影响。它们与国家的硬实力互为支撑。当然这个国家可以采用本国的一种民族语作为语言实力的体现者或承载者,也可以借用他国语言作为本国的软实力体现者。这里的选择或决定也是语言战略的一部分。例如,中国以汉族的汉语作为国家代表语言,也即作为中国的软实力体现者;印度则以英语作为国家的官方语言,也即作为印度软实力的体现者。虽然印度借助英语获得了不少语言红利,但从语言的根基看,则因为是非本国民族的,非母语的,无根或少根的,基础土壤相对松软浅薄,应用覆盖必然有大的空缺,也会相当依赖英美他国的语言发展。尤其是,这样的英语是断了文化传承的"他"语言,本民族将无法享受英语原有的许多历史文化底蕴,无法具有因此而生的微妙语感,也就无法与英美国家的英语完全等同⑤。因此,从长远看,印度这一有利不一定能超过他国而有决定性的利好。而中国的汉语植根于本国民族,根基扎实,又由于普通话的推广,已使汉语几乎覆盖所有国民,因此会有更宽广的自身语言发展。请看秦始皇"书同文"三字决策所带来的两千多年的语言红利,让汉语可以一往直前创造由它构筑的文化,并以此广阔的应用幅度与深厚文化底蕴成为联合国的正式工作语言之一。我们应对汉语软实力在未来的发展有充分的自信心。

(二)汉语战略之设立

1.现代中国汉语战略反思

现代的中国汉语战略从未以"战略"之名明确制定过。接近于此的应该是1955年10月"现代汉语规范问题学术会议"所确定的三项任务:促进汉字改革,推广普通话,实现汉语规范化。这的确是一次制定语文战略的会议。也许当时还没有明确或没有意识到:这三项任务就是那一时期的语言战略的体现。我们看到这三大任务至今60年后的效果:全国基本上推广了以北京语音为特征的普通话,使用普通话在所有的地区几乎都无所阻碍;现代汉语所有的应用文体都采用了白话文;全国都使用着汉语拼音方案作为注音、检索、输入工具,甚至局部作为准记录或表达的工具;汉字的形、音、序、量都有了规范,全国(除港澳台地区外)都使用简化字,只是简化仍存在问题。应该说,这些任务总体上取得了巨大的成果,对国家发展和民族复兴确实起到了推动作用。可惜,这次会议局限于"规范化",局限于大陆,又未明确涉及中国未来在世界上可能的地位,而略显不足。但这也难怪,因为会议授权范围如此。汉字改革与语文战略的实施应当学术主导,综合考虑国家统一和国家战略的大局。

2.今日汉语战略目标:文化语言高度的世界性语言

语言战略并不仅仅涉及语言,而是一项社会综合工程,涉及文化、科学、经济、政治,甚至军力。中国经历了一百多年的被侵略、被污辱,今天刚刚站立了起来,面对世界,为了实现中国复兴之梦。在这一关键时期,我们必须冷静估量自己与世界的距离,估计多个方面的距离。

二百年的落后,四十年的引进与学习,其中又是八年的抗击日寇,四年的解放战争;而后三十年的被封闭与被禁运,中间又被剥夺了十年,经历了被"文革"自我摧残与自我封闭。这一路,我们虽然从欧美与苏联学得了一些当时先进的科技,但到20世纪末,这些科技早已落后。我们虽然从日本侵略者手里夺回了主权,中文也成为联合国六种工作语言之一,但汉语仍只是全国性或有限国际性的文化语言,从世界角度看汉语仍不能算是一种引领世界的文化语言。中国在世界上还只有很少的话语权/话事权，承担这种权力的汉语当然也不可能有太大影响。我们必须清醒地估计自己、估计汉语。

但是，我们又必须自觉认识到：作为一个有 13 多亿人口的世界大国，有着近五千年文明历史的民族，有着深厚文化积淀而且至今从未断流的汉语，必须树立这样的战略目标：随着中国的全面复兴并和平崛起成为真正的世界大国，汉语应该依托大战略，成为世界性的文化语言。这应是"中国梦"的必有之意。中国还应当清醒并理智，应当秉持如此理念：汉语必须复兴，必须成为世界性文化语言"之一"，但绝非"唯一"。中国不排斥另一个或另几个世界性文化语言的存在。汉语应当谦恭与谨慎，决不能自我陶醉，汉语决不要也决不能称霸。中国应当倡导"和谐竞赛"理念，让汉语与其他世界性文化语言共同为世界服务。这应该是汉语战略中非常重要的内容。

在国内，我们还必须在提升并推广汉语的同时，不以挤压兄弟民族语言为代价。让他们保持并发展，让语言在不同层面和谐运行。让汉语与兄弟民族语作为不同层面的身份发挥认同作用。它们将以中国人与民族两种身份认同，维护语言和谐与语言包容的传统。这也应该是汉语战略中不可或缺的一项。

3. 汉语战略路径：以退为进，步步为营

我们必须冷静地承认汉语在目前世界上的现实地位。为了达到本世纪内的战略目标，我们宜采取"以退为进，步步为营"为核心的战略路径。"文革"以后，我们不得不为以前的政策失误、机会丧失以及长期落后付出代价。近四十年的改革与开放，我们谦恭而饥渴地学习并引进一切先进文化，我们不得不"以退为进"，让出时间学习西方语言，鼓励出国留学，不惜导致国内汉语文水平下降，任由许多人才流向国外⑥，让他们的工作语言从汉语改换为西语，与世界对接。但是，这样的退让，却也换来了此后可贵的"海归"，换来了科技水平与国力的快速提升。这样的退是为了进，是退一步进两步甚至进更多步。虽然，我们没有明文写下明确的汉语政策，但这种做法实际上已经成为一种语言战略步骤。

抗日战争时期，在敌强我弱的态势下，我们以空间换时间，终于以持久战战胜了日本侵略者。如今，在中外落后与先进明显对比的状态下，我们以局部语言的退让换取第二语言西语水平的提高，以暂时的语言让步换取文化科技全面跃进，这显然是明智的。今天，我们国家的科技已经有了很大的进步，已经开始部分跻身于世界先进，但必须清醒地认识到：我们在总体上与欧美的水平仍然有相当距离；我们在国际组织中担任领导职务还仅仅是凤毛麟角；我们的话语权还很小，还远远不够。我们必须继续改革开放。同样，先前有效的语言政策也仍应继续，并且应该加以明确化，以使全国民众自觉行动。在保持汉语教育优先、有效的前提下，让出必要的教育资源，在合适的年龄段学习"可交际"的第二语言西语⑦，培养可以在国际上直接对话的人才，以便在适当时候可以在国际上担负更多的领导职务，具有更大的发言权和影响力。也许在这一过程中，我们会流失一些人才，但随着国力的增强、国内软环境的改善，人才的回归是可以预期的。实践是检验真理的唯一标准，近四十年实践已经证明这一战略的正确性。

同时，我们应该在策略或战术层面加以自觉改进。例如，利用有限的教学资源最有效地达到汉语和外语学习目标，让语言不但成为交际要件，也成为自我人文的表征，让每一步都走得扎扎实实，更有效率。又如，鼓励选用音译或意译形式甚至字母缩略词引进外来概念与术语。术语是社会进步、科技进步的抓手与关键，也是与国际对接的要件。语言战略依靠的是文化科学技术。随着我们国力和科技文化的提升，我们也会相应调整政策对不同语言方向的用力程度。例如在汉语文教学与规范方面须要坚持"语言养护"，提升文化层次，加强传统诗文的教学，提升全民的文化素养，阻止汉语的粗鄙化与娱乐化，保卫汉语的文化体质。一个粗鄙的语言、粗鄙的民族是不会吸引世界的。又如在外语教学方面应以口语交际为基础，并在一定阶段加强实用写作，以培养与国际直接交际的能力。这就是"步步为营"。

当然，这前提应该是"以我为主"，其结果则是并无排他性的"兼容竞用"。而后者也意味着我们最终的目标：让汉语成为世界性的文化语言，与其他文化语言（例如英语、德语、法语、俄语）在世界舞台上竞演、竞赛、竞用，齐头并进，以造福人类。"以我为主，以退为进，步步为营，兼容竞用"，应该是当今中国在相当长的时期内应有的汉语战略路径。

4. 关心国外汉语与汉语祖籍语教育

今天，汉语已经走出中国，以"孔子学院"名义，在世界几十处栽种浇灌，我们期待未来开花结果。让汉语走向世界，让世界了解并学习汉语，这显然是汉语战略的一部分。但这种走出去，必须在国家"韬光养晦，有所作为"的大战略下相对平行地推进，谦恭谨慎而持之以恒地进取，不能急功近利，不能只求数量，不能借汉语的名义简单输出中国文化。文化的学习应该是完全自愿的。而且，孔子学院教学的一个重点应该是培养当地（外籍）教师。没有他们，汉语的传播是很有限的。

此外，汉语战略还有另一个重要方面，即服务于华裔子女，让中华后裔即使散播于世界各地也可以得到汉语母语/祖籍语教育。因为语言是身份认同、民族认同的重要条件。今天，远在海外的华侨华人已经高达几千万，许多海外华人到了第二、第三代，他们孩子的母语就可能被所在国的语言所替代，从而丧失对祖国/母国、对民族的认同。笔者在日本见到太多，深切感受其痛。在日本大体上只有台湾地区办的华文学校而无大陆举办的中文中小学，实在遗憾。而相对照的是日本，日本人到任何国家去从商就职，他们背后都有日本办的日语学校跟随而至。他们没有为下一代母语教育操心的后顾之忧，他们也不因说日语而感到不好意思。因此，尽最大可能让海外子弟享受汉语作为母语或祖籍语的教育，让他们永远不忘祖国/母国，永远享受汉语文化的好处，要让所有中华血脉都以汉语为母语/祖籍语而自豪。从任何一个角度看，海外汉语母语/祖籍语教育举措的意义和价值都不会比孔子学院更小。而这样的关心对于海外子弟来说更是一剂温馨的慰心、归心之良药，其价值更非孔子学院可比。

我们需要冷静地认识到，无论从国外汉语教学还是国内的二语汉语教学，我们的教学模式以及所依据的理论都还有许多可以提升之处；尤其是服务于二语汉语教学语法。这都需要我们努力探索并创新。

五　文字改革的回顾与反思

（一）中国及周边国家文字改革的回顾

19 世纪晚期到 20 世纪上半叶，中国周边在西方影响下出现一股西式拼音化尤其是拉丁化的思潮。这些国家都不同程度地掀起了文字改革运动。它们各有特色，也各有背景，一般都是尝试将民族的老文字拉丁化。较早有越南文的拉丁化[⑥]，土耳其文、马来文、印尼文的拉丁化[⑥]，还有曾经想拉丁化而没能实行的日文，甚至苏联都曾想实施俄文和其境内少数民族文字的拉丁化。在苏联的自私计谋下,蒙古(即前外蒙古)不但被分裂出中国,而且曾想跟在苏联后面实行拉丁化,却最后跟在俄文后面把自上而下的回鹘体文字搞成了西里尔字母(斯拉夫字母)化⑩。个别的还曾有拉丁字母式的线性化(如朝鲜谚文拆成字母按线性排列)的尝试。这些都很值得我们回忆并咀嚼。

19—20世纪汉字文化圈国家的文字改革其核心内容就是要废止汉字⑪。而"二战"后汉字政策的变革又造成各国的国语(标准语)改革,其中尤以日本国语改革和言文一致运动对中国的影响为最大⑫。汉字系统因为谐声(声旁)系统以及语素对应音与本民族语大相径庭而产生较大冲突,导致了越、朝、日等国"去汉字"的拼音化运动。阿拉伯字母由于表音系统不完善,不能表示元音,自右而左不符合现代科学技术的表述,加之阿拉伯字母带有严重的宗教倾向,而受到加意关注。回鹘体字母,自上而下的书写,以及复杂的表示法,难以掌握,又与现代科技表示有一定的矛盾,因而才产生改革的需求与冲动。

中国更是如此,中国的拼音化是接触西方语文以后的产物,是西方传教士在中国制定多种方言拉丁字的传染,是在鸦片战争之后的一种反应,实际进入拉丁化操作是在苏联的影响下开始的,而当时苏联本身出现的拉丁化更是受西方的影响。没有外部影响,中国很难自源地生出拼音浪潮。而且在这股初始的潮流中,西方传教士和外交官始终处于主角位置。而日本的语文运动也在近处影响着中国,为中国所借鉴。

这些改革从现代科技角度看都是可以理解的,表面上确实是一种进步,有利于书写或从事现代科技;但另一方面,从政治-文化力量的起落进退看,又几乎都是在西方思想(科技、宗教)、西方势力(包括美国和苏联)影响下发生并形成,是对民族文化的某

种打击或掩盖,也是该民族失去对传统文化信心的一种表现。因此,如今看来,亚洲所有的文字改革都有西方因素的影子,亚洲的文字改革浪潮不过是西方思想在东方的推广,其中绝不会没有西方利益的考虑。列宁说过,"采用罗马字也是东洋民族的民主主义革命的一部分"⑬。这道出了亚洲文改的深层根由。我们并不反对文字改革,也不反对文字"革命",但需要认识它们的背景,需要细细反思,才能得出正确全面的评价。

(二)中国汉字改革反思

1. 现代中国文字改革梳理

汉字要不要根本改革,关键在于汉字本身能否适应汉语,是否适应时代与人民的需要。经过这些年对过往事实的揭示与讨论,许多情况已经比较清楚,可以作如下梳理:

五四波澜。20世纪的中国文改浪潮实际上是五四新文化运动的一部分及其余波。从提倡白话文到改革汉字,是一项很自然的发展。提倡科学、废除文言文的同时,当然也就会喊出"废除汉字"。当时以及以后很长时间,"废除汉字"一直是文改运动的灵魂与理想。这个运动席卷了当时不分政治理念的许多青年学人。他们血气方刚,热血冲动,又未经周严思虑,他们的许多激进言辞大都是在这种状况下产生的⑭。现在大家都承认,五四运动有其两面性,或有两个侧面,除了科学、民主、新文化的一面,还有违反科学的一面,对民族文化盲目否定、丧失信心的一面。而革命家孙中山(1917—1919)则比较冷静,他指出:"盖一民族之进化,至能有文字,良非易事;而其文字之势力,能旁及邻国,吸收而同化之。所以五千年前,不过黄河流域之小区,今乃进展成兹世界无两之巨国。虽以积弱,屡遭异族吞灭,而侵入之族不特不能同化中华民族,反为中国所同化,则文字之功为伟矣。虽今日新学之士,间有偶废中国文字之议,而以作者观之,则

中国文字决不当废也。"(35—38)

（2）"国罗"及其理念。赵元任等一批没有明显政治背景的文化力量于20世纪20年代拟制了"国语罗马字拼音法式"（即国语罗马字，简称"国罗"）。"国罗"实际上也以未来拼音化为最终目标。该方案采用复杂的字母标调，尽量区分音节，尽量以"字"（音节）为本，不完全放弃"字"的单位。从中可以窥见他们对汉语性质的看法。这是一项比较尊重并维护汉语特点的保守方案。

（3）"北拉"及其理念。在苏联的影响下，1928—1931年中国共产党人瞿秋白等在苏联时期设计了"中国文字拉丁化的原则和规则"（即以后的"北方话拉丁化新文字"，简称"北拉"）。它不标调，甚至不区分某些声韵母，强调分词连写，从中可以窥见其所依赖的语言理念：以"词"为本，而将"字"作为一种过时的单位予以放弃。这是彻底倒向西方语言文字的一种表现。这与"国罗"对汉语本质的理解有着极大的差别。

（4）拉丁化与共产党。抗日战争时期，共产党及其领导层始终支持拼音化，支持文字改革。例如：在中共中央和毛泽东的支持下，陕甘宁边区于1936年至1938年初、1940年至1943年春先后开展了两次"北拉"新文字扫盲运动。1940年12月25日，边区政府颁发了《关于推行新文字的决定》。又如：1941年5月15日，毛泽东为《新文字报》题词"切实推行，愈广愈好"。

（5）汉字简化与国民党。近代以来，诸多文人志士致力于汉字简化。如1935年钱玄同曾独力起草"简体字表"，共1300余字。国民党政府教育部也曾以钱玄同简化字表为基础选出324字，并于1935年8月21日公布，但因戴季陶等人强烈反对而停止推行。国民党败走台湾后，蒋介石曾于1952年再度提起汉字简化之议，又遭遇以胡秋原为代表的反对派强烈抵制，终于再次搁置。

此后，台湾当局编纂包含多个简化字形的《标准行书范本》来代替，以应教育与书写急需。

（6）新中国的汉字简化。新中国成立前后，毛泽东始终关注并主导文字改革，为此并发出过多次指示。比如，1951年春，毛泽东明确提出"文字必须改革，要走世界文字共同的拼音方向"。之后发现难度太大，短期内不可能实现拼音化，毛泽东又改变主意，强调"搞文字改革不要脱离实际"，应该"首先进行汉字的简化"。这里显然有不可明言的苦衷，简化可能只是一种应对干部文化水平低下的权宜救急之策⑮。1955年5月1日毛泽东又在书信上表示："汉字太繁难，目前只作简化改革，将来总有一天要作根本改革的。"明确将推行汉字简化作为过渡，再后来又指示应该草书楷化，并采用同音替代以压缩汉字数量。这样就使传统的字形简化范围扩大到数量简化。最后形成515个简化字和54个简化偏旁，类推扩展至2235字，在3500常用字中占比达三分之二，转变为大规模简化的性质。即使如此简化，汉字依然数量庞大，加之20世纪50年代绝大多数党政军干部已经过了学习语文的最佳期，致使工农兵干部用简化字扫盲这一目标无法如意达成。

（7）文改的三项任务及其程序性问题。文字改革三项任务实际上是一种文字战略的表达。三项任务的真实含义应该是拼音化的三个阶段：先简化汉字，作为文字拼音化的过渡；同时推广普通话，作为实现拼音文字的基础；最后，在此基础上推行汉语"拼音文字"方案。无论其中哪一项都是涉及全民族长远利益的大事，理应经过全国人大的审议，应该先行试点。但大规模简化的方针未经人大讨论，简化方案也并未经人大审议，而是采取行政命令方式发布，在全国铺开使用。

（8）汉字简化与政治。汉字简化是涉及全民族及其文化传承的大事，兼听则明，理应经过尽可能广泛的迫切性与可行性的科学论证，更应尽量广泛地征求多方面的意见。然而，当时却并未充分听取各种不同意见，尤其是文化界、语言文字界的不同意见。相反，在后期将文改与汉字简化同政治倾向联系在一起，致使如陈梦家⑩等学者与民主人士蒙冤被扣上"右派"帽子，遭到"专政"。这只能有一种解释：汉字简化在当时主要不是从学术、从教学考量的，而是作为一种战略决策与政治决策推行的，由不得别人反对。在当时看来，反对简化即反对党的战略决策与政治决策，当然也就是反党、反社会主义。

（9）汉字简化与国家战略。汉字简化可以有两种安排：一是战术性简化，如日文那样仅简化一百余字，局部少量地简化，不伤整体⑰；一是战略性简化，全面大量地简化，使汉字整体有较大的改观。前者可以用行政程序发布；后者事关重大，则必须经过不同意见的专家论证，并经全国人大讨论、立法通过。当时国家、民族尚未统一，中国此时的国家战略应当是以保卫祖国、促进祖国统一为首要目标。在此情况下，对汉字采取战略性简化就显得有些操之过急。

（10）两岸汉字的相关处置。两岸对待汉字简化，初期并不带有对立之政治色彩。之所以形成目前的对立，源于 20 世纪 50 年代。大陆将反对简化作为"反党反社会主义"重要罪状之一，提高到政治取向高度。台湾便顺手牵羊，拿来当成国民党"正确"的资本，攻击大陆，却掩盖其本身也曾有二度简化之议。两岸就此问题的言战造成一种高度对立的政治气氛，大多数公众身处其中，深受影响，无法冷静观察判断。这是两岸分裂之苦果，也是中华民族之不幸。

2. 现代汉字实况梳理

（1）汉字的繁化与简化。汉字历史上历来存在繁化与简化两种趋向，两种趋向都是汉字形音义间以及汉字与社会应用需求间矛盾—平衡的结果，因此，只讲简化是片面的。

繁化的主要类型是字种繁化，原有语素被引申、比喻到一定程度就成为意义分化，变成两个语素，需要用新字形来准确表示。古代如"厤"分化为现代"歷""曆"二字；近代如"表"分化出今日的"錶"。另一种是借用造成的，如"云"本来是"雲"的本字或古字，由于借用来表示说话的"云"，只能另外改用形声法造出"雲"；"帝"本义为果实之"蒂"，被借来表示"帝王"义之后，不得不再加"艹"，生出"蒂"字。这两种都是语言使然，是语言的进步推动了文字的分化和繁化。

第二种是异体繁化，在同一字种下，由于造字法或构件的不同，书写、使用及群体的不同层次需要，产生不同的异体。如"淚"与"泪"，前为形声字，后为会意字（见《英烈传》第三三回："再四叮嚀，洒泪而别。"）；如"輝"与"煇"因形旁选择不同而造成异体；如"愛"有行草的"爱"，"書"有书法家笔下的草体"书"，"菜"有民间小贩书写的"芀"。

另有一种是笔画繁化，即笔画增多而字种未分化，甚至未产生并存并用的异体。究其原因一般都是为了"美"。因此也可称为美学繁化。例如"保"的早期形状本是"仔"（右边为"口＋十"），是会意字。为了保持右下部的平衡，而增加右下的"八"，右边改为"呆"，成为今天的"保"。再如"龙"，甲骨文中的龙是简单的，到金文就复杂了，到篆书就更繁化到如今"龍"的程度，只要对比一下，这里并无六书上的变动，几乎完全是笔画繁化。这显然是古人出于美学考虑的繁化。美化是文字发展的另一种趋向。因美学考虑改动字形是所有文字的共同规律，是有意义的。

此外，由于双音词的出现，也出现了因

选择同音近义汉字不一致而产生的词形繁化：如"交代"和"交待"；"耽搁"和"担搁"；"值勤"在八路军控制区被误写为"执勤"，将错就错至今。

至于简化，古已有之，历代均有产生。简化的种类，现今简化字已大体包括。这里需要说的是，从古代至1955年前，简体字与传承字基本上处于分层使用状态，大体互不干扰。简体形态主要存在于行书与草书中，也存在于底层人士的应用中，因此常称为"俗字"。而楷体规范字形始终基本不变，而且始终使用于正式文书、印刷方面，约定俗成，使得社会各个层次都有共同的沟通标准，因此也常被称为"正体"。

（2）传统的汉字"软规范"。秦代发布"书同文"命令与石鼓文小篆是一种行政命令式的强制规范，属于"硬规范"。秦以后，历代对传统汉字基本采用的是"软规范"，他们一般采用推崇某种字书来引导人们选择正式用字与印刷体，也即"立范"或"示范"⑱而已。期间并没有什么明确的规范法令条例。比如汉许慎的《说文解字》，实际上提出了汉代的小篆规范；唐颜元孙的《干禄字书》，分辨俗、通、正三体⑲，以明取舍，确定了宽松性的楷体正字；唐张参又在前书基础上编成《五经文字》，对楷体正字作进一步的严格化，树立了经文用字规范；又如清张玉书等奉敕所编的《康熙字典》明确了官方认定的正式字体。也有的是明确与规范相反字形的字书，标明了这些字形的非规范性质，如清赵撝叔的《六朝别字记》，近人刘复的《宋元以来俗字谱》。"软规范"的另一个特点是，不正式发布某某字是规范，可用；某某字是非规范字，不可用。也即不禁止、不废除俗字、简字、简笔草字，而是允许它们在不同层次中使用。这种规范是由汉字在长期使用中天然形成的，是对人们的一种尊重，对人性、对人的天然需要、天然变异的尊重。

这对人们、对国家、对交流没有致命的伤害，仅仅在科举考试时才会对举子们造成威胁。

今天，《汉语大词典》采用的繁简分工使用方式，虽然繁复，却道出了另一种规范形态，即对释义部分采用简化字，对应于今天的具有法律效力的"硬规范"。该词典对民国以前的书例采用繁体字，实际上也是一种擦边球式的"软规范"，因为文字法令没有禁止在特殊需要情况下使用繁体字。这说明，在"官式法令规范"之外，我们还存在一种"习惯传承规范"。现行的法令并未明令废止后者，而且也很难禁止。我们应对"软规范"加以研究。

（3）汉字的优点与缺点。汉字是世界上唯一广泛通用的非拼音文字。汉字与音节·语素（字义）直接相当，具有在确定环境中大致一字一义的表意特点，汉字的会意、形声造字法使汉字具有比较人性的学习与认知线索。汉字的大多数都具有多维度形态。其中有功能类的多维度，常见的有如下维度：表音维度的音符/声旁，表意维度的意符/形旁，模像维度的象形变异符号，提示维度的指事符号，记号维度的纯记号等五种。还有几何形态类的多维度：比如单体（"山"）、多种复体（"江、累、筍、趣、區、品、碧、器"等）等，从今天的认知科学研究得知，这样的组合方式虽然复杂，却更有利于记忆，有的也利于理解，甚至可以减轻某些认知疾病。由于汉字的多维度，因此具有较大的冗余性（羡余性），可以抗信息传输中的干扰。汉字是文字生态环境中唯一一个历史最久而且依然生气勃勃地被十多亿人现实使用的单音节·语素·多维度物种。世界文字"物种"的生态与多样性需要汉字。

汉字的缺点又是明显的：难学、难写、难认、难读、难记、书写慢与机械打字慢，而且字多量大，死而不废，生而不报，难以普及，难以推向世界，不便音译外来语，等等。但由于与汉语的匹配从古至今都较为和谐，并积累无可计量的文献，又难以抛弃，因此，历代只能以非正式场合书写简字而不触犯正式场合规定的措施来解决此一难题。今天，由于电脑输入汉字的技术有了很大的突破，打字慢已经成为一种过去式；电子转换式打字已经在电脑与手机上普及；手写机会减少；字形的繁简已经不能形成关键阻碍。至于某些人指责汉字只为封建贵族服务，是有阶级性的。这种指责当然完全是胡扯，是少数激进者未经严肃思考的言论。

（4）值得肯定的汉字整理工作。新中国成立以后，有关机构甚至个人在汉字的研究和整理方面的确做了很多工作，有很多项可以充分肯定，比如：对包括简体字内的现代汉字字形收集整理量化；对汉字部件和结构的分析；对汉字输入电脑各类型方案的研制；对汉字部首排检法的规范；对现代汉语用字用词频度的统计；对人名地名用字的调查；对汉字属性的研究；在以上基础上拟订现代汉语基本用字表和常用字表，以及最新的规范通用字表；拟订人名地名用字表；审定汉字异读、异形，先后两批整理异体字，确定了汉字的正式字形与适宜读音；确定汉字书写笔顺、笔形次序、部件、结构方式等规范；制订汉字属性国家标准，等等。以上大凡 14 大项，使现代汉语用字做到定量、定形、定音、定序，有利于教与学，有利于各行业的利用。我们现在比以前任何时期都清楚自己的汉字家底。我们必须肯定许多文字工作者为此而做的大量工作，甚至在简化过程中理清家底的工作。

（5）简化汉字所带来的利与弊。

① 简化应有所肯定。评价简化字，我们必须持客观、科学、公正的态度。简化字中有一些是非常需要的，特别是对一些特别繁复的常用汉字的简化，像"龜"简化为"龟"，"聽"简化为"听"，"糴、糶"简化为"籴、

粜"，"呼籲"简化为"呼吁"，"憂鬱"简化为"忧郁"，"挑釁"简化为"挑衅"，"臺灣"简化为"台湾"都非常受欢迎。无论从手写还是印刷、屏幕显示的角度，也无论在认知、识读方面，都应予肯定。

② 认知、识读与教学。1956—1959 年大规模推行的简化方案，确实带来了字形的简化，在电视、电脑、手机屏幕上笔画更清晰，在文本整体上也显得清朗、不浓密。的确，简体字看上去比繁体字清爽些、清晰些。但现在随着显示屏像素的增加、高清技术的出现，这已经不是问题。简单与复杂，这只是一个表象结果。从认知角度看，不能简单作为优劣的评判标准。简单也可能引起字形间差异度过小，容易引起识读混淆，例如"没"与"设"，"设有雅座"易被误认为"没有雅座"。这提醒我们：文字的识读与书写是两个不同方面，不必也不可能把二者完全统一。经验与研究告诉我们：笔画简单，容易书写的不一定容易认知、认读；字形复杂的，可能不容易书写，却往往容易认知、学习。因此，并非越简单越好。例如："震、霆、霈、霞、霾"以及"鎖、鎢、鑊、鑼、鐘"笔画繁复，却因构字理据明显，较易辨认识读。"己、已、巳"和"戊、戍、戌"以及"仓、仑"，容易书写，却难以识别[20]。至于简化是否带来识字效率与书写效率的提高，现在似乎还没有全面的科学测试与统计，但许多学者的研究却提供了与预料相反的答案，证明识读与笔画繁简并无正相关的关系[21]。此外，简化对汉字的表音度并无提高，反而下降许多[22]。简化的多方面得失比较，也相差无几，为此花费如此大的力量去推行简化，只剩下书写简便，似乎并不值得[23]。对此，我们都需要科学的测试与比较。

③ 过度简化之一：过分采用同音替代或归并，达到 96 组，使得 96 个保留字每个字形都要负担多个来源不同而且字义甚至

字音不同的语素,导致可能的混乱。如"斗、鬪"合并为"斗","里,裡/裏"合并为"里","干、幹、乾"合并为"干","制、製"合并为"制","瀋、沈"合并为"沈",切断了语素与不同原字形之间的联系,搅混了不同语素与文字表记之间的对应。

④ 过度简化之二:过多使用符号替代,使这部分汉字原有的谐声或字义理据几乎完全消失。例如"又"在"汉(漢)、仅(僅)、欢(歡)、鸡(雞)、邓(鄧)、对(對)、树(樹)、圣(聖)"等字中,替代了8个以上的部件,切断了与原有偏旁间造字理据关系。

⑤ 过度简化之三:大规模地实行简化偏旁类推,表面上使一大批同偏旁字得以类推简化,无须过多记忆,但由于偏旁字单独用字并不简化,由于简化字表的限制却出现一部分可以偏旁类推简化,另一部分同偏旁字却不允许类推简化,使人很难掌握,也使整个汉字系统失去统一性。经过多次调整,2013年发表《通用规范汉字表》,问题并没有得到根本性解决。

⑥ 过度简化之四:过分依赖草书楷化,使许多简化字在楷体层面上难以写好看,甚至不知如何起笔:如"长、马、场、尧、专、为"。像"为"字,应该从"点"起笔,可是笔者见到许多人都是从"折"起点;"长"应该从撇开始,许多人却都从横或竖起笔。让人"呜呼"。有些简化偏旁也很难写好看,例如:"钅、讠、饣"。字形美是汉字的一大特点。如果要继续使用汉字,那美学考虑是非常必要的。草书有草书的笔画走势规律与审美要求,并按此规律草化,与楷书完全不同,取前者必然破坏楷书的审美要求。

⑦ 权宜所致困扰之一。在一串同一偏旁的形声字系列中,插入一个异质符号替代的简化字,使这个系列突然断裂,如在"杨(楊)、扬(揚)、旸(暘)、炀(煬)、疡(瘍)、飏(颺)"中突然冒出"伤(傷)"和"阳(陽)",

变得不再规则。这种情况在符号替代中显露得更强烈,如与"邓"同声旁的"燈、噔、證"不能同理简化,与"仅"同声旁的"謹、瑾"也不能同理简化。

⑧ 权宜所致困扰之二。大规模简化带有明显的权宜色彩,并不完全考虑教学与全方位的文化应用,以及经济效益。因此现有的一些草书楷化字如"长、尧"在教学上、书写上并无便利可言[24]。由于没有充分考虑古文献的继承,因此在应用上,就必然出现繁简混合使用的这种更为复杂繁难的情况,例如《汉语大词典》就有难言之苦,为了避免混淆,为了让读者能与古代文献接触而又不致误解,采取释义用简化字版汉字,引民国以前的文献做例证时用传承字(繁体字)版汉字。以前,印刷厂必须制备繁简两套汉字、铅字来应对。现在,电脑字库中也必须至少制备繁简两套汉字,数量惊人,大大增加了占用国际编码信息的空间。

⑨ 记忆传承中断之虞。大规模简化使人容易中断对汉字传统使用习惯的记忆,促使人们乱简化,产生一些与传统文化接轨时的紊乱,可能造成意想不到的不规范与混乱。除了常见的因替代简化字"后"产生"后"与"後"的混淆外,因替代简化产生"中国制"究竟是"中国制式"还是"中国製造"的困扰外,还出现了因电脑简繁转换产生的新错别字,而这样的错别字导致人们对正误辨别能力的下降。例如:电视剧《红色》中上海那条弄堂从始至终挂着"同福裏"(应为"同福里")的牌子,电视剧《勇敢的心》里从头到尾地挂出"瀋公馆、瀋记茶楼"(应为"沈公馆、沈记茶楼")的匾额,却无演艺人员、导演制片等人员提出改正、撤换,可见他们已缺乏辨识能力。这非常值得警惕,显示中国人的文化素质已经到了应该重重敲响警钟的时刻。在这种情况下,你怎么能去禁止人们不写"白才"、"豆付"与"兰球"呢!人们对传

承汉字以及对传统文本认读的危害,现在已经清楚显露。文化断层已经不再仅仅是梦魇。今日简繁争论之加剧,是简繁矛盾在当代文化交流条件下的凸显,也是人们自我文化认同觉醒的一种表现,我们不能再置若罔闻、熟视无睹。

3. 几个可议观点[⑤]

观点一:国民党政府 1935 年早就提出汉字简化,1952 年,国民党到台湾后,简化问题本来台湾也赞成,国共两党都有此主张,国民党还更早,只是国民党因有强力政治人物反对而作罢。因此,不能说简化不正确。

试议一:汉字历来就存在简化,这是一个历史现实。要不要简化,并非正确与否的问题,问题是如何简化,如何简化适当。简化要慎重,要试点,要逐步并小步推进。如现在这般全国铺开,一下子多达 2236 字[⑥],确实惊人。痛快是痛快了,但问题、麻烦不断。蒋介石确实曾想简化,最终却放弃。这里的原因,可能是政治考虑,也可能是文化传承的考虑。其次,也需要客观分析汉字简化在教育普及、消除文盲中的作用,而社会制度与教育制度的改变对教育普及、消除文盲的作用也不应忽视。

观点二:简化最重要的是利于教学。小学教师都说简化字好教,都说小孩子学字、认字好认,写字好写。而且,简化字也有利于扫盲。

试议二:所谓简化字好教,是非经系统考察的感觉之言。学汉字有认、写两个方面。认读容易,不等于书写容易。书写困难,却也不等于认读也困难。简化字只是笔画简单,由于它铲除了许多构造理据,有些还合并了几个不同字种的字,因此并不一定真正好教。相对地,繁体字肯定是书写慢,但由于保留了较多的理据,却并不一定难教。过分夸大笔画减少的好,那么还保留着的常用字"疆、藏、耀、囊、蟹"等等又该如何

评说呢?此外,过去说汉字不利于工农兵学习,如果抗日时改成简化字,他们就容易学习了吗?如果容易,又容易了多少?有多少成效?那时所谓学习汉字困难,关键还是学习者已经过了学习的最佳时期,采用的教法与学习法过于传统,而且那时还缺乏坐下来安静学习的环境,都不适合成年人识字教学。教学的难易是比较的结果,严肃的科学的态度应该是将繁简两种字体做系统而充分的调查与教育测试。

观点三:联合国如果承认简化字为中文的正式用字,并决定所有文件都用简化字,这就证明简化是正确的。

试议三:很遗憾,这是一个大前提太成问题的断言。难道联合国承认就是科学的判定吗?联合国承认阿拉伯字母为阿拉伯语的正式表记体系,难道就证明阿拉伯字母表记体系是科学正确的吗?联合国的承认只是一种政治现实与国家实力的表示。此外,如果印制繁体字与简化字两种版本的联合国文件,将耗费加倍的财力,从经济考虑,改变成一种字形文本也是合理的。因此,所谓联合国承认,甚至大马、新加坡也采用简化字,那都只是出于政治现实与财政支出的关系,并非对与错的科学判定。

观点四:汉字简化的使命已经结束,两岸应实行书同文,大陆汉字应回归到"正体"。[⑦]

试议四:这是一个似是而非的观点。如果以民为本、以人为本,汉字还有不少字实在太复杂,在认、记、写各方面都不利于教学与使用,仍应在适当时机下考虑是否简化。这是一。其次,大陆推行简化字已经 60 年,很难一刀切地简单地退回到繁体字系统。第三,回归"正体"一说,并非尊重两岸现实。简化字在大陆作为正式字体通行 60 年,岂非也是一种"正体"?最后,在"两岸书同文"的前提下,只要求大陆如何,而不提台湾地

区应取何种态度,完全是推卸台湾地区方面应尽的责任。似乎台湾地区完全不必做什么。显然这是不科学、不尊重文字历史发展的态度。在操作层面上,如果没有台湾地区的配合与前行,大陆是不可能后退到繁体字的。正确的态度,应该是与时俱进,合作相向。如果以实力相较,那随着大陆的发展,两岸书刊等文化交流,简化字将为台湾地区所有人熟悉,那简化字自然而然地占据台湾地区并非不可能。这大概是台湾当局所最不愿见的。因此,和谐讨论,相向而行,应是"书同文"最佳路径。

观点五:要从世界看中国,不要从中国看世界。⑳

试议五:这的确是一组警句,其本意应该在社会、经济、文化方面,当然也可能会移用到语言方面。该句极富哲理,却颇具争议。因为世界是由全部国家构成的,"从世界看"是完全不可能的。从欧美发达世界看与从非洲不发达世界看,截然不同。因此,所谓"从世界看",实际上是"从发达的欧美西方世界看"。从这样的角度去看,必然导致以往的西方中心观。从西方社会、西方观念以及西方语言文字角度去看中国,看汉语汉字,看到的是中国的落后、汉语的贫乏和汉字落后,中国当然就应该引进西方的先进概念或观念,引进他们的某些制度,应该仿照西文实行汉语拼音化。诚然,在语言文字方面,从这里会导出类似引进科技语、外来概念词与外来词之类的许多合理结论,但也可能发生某种偏颇。尤其是,"不要从中国看世界"这一要求在实际上是不可能的。人无法摆脱自己的所属所在,就如同无法拔着自己的头发离开生养之地。只要你是在中国生活的中国人,你的思考都会不自觉地带上中国的烙印,会自动地从中国出发。这是个无法摆脱的必然。除非你更换了自我的本真属性,或长期移居外国,脱胎换骨。

另外,只有一端的思维,也会导出我们必须"与国际接轨"这种并不全面的结论。所谓"与国际接轨"实际上是"西化"的另一种表述。笔者承认,在科学技术领域,与国际接轨是基本正确的,应该引进西方的科学技术,以改造自己的体质。但在社会、哲学、文化、语言这些涉及人文的领域,却须谨慎。在这方面,中国作为一种特有文化的大体量主体,更为正确的或许应该是一种"与国际接轨"、"与国际对接"、"坚持固有轨道"三类型的混合互补模式。其中"对接"是一种坚持自力原创或传统并设置同国际接口的模式,对任何国家自强自立都极为重要。在语言文字方面,汉语拼音就是一种接口工具。因此,这后一小句确实值得商榷,有可能导致失去民族自信。笔者理解,提出这样的警句,是为了警醒国人,不要坐井观天,要更重视从世界看中国,以利于中国的发展。其出发点是极好的。但是这样的提法不够周严,太容易引起偏误。应该怎样定位才更全面、更客观、更公正呢?也许下面的表述更恰当些:要从中国看(不同的)世界,更要从(不同的)世界看中国。或者如此表达:放在世界格局中看中国。这样人们才能更理性、更全面地思考,才能看到世界的不平衡与世界的多彩,才能看到自己文化的价值。假若这样去看世界与中国,那么汉语带声调的单音节性未必就是缺点,汉语的语素—词双元机制则更非缺点,与此相匹配的汉字也未必就应该废灭,而西方语言与文字也未必全是优点。只有从多角度互动互补地看彼此,世界才是真实的,中国及其汉语汉字也才是真实的,我们也才能找到应该行动的方向与路径。

其实,任何民族、国家都应如此,即使如美国,不但要从美国看世界,也更要从世界看美国。这样美国也许才会谦恭一些,能倾听一些世界不同的声音,尊重一些世界的其他文化。

六　汉字战略试议

(一)　汉字再认识

谈汉字战略,必须先认识汉字。过去之所以发生"废灭汉字"之议,皆由汉字认识而起。汉字误识不除,难有对症之药,更难有正确战略决策。

首先,汉字之所以能够延续三千年而至今,同汉语的高匹配度息息相关。没有汉语的支持与互相适合,汉字早就会被抛弃,更不用今人费心来废灭。文改主导者显然对此缺乏研究。声调与同音异义是汉语的一大特点。对此,各种拼音方案至今没有完善解决的办法。"国罗"的字母标调过于繁难,而且难以解决语素同音问题;而"北拉"的初衷是根本甩去声调、忽视语素(字)的表示,立足于依靠复音词以及上下文。今日"汉拼"的符号标调只能用于注音,如果用于文字,很快就会被忽视或甩掉,而这正是20世纪50年代拼音化主导者的希望。上古汉语语素(字)与大部分词几乎重叠,是单音节—语素语,只有汉字才适合记录。现代汉语已经发展为语素(字)与词并重的语言,但语素(字)的重要性没有变,汉字适合汉语的基本盘依然如此。拼音化的意图是想硬套以"词"为中心的西方语言,这就如同削足适履、缘木求鱼,怎么可能达到目的呢?今日简化汉字中的同音替代也正是西方"以词为中心"的翻版,必然行之不远。因此,许多拼音化领袖人物面对此种难题,今日也只能改变某些态度或缄口无言。

其次,过去所认为的汉字难,一方面是事实,一方面也是缺乏研究。根据现代心理学、教育学的研究,只要适龄而不失时机地学习,只要根据认知习得与教育科学研究的成果,安排汉字程序与教学方式,汉字完全可以较易、较快地掌握。学者们能学会认字、写字,为什么其他人不能?底层人们之所以会有文盲,或不能完全识字,罪在政治体制、社会体制、教育体制。今日,大陆识字普及,功在体制,而非汉字简化。请看今日香港、澳门、台湾地区,依然保持着繁体,字教育却普及了,文盲消除了。因此,汉字落后、废灭汉字的立论是完全站不住脚的。

另外,文字有识读与书写两个方面,不必也不可能把二者完全统一。经验与研究告诉我们,容易识别认读的可能不容易书写,容易书写的也不一定容易认读。"震、霆、霈、霞、霾"以及"鎖、鎢、鑊、鑼、鐘"笔画繁复,却因构字理据明显,较易辨认识读。"己、已、巳"和"戊、戌、戍"以及"仓、仑",容易书写,却难以识别。尤其在电脑时代,输入已经不成问题,已经不必将识读与书写完全合一,如何保持相对"易于识读",又收获相对"易于书写",达成动态平衡,正是汉字研究者、管理者的突出任务。

再次,汉字一旦掌握之后,汉字的表意特点在表达上、交际上将远远优于拼音文字。汉字不像拼音文字仅仅是单一认知的文字,汉字是复合认知的文字,是具有模糊表音功能的音节-语素文字,是有大致规则而图像各异的文字,而且是不必完全通过语音可由字符直达意义的文字。现在,脑科学正在逐渐揭示这一脑功能秘密,而且已经获得令人惊奇的结果[20]。过去,文改前辈们曾做出汉字将在电脑中、在科学技术进步中死亡的预言[20]。现在,这个预言恰恰被电脑所击碎。现代科技不仅没有灭亡汉字,而且昭示了汉字将开辟另一与汉字有关的自然科学和智能工程技术。

最后,五四以来,人们受西方实用主义的影响,几乎完全从单纯记录语言的实用功能去看待文字,而忽视甚至忘却文字还有社会功能、认识功能和文化功能。亚洲的文字改革以及流播至今的汉语拼音化、汉字简化无不笼罩在实用主义之下。为什么20世纪50年代国内蒙古文、维吾尔文、哈萨克文、彝文的拉丁化会全部失败，而退回到传统的民族拼音形式？这就是因为，文字是民族认同的重要符号之一，一个民族需要依靠它来认同自我，认同传统文化。为什么汉语拼音化会遭到大多数人的强烈拒绝？这也是因为汉语拼音完全不具有汉字那样的社会功能、认识功能与文化功能，它仅仅停留在最基本的实用层次。汉字具有聚拢民族的功能，不会因方言的差别而很易导致分裂。人们可以欣赏、享受汉字带来的形体文化之美，形音义之妙。而拉丁字母拼写的形式却完全没有这样的功能。汉语拼音顶多只能作为一种与科技、教学的适当"接口"，只能作为一种辅助性工具，只是一种西方快餐文化在文字层面的反映，说好听一点可以勉强称之为"准文字"。为什么国内近来会兴起繁体字回潮？这不也是因为60年来简化字较大范围地损伤了汉字这样的社会、认识与文化的功能，不也是因为人们已再不满足所提供的基本实用功能。因此才会出现目前的对传承形体的追寻或追求。繁体回潮就是一种合理反弹，人民有这样的权力。政府不能漠视这样的要求与呼声，绝不能简单地扣以"不规范"而置之不理甚至一棍子打死。当人们抵达基础层次"信·达"的实用功能以后，就会追求更高的文化层次"雅·美"的认识与文化功能。当中国已经基本消灭文盲、基本普及教育、基本消除贫穷的时候，我们就应该更多地从社会功能、认识功能与文化功能去认识汉字及其形体，从社会学、心理学、文化学角度去认识汉字，关怀汉字，并以此提升文字教育与研究的层次。

汉字是世界上唯一能与西式拼音文字相对峙并为最大人群使用的文字。汉字活生生的存在本身就是经过实践过滤、检验、考验的结果。因此，它更需要我们加以爱护，不要轻易去伤毁。这样的物种能够流传使用数千年，没有被人为粗暴废止，这本身就是一种答案，也是现代科学的幸运。

（二）汉字战略：呼唤思想解放

汉字是中华文化之本位，也是汉语用以世代记录并借以发展的载体。五四运动之前，闻一多在《论振兴国学》中就说道："国于天地，必有与立，文字是也。文字者，文明之所寄，而国粹之所凭也。"这是非常睿智而深刻的一段话，值得所有人咀嚼、牢记。以此来咀嚼百年来的文改与汉字简化运动，将有极大的助益。为此，大陆需要在观念上、思想上以及制度保障上有所准备。

1. 突破禁区，解放思想

经过"文革"，我们逐渐明白：自20世纪50年代某个阶段开始，党和国家的政策就已经有"左"的表现，"文革"则是"左"的高峰；毛主席的许多话可以是一时的政策，但并不一定是真理、是科学。科学不能推翻，但政策却可以改变，可以改正。

20世纪50年代是一个封闭时代，大陆被各种人所共知的因素封闭。这种封闭有地理的、政治的，也有历史的、文化的。我们没有也很难对外开放，去接受中外的文化能量交换；我们也很难向历史开放，去与古人作文化能量的交换。在这样一个封闭环境下，简化字可以获得暂时的平衡，从而觉得地位稳定。但是，时空转换到21世纪开始前后，我们的环境已完全不同，无论两岸的政治生态、社会生态与语言文字生态已经大大不同。全方位地向世界、向传统的高度二维开放，迫使简化字不再稳定。新的文字平衡运动正在出现。这是必然的大势。

从这一历史看到，真理是有时间限度的。彼时的合理，并非永久的合理。合理是随时间、客观条件的变化而改变其核定标准的。抗日反蒋时期的合理，在新中国建立之后而全国尚未完全统一之时就可能含有不合理的过激因素。改革开放至今已经历经30多年，之前的政策都要一一重新审视，不存在不可改变之条条。宪法都可以修改，何况文字之法呢？在汉字问题上，两个"凡是"依然徘徊影响至今，未能破除。文改、简化、拼音化正确与否，始终被民众认为是个"禁区"。我们太需要与时俱进了。改革过去一切不合理之处，才能显示这个民族的强大与生命力。汉字问题当然亦复如此。汉字战略问题上，尤其是简化问题上，我们亟需一次充分的思想解放，需要自由的讨论，需要建立符合时代的"包容性"。这样才能显示我们的党和政府对自己的自信与力量，才能显示其兼听则明、从善如流的美德。这样的"退"正是一种"进"，是向正确战略目标的"进"。

2. 保护自由的学术空气

为了保证新战略的实行，我们应该从政治决策回归到学术的、教育的、应用的层次，应该让两岸专家在尽可能"去政治化"或"去意识形态化"的学术民主气氛下展开充分的自由讨论，让不同意见充分发表，展开争论或讨论。自由讨论可能会延迟决策，延迟执行。但不怕慢，只怕站；不怕慢，只怕乱。如果没有1978年"文革"后的言论自由之风吹入，那么1977年12月发布的"二简"（《第二次汉字简化方案（草案）》）就会延长生命，祸害文化。自由讨论，民主审议，是科学决策的必需保证条件。①

（三）汉字战略建言

1. 汉字战略目标

作为汉语表记的文字体系，汉字首先要支持汉语，支持汉语实现世界性文化语言的战略。

作为担负承继汉民族古今文化遗产的唯一符号体系，汉字必须在履行此项任务时能保持尽可能少的形体障碍，并减少人为设置的不合理改变。

作为中国对内对外的汉语书面符号，作为汉民族全体的书面共同表达工具，汉字要统一自身体系，要书同文，要有利于国家的统一，要铲除有碍于民族统一的文字分歧，要消除不利于国家统一的人为设置。

为此，首先必须在民族和解基础上实现汉字体系的统一。这是汉字的首要战略目标，而且是中国永远需要的战略。简言之，也即面对民族，消除繁简对立，统一体系，再度"书同文"。

其次，在统一文字的过程中必须同时实现汉语书面表达系统的"优化"与扩能。在"书同文"前提下"优化"汉字，以完善应对信息时代快速变化中的汉语。统一文字并非简单地恢复繁体，而是将所有字形放在"优化"视角加以审查、选择。简言之，即面向未来，优化字符，增加新质。这也是汉字战略中的必需内容。

具体而言，今日的汉字战略是：

（1）退后半步，从认知与现代科技角度"优化"必要汉字之字形，其中包括重新站在传承文化与未来文化发展的立场上，全面调查评价汉字字形，选择字形。

（2）让出半步，增加对非汉字字符（如拉丁字母）的兼容性，以应对更广泛的语言生活。这就是今天汉字所需的战略。

2. 汉字的战略路径

为实现战略目标，必须规划战略路径，并须为此建立新的相关理念与政策，具体是：

（1）建立诸必要新观念

① 承认现实，承认任何文字都有缺陷。目前，用于全中国的汉字体系因简化问题而分成两个版本，我们必须承认目前的文字现实，也必须承认所有文字都并非十全十美，而且也无法完美无缺。所有的文字都有在一定程度内的妥协或平衡。不必说汉字，拉丁字母、英文又何如？i的大写与l的小写，

以及同数字1，几乎完全相同；小写的d与b、q与p，因镜像缘故而在儿童学习时难以认辨；字母O与数字0更无法区分；英文字形与发音间对应之复杂更无须多言。因此，我们就可以更清醒地认识文字，并承认今天两岸的文字现状，承认大陆不可能“一风吹”地简单退回到繁体的情势，认清两岸应各自采取的态度。

② 与时俱进，以“优化”观念统率汉字问题。今天已经不是60年前两岸隔绝的状况，大陆已到处可以见到繁体字。台湾地区也到处可以买到简体字版本的大陆书刊，简体字不时现身民间甚至正式报章书籍。如“臺灣”之作“台湾”，早已见怪不怪。“识繁写简”在某种程度上已是现实。海峡两岸均应尽可能在文字问题上去政治化，因应时代与民族的愿望，与时俱进，接受文字向前发展的现实。谁也不会为了政治对立而放弃“方便”，放弃认识传承形态，除非他是冥顽不化的呆傻。管理部门则必须明察秋毫，审时度势，从善如流。两岸各界如以“优化”观念统率汉字的变动，跳出繁简争论的窠臼，以对民族长远利益负责的态度寻求解脱，则将收获两岸良性互动，最终解套困局。

③ 改变纯质化观念，接纳异质字符作为辅助。中国人历来有强烈的文字纯质化情结，很难容纳异质字符。即如“〇”此一符号，因其非楷体笔势而经历多时才获得认可。但事实是人们并非根据观念，而是依据需要行事。包容是社会和谐的要素，也是新时代的润滑剂。包容性则是新时代需要的观念。拉丁字符客观上已经进入文字体系，因此必须承认它们的辅助地位，可以作为文字辅助种类应用于书面。而且应该承认“汉语拼音”已经作为辅助性的“准文字”工具应用于多个场合，不但用于注音、检索、输入汉字，甚至也应该允许拼音作为各种应急状态下的“准文字”资格。例如允许学生作文、考试时作为非完美的临时替代。

④ 分层兼容，建立“软规范”观念。除秦始皇时代外，历代采用的是“软规范”态度(参考上文“现代汉字实况梳理”一节)。这种软规范其核心是“立范示范”、“分层兼容”，千百年来汉语雅言-方言、汉字正-俗体就是如此分层生存，兼容并行，和谐共处。所有语言文字都存在各种变异，它们也是由这些变异所构成。“分层兼容”的状态是语言文字自然发展后的人们自然选择。如果将“分层兼容”作为一种新的规范观念，那么许多现实的困扰都可以迎刃而解。过往的规范都是刚性的，说一不二，但语言文字常常不能说一不二。不同的形式除了一个替代一个，一个排斥另一个这种方式以外，更多见的是二者甚或数者并存，在使用中各有服务领域或对象，或由不同人群对此选择。这是一种顺自然之道的规范模式，却是更具人性化的规范。千百年来传承汉字存在篆隶楷行草，在同一字种下，不仅是笔势的不同，而且是构造(构件与结构法式)的不同，它们大致分别使用于不同层次的应用、不同层次的群体[32]。我们必须修正绝对标准的“硬规范”观念，在一个字种下“分层”容纳两种(或以上)不同使用层次的不同字形，形成“和谐”而“人性”的[33]软性新规范，这正是我们追求的，也许正是我们走出简化字困境的可行之路。希望今后不要因书写异体字而为难学生。

(2) 大陆先行，两岸相向靠拢。两岸多接触，多在民间、专家层次会晤，逐步消除对立情绪与误解，先专家后政府达成共识。在此过程中，大陆可以先后退半步(例如，大陆先采取“印简识繁”[34]的教育措施，以应需用)，释放文字政策善意，以开启靠拢程序。当然这必须由政府开启。既然简化是由政府决策的，那么后退这半步当然也应由政府决策。因此政府决策者的眼光与魄力将是又一关键。台湾当局也可先采取容忍简体字的适当措施以表明其善意,并开启双向靠拢互动⑱。以两岸互谅互让,各自消减对立情绪,互设回旋余地,先民间后官方,求大同存小异,相向靠拢。在这一相向过程中,务必谨慎,先易后难,局域试点,磨合成功以后再全面推行。

(3)共同选择,保留优良简体。可以保留简化得好而且确实需要简化的字形作为印刷体,例如:"挑釁"简化为"挑衅","憂鬱"简化为"忧郁","呼籲"简化为"呼吁","臺灣"简化为"台湾","龍""龓"简化为"龙""龟","糶、糴"简化为"籴、粜","聽"简化为"听",等等。在以上简化字中处理好个别同音局部替代的问题。而所谓的繁体形式也无妨存在于手头或某些印刷中。希望以长期实践来优选最终的字形。我们建议台湾当局能在两岸共同讨论、谨慎选择后,将这一部分作为相向靠拢而跨出的第一步。

(4)谨慎退回传承。部分可简化可不简化或造成字种混乱以及没有合适理据的简化字,一般可考虑逐步退回到传承体(繁体),但须一一仔细鉴定,防止一刀切。具体举例如下:

a.同音替代的调整,如:"干",恢复"干"、"乾"、"幹"三分;"斗",仍恢复"斗"与"鬥"。但考虑到大陆已经使用多年,允许手头书写时使用。

b.偏旁简化类推的调整,如:"钅"、"饣"、"讠"等恢复传承印刷体,与单字"金"、"食"、"言"等取得最大的一致。有的单字与偏旁均已经简化,但从书写美学角度看并不可取,也应恢复传承印刷体,如"马"改为"馬"。这样将使"类推到何种程度"这一难题消失。

c.鉴于美学的调整:草书楷化且书写不易美观者,应恢复传承印刷体,如:"杨"、"场"恢复为"楊"、"場";又如"专"、"传"恢复

为"專"、"傳"。同时将原简化字形作为手写行草字体,在同一字种下分别共存之。

d.符号替代字的调整:简化于理无征、隔断系列又触动较大情感者,也当恢复传承印刷体,如:"汉"恢复为"漢","邓"恢复为"鄧",等等。

(5)设置"手头可使用异体字对应表"。将保留下的简化字或退回传承体的非类推简化字都作为"手头可使用异体字"之一,与传承字形并列,制订"手头可使用异体字对应表",确定何者用于手头,何者用于印刷,并存竞用。希望以此来设计新使用规范,增强规范的弹性,体现"和谐"理念,并让使用者决定最后的结局。这样上可与古籍相连无碍,下与两岸三地用字相接和谐。当然,这些改变并不期望一次完成,而可以逐步实行,以最小震动换取民族最大的受益。笔者深信,这将极大地有利于祖国未来的统一。

(6)制订"汉字快写推荐字帖"。鉴于许多草书楷化字形与偏旁简化不但在大陆行之有年,而且自古行草已然,建议大陆或两岸共同制订类似台湾地区《标准行书范本》的快写或行书,将这些曾经作为楷体的行书字形推荐给民众,引导手写,以利使用与识别,并作为传承印刷体的一个补充,体现"和谐"大观念。

以上这些措施乃是汉语战略在文字部分的对应,是以我中华为主,以祖国统一、复兴文化为首要考虑的反应。汉字战略路径如汉语那样,也宜乎采取"以我为主;以退为进;步步为营;兼容竞用"。只要持之以恒,积以时日,相信两岸汉字必可实现新版本的"书同文"。

七 未来世界:英语世界吗? 汉语拼音化吗?

(一)英语未必

很多人都以为英语已经是世界语言,笔

者则不敢苟同。语言的不平等、不公平竞争早已是事实。在英语之前，法语、德语曾经称霸，法语、德语之前，荷兰语、西班牙语、葡萄牙语也曾称霸。它们之间的替代，证明英语同样也并非万古长青、永霸世界。被替代者的兴起与衰落或由于战争的胜败，或由于军力的起落，或由于文化的兴衰。当前英语成为世界最广使用语言，一是拜英国曾经是日不落帝国，其殖民地遍布世界各地之赐。第二拜第二次世界大战美国收取胜利之赐。当英国衰落到被纳粹德国欺凌之时，幸好美国接过接力棒，在打败德国之后升帐为新霸主。曾经流行世界的英式英语，自 20 世纪 60 年代开始已经渐渐地被美式英语所替代。而在中国，冯国璋的牛津英语优势现在也开始逐渐被美式英语所替代。而在日本，现在已经是美式英语的一霸天下。从未来学角度看，当世界各地被迫在英语帮助下发展得比较均匀时，世界发展的比较平衡又可能突显语言地位的不平衡，从而可能促发语言矛盾的加剧，促发对英语的反制或抵制，促发更多语言的崛起。在此情况下，英语的独霸地位也将因时因势而易。不变是相对的，变是绝对的。未来世界的语言会是怎样，且拭目以待。

（二）语言美元？

笔者怀疑，美国实际上是将英语当作语言中的美元。犹如美元成为世界储备货币与换算本位一样，英语也成为美国称霸世界中的一张牌。没有英语，美国就很难成为语言的霸主，以及世界的霸主。一切表达都必须通过英语，必须译成英语。世界都必须学习英语。英语则是"不动明王"⑰。使用英语的美国也就不必忙着学别国语言。让一个国家的自然语言作为全球的共同语言，显然是不平等的。英语（语音的、语法的）及其文字表达的许多缺点，有理由让人们对这种语言称霸世界产生怀疑。而语言史也告诉我

们，一种优势语言被另一种优势语言取代是经常出现的事实。我们应该对此做出预案。语言是联系着文化的，如果多语种的世界甚或某个多语言区只用一种自然语言，那么这种自然语言所依凭的族群就有可能凌驾其他族群，就可能出现"语言震慑"⑱，并把另一些语言文化消融掉。这当然是不利于语言和文化生态的。因此，最好的办法之一是有多于 1 的少数自然语言，作为具有国际性、世界性的语言，共同竞用，相互制约，为全世界服务。

（三）"辅助性"世界语言

从语言平等的角度，人们需要重新研讨，选择出一种更为理想的"辅助性"世界语言。之所以称为"辅助性"，是因为它不以消灭其他语言为目的。也许这种语言只能是人类预设计的语言，也许这是 Esperanto（世界语），或许是比它更完美的另一种新人工语言。曾宣告死亡的希伯来语在以色列的复活，Esperanto 在北欧等地实际使用⑲以及出现许许多多多种的作品或译本，都证明一种书面的语言或人工设计的语言是可以被"激活"或"活化"并运行的⑳。多种世界性文化语言并存竞用，"辅助性"世界语言沟通其间，这也许是人们对语言的一种"世界梦"。未来每个人除母语外，可能都要学会三种公用语言：所在国国语；国语以外的一种国际性或世界性语言；辅助性世界语言。他们将以如此的语言工具与语言修养去享受未来的世界生活。这也应当是语言世界梦的一部分。

（四）汉语拼音化

至于汉语汉字会不会拼音化、拉丁化，首先要看这种拼音方案能否完美承载、记录有个性的汉语。至少现在的汉语拼音正词法是没有完全体现汉语特性的。例如，正词法将中国人的姓名，按照西方办法来"词化"，把毛泽东拼成 Mao Zedong，这样毛泽

东与毛泽民的拼音缩略形式就会完全一样。汉人"名"中常常是两个特殊单字词的联合，是一种特殊词组。两个字各有含义与用途。一个字常常是排名用的，另一个才是对这个人的命名。汉语拼音正词法把汉语的特性磨灭掉了，把汉语语素（字）-词双基点磨灭、掩盖掉。这样的正词法必然行之不远、用而不广。此外，拉丁化能否实现还要看汉语会变到什么程度。声调是汉语的突出特质，至少在几百年内我们看不到汉语的声调会消失。现有拼音方案的软肋之一正好就是声调的表示；现有拼音方案的软肋之二是定型化。汉字是语素-词双定型的，与汉语的语素-词双基点恰好匹配。而目前的汉语拼音方案完全不可能实现语素-词双定型。语素-词双定型是文字功能广狭、优劣的一项很重要的衡量标准。文字会变，会发展，它将如何变？如何发展？汉语拼音方案也正经受着中西冲突的煎熬，它在长期的磨合中又将如何发展？也且待以时日，万不可过早结论。

附　注

① 新加坡法律规定马来语为国语，又规定华语、英语、马来语、泰米尔语为官方语言，并行政指定英语为行政语言和第一教育语言。行政语言在当地有多种表述，如工作语言、通用语言、第一语言。

② 关子尹（2014）将语言既养又护的事业称之为"语言作育"（language care），笔者觉得"语言养护"更容易理解，也更容易推广。

③ 2015年春，陕西考古人员披露最早下西洋的外交使节是唐代航海家、外交官、宦官杨良瑶（736—806），航海下西洋早于郑和620年。根据泾阳县出土《唐故杨府君神道之碑》的记载，杨良瑶就以"聘国使"身份携带判官和国信、诏书，率外交使团，于贞元元年（785年）四月从广州南海登舟航海，通过马六甲海峡，出使印度洋沿岸南亚、中东国家，抵达黑衣大食国首都缚达城（今伊拉克巴格达与两河流域）。同时期的唐代地理学家贾耽曾记载了此次下西洋路线。因此，实际上中国有过三次开通中西交通。

④ 在日本制作的伪满洲地图上就毫不掩饰地标明"关东

州"三字，堂而皇之地与"满洲国"三字并列，说明日本在内部早已将所谓"满洲国"当作了日本的一个"州"，与日本本土的本州、九州并列。

⑤ 据报道，曾尽力将英语作为行政语言或事实上第一语言的新加坡，已经感觉这一难以弥补的缺陷。外来语言可以作为自己的第一语言，但仅仅是实务型的语言，要在这种语言中建立厚重的文化蕴含则并非易事，须要不断地进行移植教育并长期自身培育。

⑥ 很多人担心人才流失，担心"赤字移民"。然而，即使中国仅有10%的人才回归，也对中国提升科技水平有极大助益。随着国家的逐渐强大，进入文明而发达阶段，那么赤字移民也必将逐渐转变为"黑字移民"。另外，当中国成为文化上游国时，外国的人才也会被吸纳进来。从长远看，人才流失必会得到扭转。

⑦ 徐大明在"2014海内外中国语言学者联谊会"上指出应该将外语教育改为第二语言教育，摆脱将外语沦落为考试语言、课堂语言而不能交际的困境，这无疑是正确的。现在管理当局似已意识到此问题，正在设法改变那种陷于形式主义的外语教育。（见商务印书馆2014，第13页）

⑧ 1885年法国殖民者逐渐废除汉字和字喃（或称喃字），强力推行法国传教士设计的拉丁字母方案。

⑨ 土耳其1928年决定将原用阿拉伯字母的文字改用拉丁字母表现。1904年后英国殖民者在马来亚废止Jawi字母，推行使用至今的拉丁化方案。同时，印尼的荷兰殖民者也采用相似的Rumi罗马字母书写系统；1945年印尼独立，以罗马化马来文为法定文字。两国的马来文大同小异。

⑩ 在苏联与俄文的政治影响下，蒙古国于1946年起正式启用了西里尔新蒙文。

⑪ 日本的文改运动者在1866年提出废除汉字，1872年提出改用罗马字。福泽谕吉1873年提出先限制汉字运用，往后时机成熟，就可废除汉字，并认为3000个汉字已足够应付日常。1946年3月盟军最高司令部邀请美国教育使节团来日考察，并于3月31日发表该使节团报告书。在报告中，指出学校教育中使用汉字之弊害与使用罗马字之便利，这是促使汉字-假名混合文字正式化的关键。日本的以上思潮与行动无疑影响着中国的文改人士。

⑫ 例如日本推广以东京（江户）语音为标准音的国语，并从半文半白的文体改为口语化文体；又如中国推广以北京音为标准音的普通话。日本前岛密1866年已主张"言文一致"。至1910年，已有八成出版物用"言文一致体"。蔡元培曾于《国文之将来》（1919）评价道："日本维新初年，出版的书多用汉字，到近年，几乎没有

不是言文一致的。"

⑬ 列宁这番广为引用的话语至今未查到出处。但据报道，北朝鲜就即依据此言，于 1949 年废除了用汉字表记朝鲜语的传统，不再夹杂汉字，并严格限制汉字词的使用。如果属实，可见其对思想深层影响之大。

⑭ 陈独秀指责中国文字"既难载新事新理，且为腐毒思想之巢窟，废之诚不足惜"。五四另一闯将胡适则呼喊："汉字不灭，中国必亡！"瞿秋白激烈抨击说："汉字真正是世界上最龌龊最恶劣最混蛋的中世纪的茅坑"。吴稚晖在《新世纪》第 40 号上说，"中国文字，迟早必废"。当时鲁迅也颇为激进，说："汉字和大众是势不两立的"，"方块汉字真是愚民政策的利器"。

⑮ "根据 1950 年 3 月中共中央组织部长陆定一接见苏联驻华代办谢巴耶夫时通报的材料，当时华北有 150 万党员，其中 130 万是文盲或半文盲。在区委以上领导人员中，近 50% 没有文化或文化不高。中共准备在 2—3 年的时间在党的基层干部中扫除文盲，用 5 年时间在一般党员中扫除文盲。依靠这样一支干部队伍当然是无法对偌大中国进行有效管理的。"军队的文盲情况也是严重的："据统计，1952 年中国（共产党的）军队 128 万排以上的军官，达到大学文化程度的只有 2.14%，具有高中文化水平的占 12%，还有 27.21% 的人是文盲。"（沈志华：《对在华苏联专家问题的历史考察》，载《当代中国史研究》2002 年第 1 期）

⑯ 陈梦家在鸣放中说："文字是需要简单的，但不要混淆。这些简化字，毛病出得最多的是同音替代和偏旁省略。简化后有些混淆。"（转引自《南方都市报》2006 年 3 月 20 日文章《简化字改革五十年》）

⑰ 1923 年日本公布的"常用汉字表"中含有 154 字的简体字，并未推行。1946 年日本内阁公布《当用汉字表》其中有 131 个是简体字。

⑱ 李文涛：《汉语言文字规范化问题研究》（2011 年南京师范大学硕士论文）中也提出汉语言文字"示范化"的理念，指出："规范化"与"示范化"之间存在复杂的辩证关系；两者的关系植根于"政府干预"和"民间学习"之间的关系；"政府干预"与"民间学习"存在矛盾统一。该论述颇有见地。

⑲ 参见陆锡兴（1992），作者认为："正体是写文章、对策习用的字体通体是文献中相承已久，得到广泛流行的俗字；俗体则可能是当时社会日常使用的字体。"

⑳ 王力先生（国家文字改革委员会委员）在对《第二次汉字简化方案（草案）的修订工作》中也曾说过："不要以为笔画越少越好。笔画越少，形近的字就越多。为了节省几笔，却增加了认字的困难，得不偿失。"并指出："原定十画以上的字都要简化。现在看来，这个设想是

不合理的。"（武占坤、马国凡 1988，180 页）周有光（1986）也不得不指出："简化笔画有好处，但好处不大，不是有利而无弊。从清末到解放初期，往往夸大简化的好处。近二十年来的实践，使人们认识到对简化的效果要重新进行全面的、现实的估计。"（第 183 页）但这一观点却在 2006 年有了大相径庭的改变（参见本文"几个可议观点"一节）。

㉑ 江新博士（北京语言大学对外汉语教学中心）2005 年在德国美茵茨大学宣读的论文《针对西方汉语学习者：认读分流，多认少写》中列举了汉字认知心理实验的例证，无意中证实了认读与汉字笔画数量无关的重要规律。有的实验甚至表明，北京郊区的低年级儿童反而对一些实验中出现的繁体字更容易记认。

㉒ 史有为（1983）曾逐字分析并统计简化字（非类推部分的第一表、第二表）的声旁表音度，设满分为 10，第一、第二两表平均声旁表音度为：繁体字（508 字）5.98；简化字（484 字）3.24。简化后表音度下降了 2.74。此后（史有为 1992b/1997）在引用时，改成满分为 1，则二者分别为 0.598 与 0.324。

㉓ 史有为（1991a）曾从书写速度、空间处置难度、认知难度、系统性、笔画和部件的种量、文字的稳定性、时空范围内的信息流动难度等 7 个方面粗略计算了简化的得与失，获得 6：4 的得失评价。记得最初得到的是 5.5：4.5 的结果，为了扩大"得"的分值，又修改了最初的设定。这说明该评价是粗疏的，主观性太大，应该有进一步更客观而精确的统计，以便校正评价结果。

㉔ 周有光（1992）曾指出："有些简化字比繁体字难教、难认、难写。例如简化的'长'字、'尧'字，比繁体字教起来更麻烦，写起来更困难。"（第 236 页）但这一观点却在 2006 年有了大相径庭的改变（参见本文"几个可议观点"一节）。

㉕ 本节提到的前三个观点可看《著名语言学家周有光与记者见面会文字实录》（2006.3.22），见 http://edu.people.com.cn/GB/8216/4226280.html。

㉖ 1950 年代的简化虽然经过四次推行，但相距时间很短（1956.2—1959.7，仅三年半），实际上只能算一次，而且每次都是全国铺开。

㉗ 据台湾《旺报》报道，2014 年 9 月 22 日台湾"中华文化总会"会长刘兆玄出席常熟"两岸汉字艺术节"，会后接受专访表示，汉字简化的阶段性使命已经达成，两岸应该再一次"书同文"，让汉字回归正体（即繁体）。

㉘ 参见香港《语文建设通讯》2014.10，第 107 期，第 30—33 页；《北京青年报》2015.1.11.版 13 载《汉语拼音之父"迎来 110 岁生日——谆谆告诫"要从世界看中国，不要从中国看世界"》。周有光先生是我所尊敬的一位前

輩，是他与倪海曙先生的文字引导我进入语言学领域，并促使我报考语言专业。先生是谦虚的，不争不怒，否认自己是"汉语拼音之父"，并视名利为烟云，常敢说真话，又与时俱进。他还曾经委托我指导他的研究生。我衷心祝愿先生健康长寿。但出于对科学与真理的忠诚，我仍然愿意说出心中不同的看法，以求教于先生。

㉙ 北京306医院金真、香港大学谭力海、萧慧婷对北京玉泉小学4、5年级测试得知，西文从字到音、汉文从字到义会有转换、不畅和翻译障碍。中文者语言区在额中回9、46区，接近布洛卡运动功能区；西文者则在额下回前、后侧，额上回后侧与颞枕叶联合区，是听觉的韦尼克区。西文障碍者高达7%～15%，比中文障碍者2%～7%多一倍以上。仅学说则与西语基本相同，如果同时学汉字要靠"运动"来记忆，要多看、多写、多说。（引自中国科学院网页《构建中国人大脑语言区研究的理论体系》，潘锋编译）

㉚ "方块汉字在电子计算机上遇到的困难，好像一个行将就木的衰老病人"，"历史将证明：电子计算机是方块汉字的掘墓人，也是汉语拼音文字的助产士"。（《语文现代化》1980年第1期）

㉛ 我们高兴地看到，这一从政治决策退回到学术层次的过程已经开启，报刊上已经有许多繁简问题的讨论和报道。例如《光明日报》（2015年1月28日）刊载《汉字繁简争论：眼光应向前看》。

㉜ 日本简化了少量汉字，却没有完全废止繁体字与异体字，许多繁体字与异体字仍允许人们在姓名中使用。这就是一种软规范，值得我们借鉴。日本对汉字保持了一种尊敬的态度。

㉝ 汉字"和谐"概念由香港姚德怀首先以"和谐体"形式提出（载香港《语文建设通讯》2007年12月88期），此后于93—106诸期具体化为消除"一简对多繁"的"和谐体"方案，主要就是恢复大部分同音替前的汉字，求得繁简版汉字对应的和谐。应该说，这是一个非常有创意的设计。

㉞ 袁晓园女士提出的"识繁写简"与此相似，在当时的情势下，难能可贵，值得肯定。但从大陆现实来看简体字是一个现实，首先固化于印刷方面，至于手下不必强调，因此"印简识繁"应该更符合大陆现况。

㉟ 在2007年10月召开的第八届"国际汉字研讨会"上，台湾淡江大学荣誉教授、台湾文化大学中文系兼任教授傅锡壬认为：大陆将文字的使用视为"工具"，以方便、易识为原则；台湾的学者站在教学立场，坚持文字蕴含文化内涵；但书写文字不仅是专家之事，更是庶民之事，大家应从这个层面多加思考。他还表示，两岸任何一方要抛弃现行文字去迁就另一方都是不可能的事，

建议教学应"由繁入简"，因为先学繁体要再认识简体较为简单，但台湾方面也应教学生认识简体字；而书写则"简繁由之"，依个人习惯、公文书和使用需要而定。这一认识得到广泛的支持。

㊱ 参见程星（2014），第7—9页。
㊲ 参见关子尹（2014），第5—7页。
㊳ 2012年圣马力诺共和国宣布采用世界语（Esperanto）作为其官方语言。
㊴ Esperanto的低潮是否与某种语言势力有关，是否存在反操作，这是一个"谜"，值得探究。

参考文献

程星.2014.巴别塔与国际化——国际交流中的语言障碍及解决路径.中国语言资源动态(3).

关子尹.2014.语文作育、大学教研与文化持续发展.中国语言资源动态(3).

郭锡良.1981.汉字知识.北京：北京出版社.

国语研究会所编.1923.国语月刊特刊"汉字改革号".

胡百华、陈明然.2014.和谐体与《通用规范汉字表》.语文建设通讯（总106）.

胡百华、姚德怀、陈明然.2012.汉字"和谐体"的倡议研究及成果.语文建设通讯（总100）.

李宇明.2001.中国现代的语言规划——附论汉字的未来.汉语学习.

陆锡兴.1992.唐代的文字规范和楷体正字的形成.语文建设(6).

倪海曙.1987.拉丁化新文字运动的始末和编年纪事（1987年版）.北京：知识出版社.

商务印书馆.2014.中国语言资源动态（语言教育与社会进步专辑）(3).

沈志华.2002.对在华苏联专家问题的历史考察.当代中国史研究(1).

史有为.1983.简体字与繁体字表音度比较.语文通讯建设（总11）.

史有为.1991a.汉字简化的价值评估.语文建设(3).

史有为.1991b.汉字改革的认识与文字理论的质疑——兼论汉字的共享、共识和共理.语文建设(7).

史有为.1992a.汉字辩证四题.语文建设(8).

史有为.1992b.汉字的重新发现.世界汉语教学(4).另收入史有为《汉语如是观》（北京语言文化大学出版社，1997）.

史有为.1998.新世纪汉语汉字之整合.语文建设通讯（总55）.

史有为.2002.中国的英语第二公用语化问题——兼及香港和上海的相关课题.语文建设通讯（总71）.

史有为.2014.冷眼热心说汉字——兼议"和谐体".语文建设通讯(总 107).

孙中山.1917—1919.建国方略.北京:中学图书馆文库.

王宁.2010.从汉字改革史看汉字规范和"简繁之争".云南师范大学学报哲学社会科学版(6).

吴玉章.1978.文字改革文集.北京:中国人民大学出版社.

吴玉章.1958.当前文字改革的任务.人民日报.1958 年 1 月 13 日.

武占坤、马国凡.1988.汉字·汉字改革史.长沙:湖南人民出版社.

现代汉语规范问题学术会议 1955/1956.现代汉语规范问题学术会议纪要(1956 年 4 月修订).当代中国的文字改革.北京:当代中国出版社.

许长安.2000.语文现代化先驱卢戆章.厦门:厦门大学出版社.

许寿椿.2012.从铅字机械打字到电脑打字——汉字厄运到复兴进程一窥.北京:北京时代弄潮文化发展公司.

姚德怀.2007.寻求和谐的语文生活——文字改革三大任务 50 周年反思之一:文字问题.语文建设通讯(总 88).

中国语言文字网.2012.新中国成立以来文字改革的发展历程.

周恩来.1958.当前文字改革的任务(1956.1.10 在政协全国委员会举行的报告会上作的报告).文字改革(2).

周有光.1986.中国语文的现代化.济南:山东教育出版社.

周有光.1992.新语文的新建设.北京:语文出版社.

作者简介

史有为,日本明海大学教授,博士生导师,主要研究方向为现代汉语语法、外来词、对外汉语教学等。

The Strategy of Chinese Language and the Reformation of Chinese Characters

Shi Youwei
Meikai University

Abstract:From the angle of language learning and use, language can be further categorized as cultural language, practical language, and life language. To achieve the strategic objective, Chinese needs to improve the cultural, scientific and technological, economic, and military contents of language. Domestically, Chinese has the strategic objective to standardize the variations and writing system and respond to national unity. All these call for the rethinking of the reformation of Chinese characters and the strategy of Chinese characters. At the present stage, when handling some major language issues, it is more appropriate to make concessions in order to gain advantages on the one hand, and to move forward slowly and steadily on the other hand.

Key words:strategy of Chinese language, cultural language, reformation of Chinese characters, strategy of Chinese characters, identification

字母词语收录词典需要注意规范的若干问题

于全有

提　要：近年来，陆续有现代汉语工具书将字母词语收录词典。以新近出版的中国社会科学院语言研究所词典编辑室编写的《现代汉语词典》(第 6 版)为例，在其所收录的字母词语中，仍一定程度地存在称谓的科学性问题、字母的读音及标注问题、部分词条的释义问题及相关联的其他需要研究的问题。进一步加强对这些已然存在的问题的规范性研究，对于推进字母词语与现代汉语规范化工作、维护《现代汉语词典》的规范性地位等，具有十分积极的理论意义与实践意义。

关键词：字母词语　西文字母开头的词语　字母开头的词语　《现代汉语词典》　规范

一　引言

近些年来，陆续有现代汉语工具书将字母词语收录词典。如刘涌泉《现代汉语规范词典》、中国社会科学院语言研究所词典编辑室编写的《现代汉语词典》等。其中，中国社会科学院语言研究所词典编辑室编写的《现代汉语词典》，在第 1 版(1978 年)正文词条中收录了"阿 Q""三 K 党""X 射线"等字母词 3 条，第 3 版(1996 年)正文词条中收录字母词 4 条(较前版增加了"卡拉 OK"一词)，并首次在正文词条后以附录形式收录了西文字母开头的词语 39 条。至第 4 版(2002 年)时，以附录形式收录西文字母开头的词语 142 条，正文字母词 3 条；第 5 版(2005 年)在第 4 版的基础上，附录中新增字母词语 49 条，删除 9 条；第 6 版(2012 年)正文和附录收录的西文字母词已达 242 条(正文 3 条，附录 239 条。以上计算不包括未做词条形式出现的、附属于某一汉字形式词条中的诸如"维生素 A"等形式)。显然，字母词语被收录进一般的现代汉语词典已呈不断增长之势。以新近出版的由中国社会科学院语言研究所词典编辑室编写的《现代汉

语词典》(第 6 版)为例(以下简称《现汉 6》)，作为"遵循现代汉语规范化的一贯宗旨"、力图"使这部具有广泛社会影响的语文词典与时俱进，把质量提高到一个新水平"(见第 6 版说明)的一次系统的修订，本版《现代汉语词典》对于更好地满足社会语言生活的实际需求，进一步明确词汇规范，进一步促进现代汉语规范化等，无疑具有十分积极的意义。

笔者近来因探究问题的需要，在翻阅以《现汉 6》为代表的现代汉语词典中所收录的字母词语时，陆续发现不少相关词典中所收录的字母词语，仍一定程度地存在早已出现的称谓方式的科学性问题、字母的读音及标注问题、词条的释义问题及相关联的其他问题。进一步加强对这些已然存在的问题的规范性探究，对于推进字母词语与现代汉语规范化工作、维护现代汉语词典的规范性地位等，具有十分积极的理论意义与实践意义。本文拟以《现汉 6》为例，扼要对上述问题的规范谈一些自己的认识与看法。

二　称谓的科学性问题

《现汉 6》中所收录的字母词语，共有

242 条。其中,以正文形式收录的 3 条("阿Q""三 K 党""卡拉 OK"),以附录形式收录的西文字母开头的词语 239 条。这些词语,按一般的称谓习惯,可以概括性地将其一并称之为"字母词语"。就以附录形式收录的这 239 条"西文字母开头的词语"而言,从所涉及字母的来源上看,除了二十几个未做来源说明的词条(如"AA 制""Y 染色体")外,涉及英语(如"AM""APEC")、法语(如"pH值")、日语(如"NHK")、希腊语(如"ISO")、拉丁语(如"T 淋巴细胞")等字母及汉语拼音字母(如"HSK""RMB")等多种。若将这些以字母开头的词语概称为"西文字母开头的词语",则存在不甚科学之处。

《现汉 6》在正文所收录的"西文"词条中明确说:【西文】指欧美各国的文字。①

"西文"既然是指欧美各国的文字,那么,作为像汉语、日语等非欧美国家的文字,自然应当不在"西文"的范畴内。因而,像含有汉语拼音字母等这类字母词语,理论上就不好归入属于是"西文字母开头的词语"中,尽管汉语拼音字母是从拉丁(罗马)字母中借鉴过来的。

首先,现行《汉语拼音方案》中所使用的汉语拼音字母,理论上并不是西文字母,它是汉语中所使用的一种拼写、记录汉语语音的字母,已属于我们自己民族语言的拼音字母。尽管从来源上看,现行《汉语拼音方案》中所使用的汉语拼音字母借自于世界上通行的拉丁字母,但只是借助了拉丁字母的字母形式。借过来之后,我们已经进行了不少民族形式的改造,已属于典型的"洋装虽然穿在身,我心'已然'是中国心"的状况。比方说,《汉语拼音方案》中的字母表,所用的字母虽然是拉丁字母,却已有自己的作为汉语拼音字母的名称:a(a)、b(bê)、c(cê)、d(dê)、e(e)、f(êf)、g(gê)、h(ha)、i(i)、j(jie)、k(kê)、l(êl)、m(êm)、n(nê)、o(o)、p

(pê)、q(qiu)、r(a'er)、s(ês)、t(tê)、u(u)、v(vê)、w(wa)、x(xi)、y(ya)、z(zê)(字母后面括号里为汉语拼音字母名称音。需要说明的是,《汉语拼音方案》发布当初使用的是当时人们较为熟悉的注音字母来标注这些字母的名称音,后来出现用上述新形式的字母来标注这些字母的名称音)。这些字母名称,不同于同样是使用拉丁字母的英语、法语、德语、意大利语、西班牙语等西方语言。也就是说,被吸收到汉语拼音方案中的拉丁字母,已成为我们民族语言自己的字母了,已不属于西文字母了。关于这一点,周恩来1958 年在《当前文字改革的任务》中早已说得很清楚:"现在世界上有六十多个国家采用拉丁字母来作为书写语言的符号。例如英国、法国、德国、意大利、西班牙……都是用的拉丁字母。它们接受了拉丁字母之后,都对它作了必要的调整或者加工,使它适应本民族语言的需要,因此都已经成为各个民族自己的字母了。……同样,我们采用了拉丁字母,经过我们的调整使它适应了汉语的需要之后,它已经成为我们自己的汉语拼音字母,已不再是古拉丁文的字母,更不是任何一个外国的字母了。字母是拼写语言的工具,我们用它来为我们服务,正像我们采用火车、轮船、汽车、飞机(从来源来说,这些东西也都是外来的)来为我们服务一样。"②将汉语拼音字母归于或混同于西文字母,显然是只看到了汉语拼音字母借用了拉丁字母的字母形式,而没有认识到汉语拼音字母已是属于我们自己的民族语言形式的字母了。同样,将源于日语中的字母开头的词语归入"西文字母开头的词语"中,也一定程度上存在类似问题的纠葛。

其次,作为一种称谓方式,"西文字母开头的词语"之称在称谓实际所收录的一些包括源于东西方语言中字母开头的词语在内的字母词语时,概括性差,概括度不够。前文已经说过,《现汉 6》中所收录的字母词语,从所涉及词语中字母的来源上看,除二十几个未做来源说明的词条外,已涉及英语、法语、日语、希腊语、拉丁语等字母及汉语拼音字母等多种。而这些词语中的字母,有的属于西文字母,有的不属于或不再属于西文字母。因而,以"西文字母开头的词语"之称去概括实际所收录的这些字母词语,显然是概括性差,概括度不够。

因此,学理上,在称谓一些源于包括东西方语言中字母开头的词语在内的字母词语时,称其为"字母开头的词语",显然应比称其为"西文字母开头的词语"更为科学,更为准确。

三 字母的读音及标注问题

汉语字母词语中的字母来源相对比较复杂,这使得这些字母词语中的字母的读音及其标注等问题也相应地随之复杂起来。《现汉 6》后面所附录的《西文字母开头的词语》部分,所收录的 239 条词语及正文中所收录的 3 条字母词语,对所涉及的字母均未标注读音,只是在《西文字母开头的词语》部分的脚注中说:"这里收录的常见西文字母开头的词语,有的是借词,有的是外语缩略语,有的是汉语拼音缩略语。在汉语中西文字母一般是按西文的音读的,这里就不用汉语拼音标注读音,词目中的汉字部分仍用汉语拼音标注读音。"③

表面上看,尽管这些字母词语中的字母在收录词典时虽然词条上没有一一对其进行标音,但关于这些字母词语中的字母怎么读音的问题似已通过这个脚注说得很清楚了。但实际上,这是一个非常复杂的问题,既不容易比较轻松地完全弄清楚、说明白,又在读音的实际标注上存在诸多棘手的问题,一般的读者要仅据此就完全清楚其正确的读音,谈何容易!汉语字母词语的读音及

其标注问题,目前已经成为有关字母词语入典规范方面亟需解决的一个重要的实际问题。

(一) 入现代汉语词典的字母词语中的字母,需要也应该明确标音

首先,工具书之所以成为工具书,就是要为人们掌握、使用某一方面的内容释疑解惑,提供方便。特别是作为"以确定词汇规范为目的,以推广普通话、促进汉语规范化为宗旨"的《现代汉语词典》,更应如此。给入典的字母词语同入典的其他词语一样标注读音,是现实语言生活中人们规范地掌握、使用语言的基本需要。通常而言,词语的音形义是带有基础性、规范性的。现代汉语词典类工具书在对词语进行解释时不可或缺的几个重要方面,也是现实语言生活中人们对其规范地掌握、使用最需要的几个重要方面。但在目前能够见到的相关工具书中,对入典的字母词语,却往往只有形义的解释,鲜有读音标注。即使早期存在的部分字母词语在入现代汉语词典正文内容词条时,对其字母进行过标音,也不过是以"阿Q"等为代表的几个以汉字开头的字母词语。现不论是字母词语入词典的正文还是附录,已基本上没有对其字母读音的标注。如果说这种状况出现在不是以规范为宗旨的一般字母词语词典中还尚好理解的话,那么,在以规范为宗旨的具有基础性、工具性的现代汉语词典中出现这种情况,就难免有些不甚说得过去了。

其次,不能因为给入典的字母词语标注读音的复杂与棘手,就一直这么含混模糊地、姑且由之地处理其入典中的标音问题。对入现代汉语词典的字母词语中的字母不标注读音,只笼统地说其字母"按西文字母读音",一般的读者在语言实践操作中难以据此就完全清楚其正确的读音。这是因为,一是西文字母就字母本身而言,有多种系

统,如拉丁字母、希腊字母、斯拉夫字母等诸系统,每种系统中的字母的读音均有自己的特点,并不都相同,一般人实际上难以都规范地掌握这些不同系统中的不同字母的读音;二是即使是源于同一字母系统中的字母,在不同语言中的具体读音也不尽相同。如以拉丁字母为例,现世界上数以百计的国家的语言中在使用拉丁字母,而在这诸多使用拉丁字母的民族语言中,这些字母在这些民族语言中的读音也不尽相同。一般人实际上还是很难都能具体掌握其在不同语言中的不尽相同的读音。也正因为如此,对现入典的字母词语中的字母只注明来源而不标音的方式,会导致读者在语言实践中并不一定能很好地、合乎学理地解决字母的规范读音问题。更何况,部分字母词语中的字母究竟到底是源于何种字母尚不甚明了,该按什么音去读尚处于模糊状态之状况了。例如:

【ISO】国际标准化组织。〔从希腊语 iSOS(相同的)得名,一说从英语 Intenational Organization for Standardization〕[4]

这里,作为专有名称的字母词语"ISO"的读音,到底是按希腊语读还是按英语读,就是一笔模糊状态的糊涂账,还需要进一步研究。这种状况,颇类似于早期的中国社会科学院语言研究所词典编辑室编写的《现代汉语词典》第3版之前对专有名称"阿Q"读音的两种标注"Ā Qiū,又 Ā Kiū",[5]存在专有名词不明确专有读音为哪一种的状况。

设想一般人都能清楚明白地掌握上述林林总总的不同系统、不同民族语言中的字母的读音,是不切实际的;倘若明知问题之所在,却因问题的复杂与棘手而就一直这么相对含混模糊地处理其入典中的标音问题,也不是积极面对问题并试图解决问题的理想方式。实际情况是:收入现代汉语词典的字母词语中的字母,需要也应该明确标音。

（二）入现代汉语词典的字母词语中的字母,需要研究怎样规范标音

入现代汉语词典的字母词语中的字母目前之所以鲜有标音,大概与这些字母词语中的字母的标音到底按什么标音、怎么标音问题(包括怎么排序)等问题的纠缠不清有很大的关系。这里面有不少问题需要进一步明确、厘清。源于英文字母的按英文字母的读音去标注,

理论上,按字母词语中的字母在其直接来源的具体民族语言中的读音去标音,如源于希腊字母的按希腊字母的读音去标注,源于英文字母的按英文字母的读音去标注,源于汉语拼音字母的按汉语拼音的字母读音去标注,这应该是对字母词语中的字母怎么标音最切合词语来源实际的理性选择。这种选择可能导致出现的一个现象是:纷繁多样的字母带来纷繁多样的字母读音,同一字母形式在不同的字母词语中可能因来源的不同而读不同的音。与之相应的另一种方式读音标注的选择是,大原则上按字母词语中的字母的来源读音(包括原字母直接来源系统——民族语言中的字母音、民族语言字母的直接来源系统音等)中影响相对比较大、相对较便利的某系统的读音来标注。如直接源于汉语拼音中的字母不按汉语拼音字母的读音标注,而是按同源于拉丁字母、目前影响也相对比较大的英文字母的读音来标注;或者是直接源于汉语拼音中的字母不按汉语拼音字母表中规定的字母名称音的读音标注,而是按时下影响相对较大、一般人相对更熟悉些的汉语拼音字母的呼读音来标注等(当然,这每一种选择当中都有许多值得探讨的具体问题)。这应该是现情况下对字母词语中的字母怎么标音的最切合人们惯常的实际读音习惯的习性选择。这种选择可能导致的一个现象是:字母词语

中的字母标音不一定切合词语来源的实际，却在一定程度上适合人们的某一习惯；字母读音的纷繁复杂性相对减弱。面对这两种比较主要的读音选择方式，比较而言，由于近年在字母词语中的字母读音及标注问题上，我们实际上并无比较明确、具体的理性规范来指导社会语言生活，人们在具体的社会语言生活中往往多依据已掌握的习惯形式去读字母词语中的字母音，从而使后一种选择方式呈自然上升之势。

不管这些字母的读音怎么选择，大原则上按字母词语中的字母的来源去读音（如来源于某一语种的字母就按来源语种里字母的音去读），这一点学术界的相关认识大体一致。关键是，字母读音的来源有的有直接来源与间接来源之分，有的有名称音与呼读音之别，有的有影响大与影响小之不同。在这向下再怎么选择上，大家目前的认识就不尽相同了。相比较而言，对于直接来源于某一外文的字母，按来源语种里字母音读，这一点大家的认识相对比较一致；而对于直接来源于汉语拼音的字母到底怎么读，大家的认识就不完全一致了。以字母词语中源于汉语拼音中的字母为例，目前学术界对其怎么读音，大体上就有以下几种：(1) 按《汉语拼音方案》规定的字母名称音读；(2) 按英文字母音读；(3) 按呼读音读；(4) 按元音读本音、辅音一律后加元音[O]来读；(5) 按拼读中用呼读音、引用外文时用英文音读等种种看法。⑥而社会语言生活的实际状况是：由于《汉语拼音方案》字母表中规定的字母名称没有得到相应的推行，"注音字母的名称实际上代替了拼音字母的名称。近来又有英文字母名称代替的趋势"⑦。之所以会出现这样的状况，原因是多方面的：既与自《汉语拼音方案》1958年开始推行至今，从小学开始一直重视并先教声韵调及拼音，然后再以附带的形式略带一下字母表的这种没有

认真推行字母表中字母名称教学的教学方式有关，又与传统的注音字母音的惯性影响、我们这些年来在字母词语的规范问题上的滞后及一定的社会风潮影响有关。现实的社会语言生活实际状况，迫切需要我们能够集思广益，对字母词语中字母的读音规范作出适切的选择。比较而言，笔者认为，对于字母词语里直接源于汉语拼音中的字母的读音，从这类字母的来源、读音的社会性与规范原则的一贯性上看，理应按来源读汉语拼音字母的音。具体而言，理论上，汉语拼音字母的音宜读《汉语拼音方案》字母表中规定的字母名称音。但鉴于目前社会对《汉语拼音方案》字母表中规定的字母名称音的认知相对较差的状况，推行起来难免有一定的难度，加之在一套字母里又有名称音又有呼读音的两读形式所可能带来的潜在的混乱与不经济的影响，用汉语拼音字母的字母名称音很可能比不上在中国已经完全社会化的汉语拼音字母的呼读音更容易为人们所把握、接受。而用英文字母音对于学过英语者容易掌握接受，虽然随着这些年学英语的潮流，在中国（特别是在新生代中）也有相当广泛的基础，但一是英文字母音目前在中国显然还达不到汉语拼音字母的呼读音在我们整个社会的社会化程度与普及程度，二是汉语拼音字母在拼读时读呼读音、在字母词中读英文音，汉语拼音字母中的这种一套字母两读形式同样也还有一个经济性问题。从理论上、规范原则的一致性上及现实的社会化程度、普及程度、易把握程度上等考虑，当然也包括从顺应语言文字的民族性与吸收字母词语民族化的考虑，对于字母词语里直接源于汉语拼音中的字母的读音，笔者倾向于还是用民族语言中的汉语拼音字母的音，用汉语拼音字母的呼读音。如b(bo，不是名称音 bê)、p(po，不是名称音

pê)、m(mo，不是名称音 êm)、f(fo，不是名称音 êf)等。当然，对字母词语中源于汉语拼音的字母主张用汉语拼音字母的呼读音读也好，还是主张用英文字母音读也好，各自的优长与不足都摆在那里，关键在于我们相关的规范化工作依什么样的理念来怎么决策了。

（三）由入现代汉语词典的字母词语中的字母标音所引起的相关问题

给入现代汉语词典的字母词语中的字母标音，会由此而引起一系列的需要进一步研究的相关问题。如标外文字母音无法或不宜、不便用现有的汉语拼音去标音问题，标音的方式不合现有的汉语拼音拼写规律问题，外文字母的标音方式与汉语拼音的标音方式连写问题，等等。这都是需要考虑到并注意研究的问题。以现行的《汉语拼音方案》中的汉语拼音的记音能力而言，它主要是用于对汉语普通话记音的。如用它去标注外文字母的音，难免有力所不及的时候，这当中的问题就需要研究怎么解决（前文所引《现汉 6》后面所附录的《西文字母开头的词语》部分的脚注中所说的"在汉语中西文字母一般是按西文的音读的，这里就不用汉语拼音标注读音，词目中的汉字部分仍用汉语拼音标注读音"，其中的"这里就不用汉语拼音标注读音"之表述，单独看有歧义：一是可理解为可用汉语拼音注音但没用，二是可理解为不用汉语拼音注音。从这句话的上下文看，似乎是前一种意思强一些，给人以西文字母似乎都能用汉语拼音标注读音、不过这里不做标注而已的印象。这种表述，无论从理论上还是从实践上说，都是不甚严密的、存在一定的问题的）。对于由于给入现代汉语词典的字母词语中的字母标音而来的一些标音的方式可能不一定完全合乎现有的汉语拼音拼写规律问题（如历史上《现

代汉语词典》中曾出现的"阿 Q"的读音标注"Ā Kiū"中的"Kiū"音，就是一个非普通话音节中的音）、外文字母的标音方式与汉语拼音的标音方式如何连接等问题，以及字母词语中的若干字母是否可以连读等问题，我们均应该以平和的探讨、探索问题的心态，去考虑、思索、研究这些比较特殊的问题。我们认为，因为事物的规律通常都是有一般、有特殊，外来的外文字母音本来就有它的不同于本民族语言的特殊性，对其标音也不能脱离其外来的特殊性而一概而论。

四 部分词条的释义问题及相关联的其他需要研究的问题

（一）部分词条的释义问题

《现汉 6》中，在以附录形式收录的《西文字母开头的词语》里，有部分字母词语的释义还不同程度地存在一些需要进一步研究、丰富、完善的问题。例如：

1.【α 粒子】α lìzǐ　阿尔法粒子。
2.【α 射线】α shèxiàn　阿尔法射线。
3.【β 粒子】β lìzǐ　贝塔粒子。
4.【β 射线】β shèxiàn　贝塔射线。
5.【γ 刀】γ dāo　伽马刀。
6.【γ 射线】γ shèxiàn　伽马射线。

上述词条中的解释，等于只是"西文字母汉语音译＋原词条汉字"，至于词条意义到底是什么，还是没有具体解释。其实，这些词条的汉字表示形式"阿尔法粒子""阿尔法射线""贝塔粒子""贝塔射线""伽马刀""伽马射线"等，词典的正文中都对其设有专门的词条作了解释。这里，若分别在这些词条后面能再示以"见×页×汉字词条"等类似的导引，对读者而言就更方便、更好了。这样，既对词条的具体解释作了必要的导引，又和整个词典处理类似问题的体例保持了相对一致性。这种类似的宜作同样补充

的词条还有不少,诸如"DNA""e-mail""UFO""WTO""X 刀""X 光""X 射线"等等。

还有的词条的义项,还可作必要的丰富、完善。例如:

7.【AM】调幅。〔英 amplitude moduli-ationde 的缩写〕

这里关于"AM"的解释不是不可以,而是在目前的一些汉语说明类的常见书面语言中,"AM"还经常作为"午前""上午"的意思出现(源于英文)。此义项似也应收入到词条的义项中。

（二）相关联的其他需要研究的问题

由字母开头的词语入现代汉语词典,还带来了一系列的其他相关问题需要研究。如字母词语的大小写问题、字母词语入典如何排序与编索引问题、一些作为形象表达而来的字母词语（如"T 型人才"等）中的字母到底依什么音来读合适问题,等等（似是而非的字母词语入典违法违规等问题另当别论⑧）。这些问题,从多年前的字母词语入典开始就已经存在,虽然期间也不乏一些有益的探索,但至今却仍谈不上已完全得到圆满的解决,不少问题依然存在,依然需要进一步加强相关方面的规范性探索。比方说,字母词语入典如何排序与编索引问题,这是目前有关字母词语入典迫切需要探讨、探索的重要问题之一。历史上,少量汉字打头的字母词语在进入现代汉语词典正文时,采用的是按词首汉字的音序来索引。现在一般的现代汉语词典,除了几个汉字打头的字母词语入词典正文内容依旧采用按词首汉字的音序来索引外,对大多数以字母开头的词语采用的是以正文后附录的形式收进词典。这样,同样是字母词语、同样是在一本词典中,就出现了用两种不同的收录方式收进词典,其索引的方式自然也不相同。同时,以

附录的形式收录进现代汉语词典中的字母词语,与一般的字母词词典收录的字母词语,其排序与索引目前也尚未形成相对一致的规范。像以《现汉 6》为代表的词典,在附录的字母词语的排序上,是先排希腊字母顺序的字母词语,然后再跟着排拉丁字母顺序的字母词语;而在刘涌泉编著的《字母词词典》（上海辞书出版社,2001）中,其词条的索引排序,则是先排拉丁字母顺序的字母词语,然后跟着排希腊字母顺序的字母词语。字母词语入典的规范化,亟需对上述问题进行必要的规范性的探索与引导。

附　注

① 中国社会科学院语言研究所词典编辑室编《现代汉语词典》(第 6 版)第 1389 页,商务印书馆,2012 年.
② 转引自李平《拼音人生——语文现代化文集》第 115 页,西安出版社,2008 年.
③ 中国社会科学院语言研究所词典编辑室编《现代汉语词典》(第 6 版)第 1750 页,商务印书馆,2012 年.
④ 中国社会科学院语言研究所词典编辑室编《现代汉语词典》(第 6 版) 第 1752—1753 页,商务印书馆,2012 年.
⑤ 参阅于全有《关于"阿 Q"读音的规范化问题》,《辽宁教育行政学院学报》2001 年第 11 期。另参阅于全有主编《中国语言学研究》第 48—55 页,吉林文史出版社,2006 年版.
⑥ 郭熙《汉语、汉字和汉语现行记录系统运用中的一些问题及对策》,《语言文字应用》1992 年第 3 期.
⑦ 周有光《回忆〈汉语拼音方案〉的制定过程》,《语文建设》,1998 年第 6 期.
⑧ 参阅刘婷《百学者称现代汉语词典收录 NBA 属违法,编者回应》,《北京晨报》,2012 年 8 月 29 日.

参考文献

本社编.1988.汉语拼音论文选.北京:文字改革出版社.

郭熙.1992.汉语、汉字和汉语现行记录系统运用中的一些问题及对策.语言文字应用(3).

李平.2008.拼音人生——语文现代化文集.西安:西安出版社.

刘涌泉.2001.字母词词典.上海:上海辞书出版社.

于全有. 2001.语言理论与应用研究.北京:中国社会出版社.

晁继周. 2004.树立正确的语文观念是编好规范型词典的关键. 语言文字应用(2).

中国社会科学院语言研究所词典编辑室编. 2012.现代汉语词典(第 6 版).北京:商务印书馆.

周有光. 1998. 回忆《汉语拼音方案》的制定过程. 语文建设(6).

作者简介

于全有,博士,沈阳帅范大学文学院教授,硕士生导师,主要研究方向为语言哲学、社会语言学、修辞学等。

Problems on Putting Letter Words into Dictionary

Yu Quanyou

Shenyang Normal University

Abstract: In recent years, letter words are included in many modern Chinese reference works. Take the latest published *The Contemporary Chinese Dictionary* (*version 6*) as an example, which was compiled by the dictionary editorial office of Chinese Academy of Social Sciences. Some letter words, still have terminological problems, letters' pronunciation and annotation problems, vocabulary entry's definition problems and some other related problems. These problems have existed for a long time. If we further strengthen specific research of these problems, it will be of great positive theoretical and practical significance to promote the specification of letter words and modern Chinese, and maintain the status of *The Contemporary Chinese Dictionary*

Key words: letter words, Western language letters, specification of *The Contemporary Chinese Dictionary*

Interaction between Phonological and Lexical Development of Putonghua-Speaking Children

Zhu Hua and Qi Ruying

Abstract: The paper investigates the interaction between phonological and lexical development among four Putonghua-speaking children between first-word and fifty-word stages. Using longitudinal recordings of four children's spontaneous speech collected over one year, this paper analyses the shared phonemic inventories both in the children's target words and their realisations during four-word, ten-word, twenty-word, thirty-word and fifty-word stages. It is found that children's vocabulary at four-word and ten-word stages are primarily words in syllable shapes of CV (consonant and vowel) and consist of stop or nasal consonants and open vowels. While the number of consonants and vowels in their target words begins to expand rapidly over the next twenty-word and thirty-word stages, the size of the target phonemic inventories exceeds significantly that of productive phonemic inventories. However, by the time when the children reach the fifty-word stage, there are significant individual variations as to the size of phonemic inventories and speed of development. The comparison of shared words among the children's production at different stages shows a clear preference for words with certain phonological features, i.e., syllable shapes CV or V, stop and nasal consonants and open vowels. These results support the argument that lexical and phonological development, while following their own paths of development, interact with each other in both directions in early age. Lexical development is influenced by phonological selection and phonological development is driven to some extent by the need of learning new words.

Key words: Putonghua-speaking children, lexical development, phonological development, interaction

Introduction

In a recent review article, Carol Stoel-Gammon (2011) argued that linguistic research and language acquisition studies need to pay attention to the areas of overlap rather than focusing on one separate domain. The interaction between lexical and phonological development is one important area of overlap in children's language development which deserves attention in expanding our understanding of how children acquire their native language(s).

Previous studies have found that children have certain sound preferences and avoidances up to the 50-word stage (e. g. Schwartz & Leonard 1982; Leonard et al. 1981; Kiparsky & Menn 1977; Ingram 1976). Based on their studies of seven English monolingual studying children, Ferguson and Farwell (1975) argued that young children seem more likely to produce words whose phonological characteristics are consistent with their own phonologies than words composed of sounds that are not part of their phonological systems. Similarly, Leonard et al. (1981) has shown that young children are more likely to learn a new word if the phonological characteristics of that word are consistent with the children's own existing phonological system in the mental lexicon. Young children's lexical errors often occur to those words with similar phonological features, indicating that children are relying on familiarity in the lexicon (Vihman 1981).

In addition to sound preference, evidence from experimental studies further demonstrates the effect of phonotactic probability on lexical acquisition. Friederici & Wessels (1993) found that at the age of nine months, infants prefer to listen to phonotactically legal words rather than phonotactically illegal ones. At the same age, they prefer to listen to non-words with a high-probability phonotactic pattern rather than those with a low-probability phonotactic pattern (Jusczyk, Luce & Charles-Luce 1994); they prefer to listen to unfamiliar words of their native language than words of a foreign language if the latter violates the phonotactics of their native language (Jusczyk et al. 1993). The results could be interpreted in three ways. One possibility is that phonotactic probability aids the infant in determining which sound sequences are likely to form words in their native language (Jusczyk et al. 1994; Luce & Pisoni 1998). The second possibility is that infants are sensitive to the distribution of sounds in the ambient language and may develop representations of words in phonological form without semantic knowledge (Jusczyk et al. 1994). The third possibility is that infants listen longer to high probability sound sequences because these sequences are more difficult to discriminate from other sound sequences, and therefore, high probability preference results from lexical inhibition of language processing and learning.

Analysis of the phonological features of the words among children's vocabulary inventories also supports phonological selection in operation. Stoel-Gammon (2011) reviewed studies that analysed the segmental characteristics of CDI (MacArthur Communicative Development Inventories) and the results were consistent: children's early words tend to be short, either monosyllables or disyllables, with a predominance of stops in the initial position.

The current study aims to examine the interaction between phonological and lexical development by investigating shared phonological inventories at four-word, ten-word, twenty-word, thirty-word and fifty-word stages among four Putonghua-speaking children. It re-analyses the longitudinal data of four Putonghua-speaking children which was presented at regular time intervals previously published in Zhu Hua (2002). The results on phonological development are reported in Zhu & Dodd (2000).

Study design

Participants

Four children, two boys and two girls (referred to as J. J., Z. J., H. Y. and Z. W.), in Beijing participated in the study. The subject information is summarized in Table 1. All of the children were the only child in the family. Medical records indicated that they were all healthy and had no hearing impairments. Furthermore, their motor development was reported to be within a normal range. All of the parents were Putonghua speakers. For two of the children, family relatives primarily cared for them during the day while the other two attended a private nursery.

Table 1 Subject information in the longitudinal study of normally developing children

Child	Gender	Age range	Age of four-word point	Age of reaching 50-word milestone
J. J.	girl	1;1.15-2;0.15	1;2.0	1;6
Z. J.	boy	1;0.0-2;0.15	1;4.0	1;9
H. Y.	boy	0;10.15-2;0.5	1;2.0	1;10
Z. W.	girl	1;2.0-1;8.0	1;2.15	1;6

Note: Four-word point is defined by Vihman (1996) as the approximate beginning of lexical use.

Data collection

Collection of spontaneous data took place every 15 days. In each data collection session, the mothers conversed with the children while playing together. They were instructed to repeat the child's words when they could so that the target adult forms were recorded on tape for ease of later transcription. The conversation of each child was recorded. Before the first data collection session, the mothers were trained and given detailed guidelines as to what was expected for data collection. To a certain extent, this ensured consistency in the data collection method used for the different children and between different data collection sessions for the same child.

Transcription

All the speech samples from each session were transcribed using the International Phonetic Alphabet. Inter-transcriber reliability (on 10% of the samples) for syllable-initial word-initial; syllable-initial within-word; syllable-final word-final; and syllable-final within-word consonants was 94.3%, 92.9%, 98.5% and 98.1% respectively. The children's imitated productions were marked in the data analysis. Unintelligible productions (i.e. the targets of these productions were not clear from the context) were also marked.

Results

Developmental stage

Data was analysed in terms of the

four-word, ten-word, twenty-word, thirty-word and fifty-word stages. For most children that have been studied to date, the four-word stage is the approximate beginning of lexical use (Vihman 1996) and there is usually a rapid expansion in vocabulary after reaching fifty-word stage (Stoel-Gammon 2011). There are individual differences among the subjects with regards to the age of onset of the four-word stage and the speed of lexical expansion. The development of the two boys (H. Y. and Z. J.) is much slower than that of the two girls (Z. W. and J. J.), while H. Y. and Z. J. reached the fifty-word point at the age of 1;10.15 and 1;9 respectively, Z. W. and J. J. reached the milestone at the age of 1;6. One child, Z. J, despite having a late onset, experienced a rapid expansion between the twenty-word stage and fifty-word stage.

Consonants

Table 2 shows the emergence of consonants at the four-word stage. A sound would be considered as "emerged" when the child produced the sound in realisation at least once. Target consonants are those that children attempted to produce, whereas the realisation ones are those children actually produced.

Table 2 Emergence of consonants (four-word stage)

Name	Age	No. of words	Syllable-initial target	Syllable-initial realisation	Syllable-final target	Syllable-final realisation
H. Y.	1;1.15	5	p, k, m, ts, tɕ	b, g, m, t, tɕ	n, ŋ	n, ŋ
Z. J.	1;4	5	p, m, t	b, m, tɕ		n
Z. W.	1;2	5	p, m, n	b, m, n		
J. J.	1;2	5	p, t, tɕ	b, ph, d, t	ŋ	

As Table 2 shows, all of the children tend to produce voiced syllable-initial consonants (e.g. /p/ [b]; /t/ [d]). The target repertoire consists of a small set of stops and nasals. The predominant presence of stops and nasals is also found in the children's realisations. Although an affricate sound emerged in two children's realisation repertoire at this stage, the other two did not produce this sound. The same applies to syllable-final consonants which appeared in two of the children's production.

At the ten-word stage (Table 3), the children's target repertoires expanded with the addition of some affricates and fricatives, lateral approximants and the feature of aspiration. The productive repertories, however, remain more or less the same as that of the four-word stage with the exception of the appearance of a velar fricative /x/ in two children and the disappearance of voiced stops in three out of the four children. Apart from Z.W., all of the children had one syllable-final consonant as part of the target repertoire and were able to produce it correctly.

The same trend observed for the ten-word stage also applied to the twenty-word stage. All the children by the twenty-word stage (Table 4) had the two syllable-final consonants in target, but failed to produce

the alveolar nasal /n/. More syllable-initial consonants are targeted, however, the expansion of the repertoires in production was slow. Most of the children were only able to produce stops, nasals and two fricatives. No affricates were present.

Table 3   Emergence of consonants（ten-word stage）

Name	Age	No. of words	Syllable-initial target	Syllable-initial realisation	Syllable-final target	Syllable-final realisation
H. Y.	1;4	10	p, k, m, n, l, x, ts, tɕ, tʂ, tʂʰ	p, t, m, n, l, x	n	n
Z. J.	1;7	10	p, l, x, ts	b, p, tɕ	ŋ	ŋ
Z. W.	1;2.15	10	p, t, m, n, ʂ, tʂʰ	p, t, m, n		
J. J.	1;3	11	p, t, tʰ, m, s, ts, tʂʰ	p, t, tʰ, x	ŋ	ŋ

Table 4   Emergence of consonants（twenty-word stage）

Name	Age	No. of words	Syllable-initial target	Syllable-initial realisation	Syllable-final target	Syllable-final realisation
H. Y.	1;5.15	18	p,t, tʰ, m, n, f, ɕ, tɕ, tʂ, tʂʰ	p, t,k, m, n, l, ɕ	n, ŋ	ŋ
Z. J.	1;8	21	p, tʰ,m, n, f, l, s, tʂ	p, t, m, n, s	n, ŋ	ŋ
Z. W.	1;3.15	17	p, tʰ,k, m, l, x, s, tɕ, ʂ	p, t, m, x, s	n, ŋ	ŋ
J. J.	1;3.15	17	p, t, tʰ, k, m, x, s, ts, tʂʰ, tɕ, tʂʰ	p, t, k, m, x	n, ŋ	ŋ

Z. J. was the only child whose word production went directly from the twenty-word stage to the fifty-word stage. For H. Y. and Z. W., there was a noticeable development in the production of syllable-initial consonants: affricates, fricatives and lateral approximants (/l/, /x/, /s/, /ɕ/, /tɕ/,/tʂ/) were introduced to the repertoire. J. J. saw little change in both her target and realised repertories.

When all the children produced at least fifty words (Table 6), both of the syllable-final consonants were present in their productive inventories. All the children either began or continued the rapid expansion which started in thirty-word stage in target and realised repertoires. All the children shared (/p/, /t/, /k/, /m/, /n/, /l/, /ts/, /ɕ/, /tɕ/, /ʂ/) in target and ([p], [t], [k], [m], [n], [ts], [ɕ], [tɕ],

76

[tʂ]) in realisation. There are significant individual variations as to the size of phonemic inventories and speed of development: two children have almost all of the consonants and vowels in their target words and matching their productive phonemic inventories, while the other two only have 15 or 16 out of 21 possible syllable-initial consonants in their target words.

Table 5 Emergence of consonants (thirty-word stage) *

Name	Age	No. of words	Syllable-initial target	Syllable-initial realisation	Syllable-final target	Syllable-final realisation
H. Y.	1;8	31	p, pʰ, t, k, m, n, l, x, s, ɕ, tɕ, tɕʰ, ʂ, tʂ, tʂʰ	p, pʰ, t, tʰ, k, m, n, l, x, s, ɕ, tɕ	n, ŋ	n, ŋ
Z. W.	1;5	32	p, t, t, k, m, n, f, tɕ, tɕʰ, ɕ, tɕ, ʂ, tʂ, tʂʰ	p, t, k, m, n, s, ɕ, tɕ, ʂ, tʂ	n, ŋ	n, n
J. J.	1;5	27	p, t, tʰ, k, m, n, ts, tɕ, tɕʰ, tʂ	p, t, k, m, n, tɕ	n, ŋ	n, ŋ

* Note: Z. J. skipped the thirty-word stage and therefore his data is not included in the table.

Table 6 Emergence of consonants (fifty-word stage)

Name	Age	No. of words	Syllable-initial target	Syllable-initial realisation	Syllable-final target	Syllable-final realisation
H. Y.	1;10.15	54	p, pʰ, t, tʰ, k, kʰ, m, n, f, ɹ, i, x, ɛ, tɛ, ɕ, tɕ, ʂ, tʂ, tʂʰ	p, pʰ, t, tʰ, k, kʰ, m, n, f, l, ɹ, x, s, ts, ɕ, tɕ, ʂ, tʂ, tʂʰ	n, ŋ	n, ŋ
Z. J.	1;9	50	p, t, k, kʰ, m, n, f, l, ɹ, x, s, ts, tsʰ, ɕ, tɕ, ʂ	p, t, k, m, n, f, ɹ, ts, ɕ, tɕ, tʂ	n, ŋ	n, ŋ
Z. W.	1;6	52	p, pʰ, t, tʰ, k, kʰ, m, n, f, l, x, ts, tsʰ, ɕ, tɕ, tɕʰ, ʂ, tʂ, tʂʰ	p, pʰ, t, tʰ, k, kʰ, m, n, f, l, x, ts, ɕ, tɕ, tɕʰ, ʂ, tʂ, tʂʰ	n, ŋ	n, ŋ
J. J.	1;6	52	p, t, tʰ, k, m, n, l, ts, tsʰ, ɕ, tɕ, tɕʰ, ʂ, tʂ, tʂʰ	p, t, tʰ, k, m, n, l, ɕ, x, ts, tɕ, tʂ	n, ŋ	n, ŋ

The emergence of vowels both as targets and realisations is summarized in Tables 7 – 11. Compared to the rate of development of consonants, vowels developed faster than consonants. At the four-word stage, simple vowels and diphthongs have emerged in both target and realisation among the four children, while triphthongs only appeared in Z. J. Although there is a gap between the target and realisation, the differences are small.

At the ten-word stage, the size of vowels in realisation almost doubled compared with the four-word stage. The gap between the target and realisation repertories remains small in all the children. Three out of the four children shared /i/, /u/, /ao/, /uA/ in target and [i], [u], [uA] in realization. Diphthongs began to appear in the realisation repertoire.

Table 7　Emergence of vowels (four-word stage)

Name	Age	No. of words	Vowel (target)	Vowel (realisation)
H. Y.	1;1.15	5	u, ɤ, A, a, ae, iɛ	u, ɤ, A, iɛ
Z. J.	1;4	5	i, u, y, A, ei, iow, uei	i, A, a, ei, iow
Z. W.	1;2	5	i, A, uA, iow	i, A, uA
J. J.	1;2	5	u, A, ʌ, ae, iA, iao	u, ɤ, A, a, iA

Table 8　Emergence of vowels (ten-word stage)

Name	Age	No. of words	Vowel(target)	Vowel(realisation)
H. Y.	1;4	10	u,ɤ,A,a,ae,iɛ,uA	u,ɤ,A,ae,ei,ia,iɛ,uA
Z. J.	1;7	10	i,u,A,iA,ao,uei	i,u,A,ə,iow
Z. W.	1;2.15	10	i,ɤ,A,ae,ao,iɛ,uA	i,ɤ,A,ao,iɛ,uA
J. J.	1;3	11	i,u,A,ao,ei,ow,uA	i,u,A,a,ao,ei,ow,uA

At the twenty-word stage (Table 9), individual differences were noticeable among the children. H. Y. and Z. W. developed more diphthongs and triphthongs in both their target and realisation inventories. Z. J. had more simple vowels in his inventory, whereas J. J. had fewer additions compared to the other three. At this stage, all the children shared /i/, /A/, /a/ in target and [i], [ɤ], [A], [a], [iɛ] in realisation.

Table 9　Emergence of vowels (twenty-word stage)

Name	Age	No. of words	Vowel (target)	Vowel(realisation)
H. Y.	1;5.15	18	i, ɤ, A, a, ʌ, ae, ao, iA, uA, iao, iow, uei	i, ɤ, A, a,ə, ae, ei, ao, iA, iɛ, uA, iow, uaei, uei
Z. J.	1;8	21	i, u, y, A, a, ɚ, ae, ei, ao, iɛ, iao, iow	i, u, y, ɤ, A, a, ɚ, ei, ao, iɛ, iao
Z. W.	1;3.15	17	i, ɤ, A, a,ɚ, ei, iA, iɛ, uA, iow	i, ɤ, A, a, ɚ, iA, iɛ, uA, uo, iow, uei
J. J.	1;3	17	i, u, ɤ, A, a, ɚ, ae, ei, ao, ow,iɛ, iao, uei	i, u, ɤ, A, a, ae, ei, ow, iA, iɛ

Little vowel development was evident in the thirty-word stage (Table 10), apart from the presence of more shared vowels in both target (/i/, /u/, /ɤ/, /A/, /ei/, /ao/, /iow/) and realization ([i], [u], [ɤ], [A], [ao], [ow], [uA]) in all the three children.

Table 10   Emergence of vowels (thirty-word stage)

Name	Age	No. of words	Vowel (target)	Vowel (realisation)
H. Y.	1;8	31	i, u, ɤ, A, a, ɚ, ae, ei, ao, iɛ, uA, uo, yɛ, iao, iow	i, ɤ, A, a, ə, ae, ei, ao, iA, iɛ, uA, iow, uaei, uei
Z. W.	1;5	32	i, u, ɤ, A, a, ʌ, ɚ, ae, ei, ao, ow, iA, iɛ, uA, uo, iow, uei	i, u, ɤ, A, a, ae, ao, ow, iɛ, uA, uo, iow, uei
J. J.	1;5	27	i, u, ɤ, A, ə, ʌ, ɚ, ei, ao, ow, iA, uA, iao, iow	i, u, o, ɤ, A, ə, ʌ, ei, ao, ow, iA, uA, iao, iow

At the fifty-word stage (Table 11), similar to the consonant development, there was a rapid expansion in the size of target and produced vowel repertoires. All of the children have developed most of the simple vowels, two thirds of the diphthongs, and half of the triphthongs. For target repertoires, they had in common six simple vowels (/i/, /u/, /ɤ/, /A/, /a/, /ʌ/), six diphthongs (/ae/, /ei/, /ao/, /ow/, /iA/, /uA/) and two triphthongs (/iao/, /iow/). There was a small gap between the target and the realised repertories.

Table 11   Emergence of vowels (fifty-word stage)

Name	Age	No. of words	Vowel (target)	Vowel (realisation)
H. Y.	1;10.15	54	i, u, ɤ, A, a, ɚ, ʌ, ae, ei, ao, ow, iA, iɛ, uA, uo, iao, iow, uae, uei	i, u, ɤ, A, a, ə, ʌ, ae, ei, ow, iA, iɛ, uA, uo, yɛ, iao, iow, uei
Z. J.	1;9	50	i, u, ɤ, y, A, a, ə, ʌ, ɚ, ae, ei, ao, ow, iA, uA, uo, iao, iow	i, u, ɤ, A, a, ʌ, ɚ, ae, ei, ao, ow, iA, uA, iə, uə, iao, iow
Z. W.	1;6	52	i, u, y, ɤ, A, a, ʌ, ae, ei, ao, ow, iA, iɛ, uA, uo, iao, iow, uei	i, u, y, ɤ, A, a, ə, ae, ei, ao, ow, iA, iɛ, uA, uo, iao, iow, uei
J. J.	1;6	52	i, u, ɤ, y, A, a, ə, ʌ, ɚ, ae, ei, ao, ow, iA, iɛ, uA, iao, iow, uei	i, u, ɤ, A, ə, ae, ao, ow, iA, iɛ, uA, iao, iow, uei

Shared words and lexical development

The children's vocabulary size developed slowly during the first few weeks of word production, and began to expand significantly before they reached the fifty-word stage. It took H. Y. and Z. J. about three months to reach the ten-word stage, a month and a half to the twenty-word stage, two and a half months for H. Y. to the thirty-word stage and then the same time to reach the fifty-word stage. Z. J. skipped the thirty-word stage and reached the last stage in a month. In this section, shared words among the children at various stages are pooled together in order to examine whether they have any shared phonological features. Table 12 shows the two words shared by the children at the four-word stage. Not surprisingly, they are the terms referring to mum and dad. At the ten-word stage (Table 13), as children's vocabulary size grew, the shared words reached five. They predominantly have a syllable shape of CV (Consonant+Vowel), with the consonants being limited to stops. The diphthongs also began to emerge.

Table 12　Shared words in four-word stage

No.	Chinese pinyin	English translation	IPA	Realisation			
				H. Y.	Z. J.	Z. W.	J. J.
1	baba	father	pApA	bAbA		bAbA	bAbA
2	mama	mother	mAmA	mAmA	mAmA	mAmA	

Table 13　Shared words in the ten-word stage

No.	Chinese pinyin	English translation	IPA	Realisation			
				H. Y.	Z. J.	Z. W.	J. J.
1	baba	father	pApA	bAbA		bAbA	bAbA
2	bao	hug	pao		pA	pao	pao
3	mama	mother	mAmA	mAmA	mAmA	mAmA	
4	nainai	grandma	naenae	naenae		nene	
5	yeye	grandpa	iɛ	iaia		iɛ	

The same trend continued at the twenty-word stage (Table 14) and thirty-word stage (Table 15). The syllable shape of the shared words is still CV or V with the exception of one word (*san*, meaning three) and the consonants are largely stops and nasals. However, the range of phonological features began to expand. The words contain several new vowels and phonological features including aspiration and affricates, as the children were learning numerals (e.g. two, three, five) and kinship terms (e.g. younger brother, aunt), which are the main categories of lexicons at these stages.

Table 14　Shared words in twenty-word stage

No.	Chinese pinyin	English translation	IPA	Realisation			
				H. Y.	Z. J.	Z. W.	J. J.
1	a'yi	aunt	Ai	A	i		
2	ba	eight	pA		pA		pa
3	baba	father	pApA	bAbA		bAbA	bAbA
4	bao	hug	pao		pA	pao	pao

Continued

No.	Chinese pinyin	English translation	IPA	Realisation			
				H. Y.	Z. J.	Z. W.	J. J.
5	er	two	ɚ		ɚ	ɚ	A
6	gege	elder brother	kɤkɤ			xɤxɤ	kɤkɤ
7	mama	mother	mAmA	mAmA	mAmA	mAmA	
8	nainai	grandma	naenae	naenae		nene	
9	san	three	san		sao	Se	ta
10	tu	rabbit	tʰu		tu		tu
11	yeye	grandpa	iɛ	iaia		iɛ	
12	yi	one	i		i	I	i

Table 15 Shared words in thirty-word stage

No.	Chinese pinyin	English translation	IPA	Realisation		
				H. Y.	Z. W.	J. J.
1	a'yi	aunt	Ai	A		
2	ba	eight	pA			pa
3	baba	father	pApA	bAbA	bAbA	bAbA
4	didi	younger brother	titi	titi	titi	
5	bao	hug	pao		pao	pao
6	er	two	ɚ		ɚ	A
7	gege	elder brother	kɤkɤ		xɤxɤ	kɤkɤ
8	gugu	aunt	kuku	kuku	kuku	
9	jiejie	elder sister	tɕiɛtɕiɛ	tɕiɛtɕiɛ	tɕiɛtɕiɛ	
10	jiujiu	uncle	tɕiowtɕiow	tɕowtɕow	tɕiowtɕiow	
11	mama	mother	mAmA	mAmA	mAmA	
12	meimei	younger sister	meimei	meimei	meimei	
13	nainai	grandma	naenae	naenae	nene	
14	san	three	san		se	ta
15	tutu	rabbit	tʰutʰu		towtow	towtow
16	yeye	grandpa	iɛiɛ	iɛiɛ	iɛiɛ	
17	yi	one	i		i	i

At the fifty-word stage (Table 16), the shared words increase to 29. This is over half of the size of the children's vocabulary which highlights similarities in lexical development among the children. More phonemes and phonological features appeared in the shared word list. Similar to the previous stages, there are individual differences in the way children produced these shared words, owing to the children's different phonological productive ability and strategies in learning.

Table 16   Shared words in the fifty-word stage

No.	Chinese pinyin	English translation	IPA	Realisation			
				H. Y.	Z. J.	Z. W.	J. J.
1	baba	father	pApA	bAbA		bAbA	bAbA
2	chuang	bed	tʂʰuaŋ	kuaŋ			ue
3	dao	knife	tao	tao	tao		
4	deng	lamp	tʌŋ	tʌŋ	te		
5	gou	dog	kow			kow	kow
6	hua	flower	xuA	kuA	uA		
7	jiazi	clip	tɕiAtsi	tAtʂi	tAtʂi		
8	kuaizi	chopstick	kʰuae tsi	kʰatsi	taetsɤ		
9	laba	horn	lApA			lApA	lApA
10	mama3	horse	mAmA			mAmA	mAmA
11	mama1	mother	mAmA		mAmA		mAmA
12	maomao	hat	maomao		maomao	maomao	maomao
13	meimei	younger sister	meimei		meimei	meimei	mueimuei
14	men	door	mən	me	mɤ		mən
15	nainai	grandma	naenae	naenae			niannia
16	niao3	Bird	niao		nao	niao	
17	Niao4	Piss	niao	liao	nao	niao	
18	qin	piano	tɕʰiŋ	tɕiŋ	tɕi		
19	san	umbrella	san	ʂei	tan		
20	taiyang	sun	tʰaeiaŋ	tʰaeiaŋ		teiaŋ	
21	wawa	sock	uAuA		uAuA		uAuA
22	wu	five	u		u		u
23	xigua	watermelon	ɕikua	ɕitA	ɕituA	ɕikuA	
24	xiangjiao	banana	ɕiaŋtɕiao	ɕiaŋtɕiao			tɕiao

Continued

No.	Chinese pinyin	English translation	IPA	Realisation			
				H. Y.	Z. J.	Z. W.	J. J.
25	xie	shoe	ɕiɛ	ʂei			ɕiɛ
26	yao	want	iao		iow		iao
27	yaoshi	key	iaoʂi	iaosi	iaotow		
28	yeye	Grandpa	iɛ iɛ			iɛ iɛ	iɛ iɛ
29	yi	one	i		i		i

Discussion and conclusion

The paper investigates the interaction between phonological and lexical development among four Putonghua-speaking children between the first-word and fifty-word stages. The analysis of shared consonants and vowel inventories in the children target words and their realisations shows the following:

• The children's vocabulary at the four-word and ten-word stages are primarily words in CV (consonant + vowel) syllable shapes and consist of stop or nasal consonants and open vowels only.

• While the number of consonants and vowels in their target words begins to expand rapidly over the next twenty-word and thirty-word stages, the size of the target phonemic inventories exceeds significantly that of the productive phonemic inventories.

• By the time the children reach the fifty-word stage, there are significant individual variations as to the size of phonemic inventories and the speed of development: two children have almost all the consonants and vowels in their target words and matching productive phonemic inventories, while the other two have only 15 or 16 out of 21 possible syllable-initial consonants in their target words.

The comparison of shared words among the children's production at different stages shows that the children shared similar paths in their lexical development: with the predominance of kinship terms and numerals in early stages, followed by an expansion of object labels at the fifty-word stage. Among the shared words at the early stages, there is a clear preference for words with certain phonological features, i.e. CV or V syllable shapes, stops and nasal consonants and open vowels, which triangulates the first finding in the analysis of target and realisation inventories.

These findings suggest that phonological selection is evident in children's lexical development in early stages. In the case of Putonghua-speaking children, they tend to learn and produce words with a CV shape, made up of stops or nasals and open vowels. The findings show that the phonemic inventories in the target words exceed significantly those of the children's production at the twenty- and thirty-word stages and that there are significant individual differences among the four children in terms of size of target and realised phonemic repertories. This suggests that the introduction of new phonemes and syllable shapes in the children's phonology may be driven, or sped up at least, by the need to learn more words, another area where lexical and phonological development interact. They also suggest that phonological selection is not correlated with production alone. Whether the phonological selection takes place on the basis of the children's productive or perceptual ability or both needs further research.

In sum, these results support the argument that while lexical and phonological development each follow their own paths of development, they also interact with each other in both directions in an early age. Lexical development is influenced by phonological selection and phonological development is driven to some extent by the need to learn new words.

Acknowledgements

The authors are grateful to Wang Qian, who assisted with the data analysis as part of her postgraduate dissertation.

References

Ferguson, C. A., & Farwell, C. 1975. Words and Sounds in Early Language Acquisition. *Language* 51, 419 – 439.

Friederici, A., & Wessels, J. 1993. Phonotactic Knowledge of Word Boundaries and Its Use in Infant Speech Perception. *Perception and Psychophysics* 54, 287 – 295.

Ingram, D. 1976. *Phonological Disability in Children*. London: Edward Arnold.

Jusczyk, P., Friederici, A., Wessels, J., Svenkerud, V., & Jusczyk, A. 1993. Infants' Sensitivity to the Sound Pattern of Native Language Words. *Journal of Memory and Language* 32, 402 – 420.

Jusczyk, P., Luce, P., & Charles-Luce, J. 1994. Infants' Sensitivity to Phonotactic Patterns in the Native Language. *Journal of Memory and Language* 33, 630 – 645.

Kiparsky, P., & Menn, L. 1977. On the Acquisition of Phonology. In: *Language Learning and Thought*, J. Macnamara ed. New York: Academic Press.

Leonard, L. B., Schwartz, R. G., Morris, B., & Chapman, K. 1981. Factors Influencing Early Lexical Acquisition: Lexical Orientation and Phonological Composition. *Child Development* 52, 882 – 887.

Luce, P., & Pisoni, D. B. 1998. Recognizing Spoken Words. The Neighborhood Activation Model. *Ear and Hearing* 19 (1), 1 – 36.

Schwartz, R., & Leonard, L. 1982. Do Children Pick and Choose: An Examination of Phonological Selection and Avoidance in Early Lexical Acquisition. *Journal of Child Language* 9, 319 – 336.

Stoel-Gammon, C. 2011. Relationships Between Lexical and Phonological Development in Young Children. *Journal of Child Language* 38 (1), 1 – 34.

Vihman, M. M. 1981. Phonology and the Development of the Lexicon: Evidence from Children's Errors. *Journal of Child Language* 8 (2), 239 – 264.

Vihman, M. M. 1996. *Phonological Development*. Oxford: Blackwell.

Vihman, M. M., & McCune, L. 1994. When Is a Word a Word? *Journal of Child Language* 21, 517 – 542.

Zhu, H. 2002. *Phonological Development in Specific Contexts: Studies of Chinese-Speaking Children*. Clevedon: Multilingual Matters Ltd.

Zhu, H., & Dodd, B. 2000. The Phonological Acquisition of Putonghua (Modern Standard Chinese). *Journal of Child Language* 27, 3 – 42.

Notes on contributors

Zhu Hua (Email: zhu.hua@bbk.ac.uk), PhD, Professor and head of the Department of Applied Linguistics and Communication, Birkbeck, University of London. Her research interests: intercultural communication, discourse and conversation analysis, bilingualism, and child language development and disorder.

Qi Ruying (Email: r.qi@uws.edu.au), PhD, Senior Lecturer and PhD supervisor in Bilingualism and Chinese of the School of Humanities and Communication Arts at the University of Western Sydney. She is also Director of Bilingualism Research Lab @ UWS-JNU and Leader of the China Liaison Unit (Language and Culture) and an adjunct member of ARC Centre of Excellence for the Dynamics of Language. Her research interests: Mandarin-English bilingual children's language acquisition, early bilingual education, bilingualism and biculturalism, language acquisition, Chinese language and cultural teaching and learning.

幼儿普通话习得过程中音系和词汇发展的双向互动

Zhu Hua

Birkbeck College, University of London, UK

Qi Ruying

University of Western Sydney, Australia

提　要:本文探讨了四名汉语普通话儿童在最初的几个词汇至五十个词阶段音系和词汇发展的互动关系。本文的语料来自于对四名儿童的自然语言历时一年的纵向录音。文中分析了儿童在四个词、十个词、二十个词、三十个词和五十个词各阶段目标词语及实际产出词语所共有的音位总量。研究结果表明,儿童在四个词和十个词阶段的词汇主要是 CV(辅音和元音)的音节结构,由塞音或鼻辅音加开元音组成。在二十个词至三十个词阶段,目标词汇中的辅音和元音数量开始快速增长的时候,目标音位总量会显著超过儿童实际产出的音位总量。然而,当儿童达到五十个词阶段的时候,音位总量和发展速度体现出显著的个体差异。通过比较儿童在不同阶段所产出的共同的词汇,发现他们明显倾向于据有某一些音系特征的词汇,即由 CV 或 V 构成的音节,塞音,鼻辅音和开元音。研究结果支持词汇和音系在儿童早期语言发展中虽然遵循各自的发展路径但两者之间存在双向互动关系。音系的选择影响词汇的发展,学习新词的需求在一定程度上也促进音系的发展。

关键词:普通话儿童　词汇发展　音系发展　互动

Input and Acquisition of Mandarin Classifiers by English-Mandarin Bilingual Children in China

Qi Ruying and Wu Wanhua

Abstract: Previous studies on acquisition of classifiers by Mandarin-speaking monolingual children report that in comprehension studies the children often correctly select referents on the basis of classifiers, but in production they often use "general" classifiers like *ge* "个" and *zhi* "只" instead of the correct and specific classifiers. This study reports two tests adopted from Ning & Gu 2013 on how successive English-Mandarin bilingual children comprehend and produce classifiers while they are acquiring English at the same time. Five English-Mandarin bilingual children whose parents are native English speakers and nine monolingual Mandarin-speaking children from the same kindergarden in Xi'an China are recruited. Their input information is collected through questionnaires and recordings from parents, childcare givers and observational data. Both bilingual children and monolingual children participated in the elicited tasks for comprehension and production of Mandarin classifiers. The results show that the bilingual subject group, though with only half or even less exposure time in comparison to their monolingual peers, have achieved a similar pattern of classifier acquisition in comprehension and production. There are no qualitative differences between these two groups, although individual differences are found within these two groups. The findings on bilingual children's comprehension of Mandarin classifiers are consistent with the previous monolingual research. Bilingual children even perform better than monolingual peers in production for certain classifiers. It seems that limited input does not affect bilingual children's acquisition of Mandarin classifiers and their syntactic combinations.

Key words: classifier, English-Mandarin bilingual children, input

1. Introduction

There are contrastive viewpoints for the effect of input on the development of grammar. Usage-based language acquisition approaches argue that input plays a major role (e.g. Tomasello 2003), while nativist approaches hold that it is the innate knowledge rather than the input that determines grammatical development (e.g. Chomsky 1986; Crain 1991).

Comparisons of different learner groups can be used to test the predictions put forward by these two approaches because the amount of input available often differs and can sometimes be manipulated systematically (Unsworth 2014). For bilingual children, they are likely to have less exposure to each of their languages than their monolingual peers in either language

(Paradis & Genesee 1996; Zhu & Li 2005). Such children are the perfect natural experimental context when testing for input effects (Unsworth 2014).

Blom (2010) investigated the early development of four Turkish-Dutch bilingual children with different input conditions, and found that input quantity led to the differences between bilingual and monolingual children in grammatical development. Unsworth (2014) compared acquisition across domains (grammatical gender and scrambling) within a group of Dutch-English bilingual children and found input effects for gender but not for scrambling. She concluded that the domain of scrambling constitutes a poverty of stimulus problem that input does not play a major role. Meisel (2007) also contended that in early child bilingualism reduced input is unlikely to cause acquisition failure even for the weaker language. According to usage-based theory of language acquisition (Tomasello 2003), children acquire language by piecemeal fashion as input is the driving force that helps the child to get the target.

Previous researches for the input effects on the grammatical development mostly focus on bilingual children in European settings where two languages might be similar typologically (Qi 2011). The pair of two typologically different languages like Mandarin and English in bilingual acquisition research is needed to further test the input effect on the development of grammar.

Mandarin classifier is an interesting domain that has attracted attention not only in theoretical studies (Chao 1968; Li and Thompson 1981; Cheng and Sybesma 1998, 1999) but also in child language acquisition research (Fang 1985; Hu 1993; Chien et al. 2003; Li et al. 2010). Previous studies on acquisition of classifiers by Mandarin-speaking monolingual children report that children often correctly select referents on the basis of classifiers in comprehension studies (Fang 1985; Hu 1993; Chien et al. 2003; Li et al. 2010), but that in production they tend to use "general" classifiers like ge and zhi instead of the specific classifiers normally used by adults (Hu 1993; Myers and Tsay 2000). These studies show that on the one hand children as young as 3 or 4 already demonstrate knowledge of the relatively fixed relationship between classifiers and an entity denoted by a noun and acquire basic syntactic knowledge of Mandarin classifiers, but the use of classifiers still shows overextension of general classifiers (Lee 1996).

Should classifiers bring about greater difficulties for bilingual children whose input is likely to be much reduced compared to their monolingual peers? Yip and Matthews (2010) point out that classifier systems, a salient typological property of Chinese languages, may pose problems for bilingual children when paired with a non-classifier language such as English. One study concerning acquisition of Cantonese classifiers appears in Li and Lee (2001) who examined the use of Cantonese classifiers by 34 young British-born Chinese aged between 5 and 16. The result shows that the bilinguals have difficulties with specific Cantonese classifiers, which is interpreted as incomplete Cantonese learning and the influence from English. Gao (2010), using a group of 30 Chinese-Swedish bilinguals aged between 5 and 16 as controls, tested the learning strategies differences between adult L2 learners and bilingual children's production of Mandarin classifiers, finds that bilingual children perform better than adult L2 learners. The contexts of the two researches are both in Europe where Chinese (either Cantonese or Mandarin) is home language for the bilingual children.

There has been an ever increasing number of native English speaking people working or studying in mainland China since the 1980s when China started the reform and open policy. Many of them live in China with their families for years. Their children acquire Mandarin in the wider community and English at home where both parents speak English. However, little has been reported in the literature on how these English-Mandarin bilingual children growing up in mainland China acquire Mandarin classifiers (Qi 2011; Xu 2010).

The present research will test whether English-Mandarin bilingual children have greater difficulties than monolingual children both for comprehension and production of Mandarin classifiers. We will ask whether, given the reduced Mandarin input, English-Mandarin bilingual children in China show similar or different competence in comprehension and production of Mandarin classifier compared to their monolingual peers. More specifically, the questions are:

(1) Do English-Mandarin bilingual children demonstrate knowledge of the relatively fixed relationship between a classifier and an entity denoted by a noun?

(2) Do English-Mandarin bilingual children with Mandarin as their weaker language have basic syntactic knowledge of Mandarin classifiers?

(3) Do English-Mandarin bilingual children show a similar overuse of general classifiers in Mandarin as their monolingual peers?

The results of this study will shed some light on the persisting debate between generative/nativist and usage-based approaches to language acquisition. In what follows, section 2 is a brief introduction to Mandarin classifiers; section 3 explains the methodology employed in the present investigation including a detailed description of the bilingual children's input conditions; section 4 presents the results of our investigation. The final section offers a discussion and draws a conclusion.

2. Classifiers in Mandarin

Li and Thompson (1981: 104) give a detailed definition of Mandarin classifier as follows:

"A classifier is word that must occur

with a number (e.g., *yi* 'one', *ban* 'half', *shi* 'ten') and/or a demonstrative (i.e., *zhe* 'this', *na* 'that', *nei* 'which'), or certain quantifiers (such as *zheng* 'whole', *ji* 'how many/a few', *mou yi* 'a certain', *mei* 'every') before the noun."

For example:

(1) san – ge pinguo
    three – CL apple
    three apples

(2) liang – ben shu
    two – CL book
    two books

(3) si – bei shui
    four – CL(cup) water
    four cups of water

(4) wu – wan fan
    five – CL(bowl) rice
    five bowls of rice

Li and Thompson (1981) also say that to a speaker of English one of the most striking features of the Mandarin noun phrases is the classifier. English differs from Mandarin on the point that count nouns can be quantified directly by a numeral or quantifier determiner (e. g. three books); however non-count (mass) nouns must take a classifier when they are quantified (e. g. a few pieces of bread), which is similar to Mandarin (cf., McEnery and Xiao 2007).

Cheng and Sybesma (1998) argue that Chinese count-mass distinction is reflected at the level of classifier. One of the strong arguments is the insertion of the particle *de* after the classifier. The classifiers *ge* and *ben* in (1) and (2) are count classifiers not permitting the insertion of *de* while *bei* and *wan* in examples (3) and (4) are mass classifiers accepting the insertion of *de* for the purpose of measure.

Chien et al.'s (2003) study of Chinese children's comprehension of count-classifiers and mass-classifiers adds evidence that count-mass distinction is relevant in Chinese grammar as children as young as 3 grasp the grammatical count-mass distinction.

3. Methodology

The methodology of this study makes use of two elicited production tasks to test children's comprehension and production of some commonly used classifiers. The two instruments for this study are adopted from classifiers tests of Ning & Gu's (2013) book—*Linguistic Ability Test for Preschool Children*. According to Cheng and Sybesma (1998), there is count-mass distinction between mandarin classifiers. In Chien et al.'s (2003)study, 14 count classifiers(支 zhi,张 zhang ,棵 ke, 顶 ding, 辆 liang, 条 tiao, 个 ge, 件 jian, 只 zhi, 本 ben, 朵 duo, 块 kuai, 根 gen, 片 pian) and 4 mass classifiers/container measure words (杯 bei, 碗 wan, 瓶 ping, 包 bao) were selected from a pool of Chinese count- and mass-classifiers. In Ning & Gu (2013)'s book, 11 count-classifiers and 6 mass-classifiers were selected, among which the majority also appear in Chien et al's (2003) study. The following table shows the count-classifiers, mass classifiers and their corresponding nouns designating the pictures in each experiment, adapted from Chien et al (2003).

Table 1

Count-classifiers	Meanings	Nouns
双 shuang	CL for a pair of something	socks
片 pian	CL for something thin or a slice of something	feather
张 zhang	CL for something with a thin, flat, rectangular, and two-dimensional extended surface	photo
棵 ke	CL for plants	tree
匹 pi	CL for horse	horse
辆 liang	CL for vehicles	car
条 tiao	CL for something (animate or inanimate) long, thin, cylindrical, and flexible	fish
支 zhi	CL for something long, thin, cylindrical, and rigid	pen
块 kuai	CL for a chunk, a lump, or a piece of something	soap
朵 duo	CL for flowers or clouds	flower
本 ben	CL for bound volumes	book
Mass-classifiers	Meanings	Nouns
杯 bei	cup or mug	water
瓶 ping	bottle or jar	drinks
碗 wan	Bowl	steamed rice
包 bao	Bag	sugar
串 chuan	Bunch	grapes
堆 dui	Pile	soil

Five bilingual children and nine monolingual children recruited from the same kindergarten participated in the classifiers comprehension and production tests. Each child is tested separately by the researcher (the second author of this paper) in a room of the kindergarten attended by the children, who are very familiar with that environment and with the researcher, since he has been a volunteer helper in that same kindergarten for more than two years prior to this study. All children except for B2, M1 and M6 were tested only once as all of them were very eager to participate. B2, M1 and M6 were tested twice because they demonstrated different patterns from others. However, the second test for these three children resulted in the same patterns. In order to ensure the child knew the noun for each entity in the picture, the researcher presented the noun of each picture to the child, intentionally avoiding using classifiers as in (1) below:

(1) zhe shi wazi, zhe shi yumao, zhe shi xiangpian, zhe shi shu

this is sock, this is feather, this is photo, this is tree

"These are socks; this is feather; this is a photo; this is a tree"

There are two parts of the experiment: the comprehension test and the production test. The experiment is audio recorded, and then transcribed by the researcher and later double checked by a teacher of the kindergarten who is very familiar with every child.

3.1 Participants

Five Mandarin-English bilingual children (4 to 6 years old mean age 5;3) and nine monolingual Mandarin-speaking children from the same kindergarten (4 to 6 mean age 4;8) were recruited with the consent from the parents and teachers. All the bilingual children's parents are native speakers of English from US or Australia, with different proficiency in L2 Mandarin. Most of the children's (bilingual or monolingual) parents hold higher education degrees. At home the bilingual children are mostly exposed to English in communicating with their parents and siblings but in their kindergarten they are mainly exposed to Mandarin as spoken by teachers and peers. All the children are known to be developing normally with no apparent speech or hearing problems according to their health check reports required by the school. The monolingual children in this study are observed for the purpose of comparison. The five bilingual children are code named from B1 to B5 in ascending order of age. B1 (boy) and B5(boy) are siblings from Australia; B2(boy) and B4(girl) are siblings from US, and B3(boy) is also from US. The nine monolinguals are code named from M1 to M9 in the same age order. Tables 2 and 3 show a brief profiles of the two sets of children.

Table 2   Bilingual group

Code name	Gender	Age	Country of citizen	Sibling	Class
B1	M	4;2	Australia	B5	Moon
B2	M	4;5	US	B4	Moon
B3	M	5;1	US		Sun
B4	F	6;2	US	B2	Sun
B5	M	6;5	Australia	B1	Sun

Table 3   Monolingual group

Code name	Gender	Age	Class
M1	M	4;3	Moon
M2	M	4;4	Moon
M3	M	4;5	Moon
M4	M	4;7	Moon
M5	F	4;8	Moon
M6	M	4;9	Sun
M7	M	5;1	Sun
M8	F	5;2	Sun
M9	M	6;2	Sun

3.1.1 The kindergarten setting

All the English-Mandarin bilingual children and the Mandarin monolingual children participants were recruited from the same kindergarten in mainland China. There are all together about 25 children in

91

the kindergarten among which the bilingual children make up about one third of the population. All the parents hold degrees of higher education. The children are divided into four different classes (dots, star, moon and sun) according to their age. The kindergarten is not intended to be a bilingual one although there are some bilingual children. The bilingual children come to school to learn Mandarin, so teachers are required to speak Mandarin to kids of English background at school. In particular occasions English may be used, e.g., for explanations, especially for safety reasons. All the kindergarten teachers have basic communicative skills in English. Each teacher takes care of 5 or 8 children in her class.

The schoolday goes from 8:30 am to 5:30 pm, but the bilingual children only attend the morning sessions from 8:30 to 11:30 (those who do not have lunch at school) or up to 12:30 (those who have lunch and listen to Mandarin story after lunch). All monolingual children attend whole day schooling from Monday to Friday except for occasional absence if they are being sick or for other particular reason.

The monolingual children are exposed to Mandarin both at school and at home. All the parents of monolingual children speak Mandarin at home. The grandparents, who may speak some dialect of Shaanxi province, are only occasional visitors. The monolingual children's mandarin productions do not show any influence from dialects according to teachers and observation. The monolingual children have two

English classes (20 minutes each time) based on local kindergarten English books for learning some words and very basic sentences. They may overhear the bilingual children talking to each other in English; however, almost no English production was observed from them, with the exception of "yes" and "no" occasionally.

3.1.2 Profiles of English-Mandarin bilingual children and their input conditions

The five bilingual children in this study are from three different families. Following Qi (2011), all the bilingual children's sociolinguistic settings and input conditions are described (see the Appendix for detailed information in tables). Siblings are put together. The bilingual children's input information is collected through questionnaires and recordings from parents, childcare givers and observational data. All the children recruited attended the same kindergarten in Xi'an China, and all the children have normal intellectual and interpersonal development.

B1 and B5

B1 and B5's parents are native Australians who have been studying and working in Xi'an China for about 4 years. Both Father and Mother received higher education from Australia majoring in Science and Engineering. They started to learn Mandarin soon after their arrival. They first arrived in China when their elder son B5 was 2 years and 6 months and their second son B1 was about 2 months old. B5 was then sent to the kindergarten when he was 3 years old. Their parents immediately started to learn Mandarin after having settled down. They are very motivated Mandarin learners as they always try every chance to speak Mandarin with teachers and other Chinese parents. The parents also practise their Mandarin at home with each other, and they speak Mandarin to their children sometimes. A Chinese house-helper comes four times a week (four hours each time) to help with housework. The children watch both English and Chinese educational cartoons and movies regularly.

B2 and B4

B2 and B4's parents are Americans, and have been learning Chinese and working in China for about 7 years. Both of the children were born in Beijing. The parents have received higher education in US. The mother holds a BA of linguistics, and Father holds a BA of history and education. Their Mandarin level is the highest among the three families in this study according to ratings by the kindergarten teachers. They keep speaking English to their kids almost all the time except when Chinese friends visit their home occasionally. Although they speak good Mandarin, they do not speak Mandarin to their children as they don't want their children to pick up their foreign accent. They sent their children to kindergarten from an earlier age for 5 mornings sessions each week, and do home schooling in English at home in the afternoon. They returned to America twice for half a year each time. There are four children in this family. B4 is the second child,

and B2 is the third one. The first child of this family is a boy, and the fourth one is a girl. Before this family moved to Xi'an, B4 (from 2;6 to 3;6) and her elder brother were the only foreign children in the Mandarin preschool in Beijing where they went to school five mornings each week. A Chinese house-helper came to their home to help with housework two afternoons per week. The children watched both English and Chinese educational cartoons and movies regularly.

B3

B3's parents have also been living in China for about seven years. They keep speaking English but not Mandarin to their children as they believe non-native input is not beneficial for children's language development (data from the interview). B3 has an elder sister who is seven years old at the time of the study. His sister goes to a local Chinese primary school five days a week. According to his parents, the girl is good at both Mandarin and English in both speaking and literacy. She sometimes speaks Mandarin to the younger ones.

3.2 Comprehension test

The test assesses whether the children know that the relationship between a classifier and an entity denoted by a noun is a relatively fixed one. The classifiers are organized into groups with four pictures denoting different entities depicted on one page. Five classifiers are tested on five pages of 20 pictures (four picture entities per page) as the table 4 shows:

Table 4

Classifier tested	Pictures on the page	Corresponding classifiers
杯 bei	a cup of water, a bottle of drink, a bowl of steamed rice, a bag of sugar	杯 bei, 瓶 ping 碗 wan, 包 bao
棵 ke	a pair of socks, a feather, a photo, a tree	双 shuang, 片 pian 张 zhang, 棵 ke
条 tiao	a horse, a car, a fish, a bunch of grapes	匹 pi, 辆 liang 条 tiao, 串 chuan
本 ben	a pen, a soap, a flower, a book	支 zhi, 块 kuai 朵 duo, 本 ben
碗 wan	a cup of water, a bottle of drinks, a bowl of steamed rice, a bag of candies	杯 bei, 瓶 ping 碗 wan, 包 bao

Each child is presented with a group of four pictures representing different entities on a page each time, and they are prompted to speak out a specific entity required by a specific classifier as (2) below exemplifies.

(2) ni kan, zheli you yi-ke shenme?

you look, here have one-CL what?

"Look, which CL is here?"

The child can see four pictures on one page: a pair of socks, a feather, a photo and a tree. The child is expected to say "shu" (tree) or "yi-ke shu" (one-Cl tree) if he has the knowledge of the relatively fixed relationship between a classifier and an entity represented by a noun. If the child says "shu" (tree) or "yi-ke shu" (one-CL tree), he/she gets 1 score. If he pairs the classifier with the wrong entity or says nothing, he gets 0.

3.3 Production test

The production test investigates whether the children demonstrate a knowledge of basic syntactic nature of Mandarin classifiers, and whether they show overgeneralization in production. The same children are tested separately to elicit their

production of Mandarin classifiers. Five classifiers are tested as shown in the Table 5.

Table 5

Classifier	Pictures on each page
棵 ke	Two trees
条 tiao	Three fish
杯 bei	Three cups of water
本 ben	Five books
堆 pile	Two piles of soil

A child is presented with a picture of a number of tokens of the same item (usually from two to five tokens). Then the child is asked a question as (3) exemplifies:

(3) Zhe shi yu, qing ni gaosu wo, you duoshao ya?

This is fish, please you tell me, have how many SFP.

"These are fish; please tell me, how many?"

If the child says "san-tiao" (three Cl) or "san-tiao yu" (three-Cl fish), he/she scores 1. If the child says "san-ge" or "san-zhi" using general classifiers or other classifiers, he/she gets 0. 5 score as using general classifiers is inappropriate but still shows basic syntactic knowledge of of Mandarin classifiers. If the child says only a number, he/she gets 0.

4. Results

The first research question asks whether English-Mandarin bilingual children demonstrate knowledge of the relatively fixed relationship between a classifier and an entity denoted by a noun. In the comprehension test, the bilingual children showed a very good command of this knowledge (1 refers to correctly matching a classifier and a noun, 0 refers to incorrectly matching). As Table 6 shows, except for B2, who made mistakes on *ke* and *ben*, all other bilinguals accurately matched the nouns corresponding to the classifiers. B2 said *ren* (person) when he was asked to match the classifier *ke*, and he said *bi* (pen) to match the classifier *ben*. Although "yi ke ren" (one man) and "yi ben bi" (one pen) are not accepted in adult speech, B2 matched them with his certain understanding for the features of nouns shown in the picture and their relationship with classifiers. The feature of man and tree does show similarity with a Chinese simile "a man standing like a pine tree" (站似一棵松) as an example. He wrongly matched classifier

ben with a pen possibly because its closeness to a book in use for schooling. For monolingual controls, the same test result as shown in Table 7, most monolinguals are able to match the classifiers and their corresponding nouns with the exception of M1 who matched each classifier to all four nouns. We cannot say M1 completely lacked the knowledge of the fix relationship between these classifiers and nouns although he was tested twice and was clear about the task. One tentative explanation might be that this knowledge is not very sound in his mind at this age (4;3) for him. The result showed that most bilinguals and monolinguals demonstrated a sound knowledge of the relatively fixed relationship between a classifier and an entity denoted by a noun for the tested classifiers.

The second research question asks whether English-Mandarin bilingual children have basic syntactic knowledge of Mandarin classifiers. Results from the production test as shown by Table 8 below, except for B2, all other bilingual children use classifiers in the noun phrase though they frequently use general classifiers inappropriately (1 refers to using correct classifiers, 0.5 refers to using general classifiers, 0 refers to omitting classifiers).

Table 6　Test 1—Classifier comprehension test on bilinguals

Subject	Age	杯 Bei	棵 Ke	条 Tiao	本 Ben	碗 Wan
B1	4;2	1	1	1	1	1
B2	4;5	1	0	1	0	1
B3	5;1	1	1	1	1	1
B4	6;2	1	1	1	1	1
B5	6;5	1	1	1	1	1

Table 7   Test 1—Classifier comprehension test on monolinguals

Subject	Age	杯 Bei	棵 Ke	条 Tiao	本 Ben	碗 Wan
M1	4;3	0	0	0	0	0
M2	4;4	1	1	1	1	1
M3	4;5	1	0	0	1	1
M4	4;7	1	1	1	1	1
M5	4;8	1	1	1	1	1
M6	4;9	1	1	1	1	1
M7	5;1	1	1	1	1	1
M8	5;2	1	1	1	1	1
M9	6;2	1	1	1	1	1

Table 8   Test 2—Classifier production test on bilinguals

Subject	Age	杯 Bei	棵 Ke	条 Tiao	本 Ben	堆 Dui
B1	4;2	0.5	0.5	0.5	0.5	0.5
B2	4;5	0	0	0	1	0
B3	5;1	0.5	0.5	0.5	0.5	0.5
B4	6;2	0.5	1	0.5	0.5	0.5
B5	6;5	0.5	1	1	0.5	0.5

Table 9   Test 2—Classifier production test on monolinguals

Subject	Age	杯 Bei	棵 Ke	条 Tiao	本 Ben	堆 Dui
M1	4;3	0.5	1	0.5	0.5	0
M2	4;4	0.5	0.5	0.5	0.5	0.5
M3	4;5	0.5	0.5	0.5	0.5	1
M4	4;7	1	1	1	1	0.5
M5	4;8	0.5	0.5	0.5	0.5	0.5
M6	4;9	0	0.5	0.5	0	0
M7	5;1	0.5	0.5	0.5	0.5	0.5
M8	5;2	0.5	0.5	0.5	0.5	0.5
M9	6;2	0.5	0.5	0.5	0.5	0.5

The third question asks whether English-Mandarin bilingual children showed similar developmental patterns as monolingual peers by overextending general classifiers. Results showed that bilingual children have a similar pattern of over extending general classifiers *ge* and *zhi* as monolingual peers as shown by Table 10 and 11.

Table 10   Test 2—Classifier production test on bilinguals

Subject	Age	杯 Bei	棵 Ke	条 Tiao	本 Ben	堆 Dui
B1	4;2	ge	ge	ge	ge	ge
B2	4;5	0	0	0	ben	0
B3	5;1	zhi	zhi	zhi	zhi	zhi
B4	6;2	ge	ke	ge	ge	ge
B5	6;5	ge	ke	tiao	ge	ge

Table 11   Test 2—Classifier production test on monolinguals

Subject	Age	杯 Bei	棵 Ke	条 Tiao	本 Ben	堆 Dui
M1	4;3	ge	ke	ge	ge	0
M2	4;4	ge	ge	ge	ge	ge
M3	4;5	ge	ge	ge	ge	kuai
M4	4;7	bei	ke	tiao	ben	ge
M5	4;8	ge	ge	ge	ge	ge
M6	4;9	0	ge	ge	0	0
M7	5;1	ge	ge	ge	ge	0
M8	5;2	ge	ge	ge	ge	ge
M9	6;2	ge	ge	zhi	ge	ge

5. Discussion and conclusions

We have tested 5 English-Mandarin bilingual children and 9 Mandarin monolingual children's comprehension and production of certain Mandarin classifiers. The bilingual children whose home language is English have reduced input to Mandarin (see the appendix). Do they show similar or different competence in comprehension and production of Mandarin classifier compared to their monolingual peers? The preliminary results showed that the bilingual children though with only half or even less exposure time of the monolingual children, demonstrated the same pattern as their monolingual peers. Most bilingual children demonstrate a sound knowledge of the relatively fixed relationship between a classifier and a noun; they also seldom omit a classifier that is obligatory in a noun phrase, and they also overextend the general classifiers. The results of both bilingual children and monolingual children are consistent with previous research on Mandarin monolingual children (Chien et al. 2003; Erbaugh 1986; Fang 1985; Hu 1993; Li et al. 2010; Myers & Tsay 2000).

For the bilingual children with more English exposure than Mandarin, it poses challenges to them as English does not require a classifier or measure word for count nouns. They are likely to omit classifiers in count noun phrases. One bilingual child (B2) does omit classifiers in four of the five classifiers tested. It appears to show the influence from English that a classifier/measure word is not required. However, this interpretation does not stand as we also find one monolingual child (M6) who omitted classifiers in three out of five classifiers tested. Thus, omitting classifiers should be regarded more as a developmental pattern rather than transfer from the other language. Overextending general classifiers applies to both bilinguals and monolinguals.

How can the bilingual children achieve the same milestones as monolingual peers? One possible explanation is in line with the Bilingual Bootstrapping Hypothesis, proposed by Gawlitzek-Maiwald and Tracy (1996: 903), which is defined as "something has been acquired in language A fulfils a booster function for language B". Paradis, Genesee & Crago (2011) also point out that a bilingual child's development in one language can be advanced by the other, and the two languages can be mutually advanced for sharing some linguistic-conceptual knowledge. It is possible that the bilingual children make use of the linguistic-conceptual knowledge acquired from English to acquire Mandarin, thus facilitating the learning.

In terms of input effect, the results in this study that bilingual children showed similar knowledge and skills in the use of classifier in Mandarin seem to support the nativist approaches of language acquisition in the point that input effects are not evident. However, this claim is only tentative due to a small number of bilingual children and limited Mandarin classifiers examined in this study. Future studies may be directed to recruit more bilingual subjects with different input conditions to test the effect of input on classifier acquisition.

Acknowledgements

We thank the participating children and their parents for consenting to the experiments. We are also thankful for the insightful feedback received from participants at the Second Symposium of Bilingualism and Intercultural Communication as well as the Workshop on Research Methods held at UWS, August 2014.

References

Blom, E. 2010. Effects of Input on the Early Grammatical Development of Bilingual Children. *International Journal of Bilingualism.*

Cheng, L. L. S., &.Sybesma, R. 1998. Yi-wan Tang, Yi-ge Tang: Classifiers and Massifiers. *Tsing Hua Journal of Chinese studies* 28(3), 385 – 412.

Chien, Y. C., Lust, B., & Chiang, C. P. 2003. Chinese Children's Comprehension of Count-classifiers and Mass-classifiers. *Journal of East Asian Linguistics* 12 (2), 91 – 120.

Chomsky, N. 1986. *Knowledge of Language: Its Nature, Origin, and Use.* Dordrecht: Foris.

Crain, S. 1991. Language Acquisition in the Absence of Experience. *Behavioral and Brain Sciences* 14 (04), 597 – 612.

Erbaugh, M. S. 1986. Taking Stock: The Development of Chinese Noun Classifiers Historically and in Young Children. In: *Noun Classes and Categorization*, C. Craig ed. Amsterdam: J. Benjamins.

Fang, F. 1985. An Experiment on the Use of Classifiers by 4-to 6-year-olds. *Acta Psychologica Sinica.*

Gawlitzek-Maiwald, I., & Tracy, R. 1996. Bilingual Bootstrapping. *Linguistics* 34(5), 901 – 926.

Hu, Q. 1993. *The Acquisition of Chinese Classifiers by Young Mandaring Speaking Children*. Unpublished Doctoral Dissertation, Boston University.

Lanza, E., & Svendsen, B. A. 2007. Tell Me Who Your Friends Are and I Might Be Able to Tell You What language(s) You Speak: Social Network Analysis, Multilingualism, and Identity. *International Journal of Bilingualism* 11(3), 275 – 300.

Li, C. N., & Thompson, S. A. 1981. *Mandarin Chinese: A Functional Reference Grammar*. Los Angeles: University of California Press.

Li, P., Huang, B., & Hsiao, Y. 2010. Learning That Classifiers Count: Mandarin-speaking Children's Acquisition of Sortal and Mensural Classifiers. *Journal of East Asian Linguistics* 19(3), 207 – 230.

Li, W., & Lee, S. 2001. L1 Development in an L2 Environment: The Use of Cantonese Classifiers and Quantifiers by Young British-born Chinese in Tyneside. *International Journal of Bilingual Education and Bilingualism* 4(6), 359 – 382.

Lim, V. P.,Liow, S. J. R., Lincoln, M., Chan, Y. H., & Onslow, M. 2008. Determining Language Dominance in English-Mandarin Bilinguals: Development of a Self-report Classification Tool for Clinical Use. *Applied Psycholinguistics* 29(3), 389 – 412.

McEnery, T., & Xiao, R. 2007. Quantifying Constructions in English and Chinese: A Corpus-based Contrastive Study. In: *The Fourth Corpus Linguistics Conference*(pp. 27 – 30).

Meisel, J. M. 2007. The Weaker Language in Early Child Bilingualism: Acquiring a First Language as a Second Language?. *Applied Psycholinguistics* 28(3), 495 – 514.

Myers, J., &Tsay, J. 2000. The Acquisition of the Default Classifier in Taiwanese. In: *Proceedings of the 7th International Symposium of Chinese Languages and Linguistics*(pp. 87 – 106).

Ning, C., & Gu, G. 2013. *Xuelingqian Ertong Yuyan Nengli Ceshi* [*Linguistic Ability Test for Preschool Children*]. Tianjin: Tianjin University Press.

Paradis, J., & Genesee, F. 1996. Syntactic Acquisition in Bilingual Children: Autonomous or Interdependent?. *Studies in Second Language Acquisition* 18(1), 1 – 25.

Paradis, J., Genesee, F., & Crago, M. B. 2011. *Dual Language Development and Disorders: A Handbook on Bilingualism and Second Language Learning*. Brookes Publishing Company.

Qi, R. 2011. *The Bilingual Acquisition of English and Mandarin: Chinese Children in Australia*. New York: Cambria Press.

Tomasello, M. 2003. *Constructing a Language: A Usage-based Theory of Language Acquisition*. Cambridge, MA: Harvard University Press.

Unsworth, S. 2013. Current Issues in Multilingual First Language Acquisition. *Annual Review of Applied Linguistics* 33, 21 – 50.

Unsworth. S. 2014. Amount of Exposure as a Proxy for Dominance in Bilingual Language Acquisition. In: *Language Dominance in Bilinguals: Issues of Measurement and Operationalization*, C. Silva-Corvalan & J. Treffers Daller eds. Cambridge: Cambridge University Press.

Xu, D. 2010. *Sociolinguistics Experimental Course*. Beijing: Peking University Press.

Yip, V., & Matthews, S. 2007. *The Bilingual Child: Early Development and Language Contact*.Cambridge, UK: Cambridge University Press.

Yip, V., & Matthews, S. 2010. The Acquisition of Chinese in Bilingual and Multilingual Contexts.*International Journal of Bilingualism* 14(1), 127 – 214.

Zhu, H., & Li, W. 2005. Bi-and Multi-lingual Acquisition. In: *Clinical Sociolinguistics* (pp. 165 – 179), M. Ball ed. Oxford, UK: Blackwell.

Appendix: Bilingual children's sociolinguistic settings and input conditions

B1's sociolinguistic settings and input conditions

Age period	Place of residence	Sociolinguistic settings	Context	Carers	Input	Amount (hrs/day)
0 – 0;3	Australia	Family	Daily routine English TV English story-telling	Mother Father Sibling	E	8
0;3 – 1;3	China	Family	Daily routine English TV English story-telling Chinese TV Chinese househelper Other activities	Mother Father Sibling	E M	6 2
1;3 – 1;4	Thailand	Family Friends	Holiday Meetings	Mother Father Sibling Others	E M T	7 1 1
1;4 – 2;6	China	Family	Daily routine English TV English story-telling Chinese TV Chinese househelper Other activities	Mother Father Chinese Househelper Sibling	E M	6 2
2;6 – 2;9	China	Family Kids story club	Daily routine English TV English story-telling Chinese TV Chinese househelper Other activities Chinese story-telling	Mother Father Sibling Teachers & peers	E M M	6 2 0.5
2;9 – 3;5	China	Family Kindergarten	Daily routine English TV English story-telling Chinese TV Chinese househelper Other activities Kindergarten life (3 mornings/w)	Mother Father Sibling Teachers and peers	E M M	5 2 1.5

Continued

Age period	Place of residence	Sociolinguistic settings	Context	Carers	Input	Amount (hrs/day)
3;5 – 4;2	China	Family	Daily routine English TV English story-telling	Mother Father Sibling	E	5
			Chinese TV Chinese househelper Other activities		M	2
		Kindergarten	Kindergarten Life (4 mornings/w)	Teachers and peers	M	2

B5's sociolinguistic settings and input conditions

Age period	Place of residence	Sociolinguistic settings	Context	Carers	Input	Amount (hrs/day)
0 – 2;5	Australia	Family	Daily routine English TV English story-telling	Mother Father	E	8
2;5 – 3;0	China	Family	Daily routine English TV English story-telling	Mother Father	E	6
			Chinese TV Chinese guests visiting Other activities		M	2
3;0 – 3;4	China	Family	Daily routine English TV English story-telling	Mother Father	E	6
			Chinese TV Chinese guests visiting Other activities		M	2
		Kindergarten	Kindergarten life (2 mornings/w)		M	1
3;4 – 3;5	Thailand	Family Friends	Holiday Meetings	Mother Father Others	E M T	7 1 1
3;5 – 4;5	China	Family	Daily routine English TV English story-telling	Mother Father Sibling	E	6
			Chinese TV Chinese househelper Other activities		M	1.5
		Kindergarten	Kindergarten life (3 mornings/w)	Teachers and peers	M	1.5

Continued

Age period	Place of residence	Sociolinguistic settings	Context	Carers	Input	Amount (hrs/day)
4;5 – 6;1	China	Family	Daily routine English TV English story-telling	Mother Father	E	6
			Chinese TV Chinese househelper Other activities		M	1.5
		Kindergarten	Kindergarten life (4 mornings/w)	Teachers and peers	M	2
6;1 – 6;5	China	Family	Daily routine English TV English story-telling	Mother Father	E	5
			Chinese TV Chinese househelper Other activities		M	1
		Chinese primary school	School life (4 days/w)	Teachers & peers	M	4

B2's sociolinguistic settings and input conditions

Age period	Place of residence	Sociolinguistic settings	Context	Carers	Input	Amount (hrs/day)
0 – 1;7	Beijing China	Family	Daily routine English TV English story-telling	Mother Father	E	7
			Chinese TV Chinese househelper Other activities		M	1
1;7 – 2;2	Xi'an China	Family	Daily routine English TV English story-telling Various activities	Mother Father Siblings	E	6
			Chinese TV Chinese househelper Other activities		M	2

Continued

Age period	Place of residence	Sociolinguistic settings	Context	Carers	Input	Amount (hrs/day)
2;2 – 3;3	Xi'an China	Family	Daily routine / English TV / English story-telling	Mother Father Siblings	E	5
			Chinese TV / Chinese househelper / Other activities		M	1
		Kindergarten	Kindergarten life (5 mornings/w)	Teachers & peers	M	3
3;3 – 3;9	America	Family	Daily routine / English lessons & TV / Activities with extended families, relatives, and friends	Mother Father Grandma Grandpa Siblings	E	9
3;9 – 4;5	Xi'an China	Family	Daily routine / English lessons & TV	Mother Father Siblings	E	5
			Chinese TV / Chinese househelper / Other activities		M	2
		Kindergarten	Kindergarten life (5 mornings/w)	Teachers and peers	M	3

B4's sociolinguistic settings and input conditions

Age period	Place of residence	Sociolinguistic settings	Context	Carers	Input	Amount (hrs/day)
0 – 2;0	Beijing China	Family	Daily routine / English TV / English story-telling	Mother Father	E	6
			Chinese TV / Chinese househelper / Other activities	2	M	2
2;0 – 2;6	America	Family	Daily routine / English TV / English story-telling / Various activities	Mother Father Grandpa Grandma Peers	E	8

Age period	Place of residence	Sociolinguistic settings	Context	Carers	Input	Amount (hrs/day)
2;6 – 3;6	Beijing China	Family	Daily routine English TV English story-telling	Mother Father	E	5
			Chinese TV Chinese househelper Other activities		M	1
					M	3
		Kindergarten	Kindergarten life (5 mornings/w)			
3;6 – 5;1	Xi'an China	Family	Daily routine English lessons English TV	Mother Father	E	5
			Chinese TV Chinese househelper Other activities		M	1
					M	3
		Kindergarten	Kindergarten life (5 mornings/w)			
5;1 – 5;7	America	Family	Daily routine English lessons & TV Activities with extended families, relatives and friends	Mother Father Grandma Grandpa	E	9
5;7 – 6;1	Xi'an China	Family	Daily routine English lessons & TV	Mother Father	E	5
			Chinese TV Chinese househelper Other activities		M	2
		Kindergarten	Kindergarten life (5 mornings/w)	Teachers and peers	M	3
6;1 – 6;5	China	Family	Daily routine English TV English story-telling	Mother Father	E	5
		Home school in English & Chinese	Chinese TV Chinese househelper Other activities		M	2
			Chinese class	Teachers & sibling	M	3

B3's sociolinguistic settings and input conditions

Age period	Place of residence	Sociolinguistic settings	Context	Carers	Input	Amount (hrs/day)
0 – 1.6	Xi'an China	Family	Daily routine English TV English story-telling	Mother Father Sister	E	6
			Chinese househelper Other activities		M	2
1.6 – 2.0	America	Family	Daily routine English TV English story-telling Various activities	Mother Father Grandpa Grandma	E	6
			Chinese church Chinese friends visiting twice a week		M	2
2.0 – 3.0	Xi'an China	Family	Daily routine English TV English story-telling	Mother Father Sister	E	5
			Chinese TV Chinese househelper Other activities		M	2
					M	1
3.0 – 4.7	Xi'an China	Family	Daily routine English lessons & TV English story-telling	Mother Father Sister	E	5
			Chinese TV Chinese househelper Other activities		M	2.5
		Kids club	Kids club activities (3 times/w)	Teachers & peers	M	1.5
4.7 – 5;1	Xi'an China	Family	Daily routine English lessons & TV English story-telling	Mother Father Sister	E	5
			Chinese TV Chinese househelper Other activities		M	2
		Kindergarten	Kindergarten life (5 mornings/w)	Teachers & peers	M	3

Notes on contributors

Qi Ruying(Email：r.qi@uws.edu.au)，PhD，Senior Lecturer and PhD supervisor in Bilingualism and Chinese with the School of Humanities and Communication Arts at the University of Western Sydney. She is also Director of Bilingualism Research Lab @ UWS-JNU and Leader of the China Liaison Unit (Language and Culture) and an adjunct member of ARC Centre of Excellence for the Dynamics of Language. Her research interests are Mandarin-English bilingual children's language acquisition, early bilingual education, bilingualism and biculturalism, language acquisition, Chinese language and cultural teaching and learning.

Wu Wanhua(Email：wanhua.wu@uws.edu.au)，PhD candidate, School of Humanities and Communication Arts, Bilingualism Research Lab @ UWS-JNU, University of Western Sydney. His research interests：bilingual acquisition of Mandarin and English, Chinese linguistics, language teaching and learning.

英汉双语儿童习得汉语量词的测试研究

齐汝莹　吴万华

西悉尼大学

提　要：汉语普通话儿童量词习得的研究表明 3 至 4 岁的儿童已掌握普通话量词的基本句法结构，但仍然普遍存在通用量词如"个"和"只"的泛化使用现象。然而以往的研究并未涉及在中国的英汉双语儿童汉语量词的习得。本文探讨了英汉双语儿童对普通话量词的理解和产出，并以普通话单语儿童作为对照。本文使用宁春岩和顾钢（2013）的两个关于儿童量词习得的测试，试图了解英汉双语儿童在普通话输入量相当于单语儿童一半或更少的情况下是否表现出和同龄单语儿童相似的习得模式。来自同一所幼儿园的 5 名英汉双语儿童（4 至 6 岁）和 9 名普通话单语儿童（4 至 6 岁）参加了量词理解和产出的实验。双语儿童的父母均为英语本族语者。语言输入信息是通过对父母及老师的问卷和访谈获得。初步研究结果表明，虽然英汉双语儿童的普通话输入量只是同龄的普通话单语儿童的一半或更少，但他们在量词的习得和单语儿童并无差异。语言输入的作用在双语儿童习得普通话量词方面并不明显。研究结果在双语相互提升假说（bilingual bootstrapping）和语言输入效应背景下展开讨论。

关键词：量词　英汉双语儿童　输入

Development of English Lexicon and Morphology in 5-year-old Serbian-English Bilingual Children Attending First Year of Schooling in Australia

Satomi Kawaguchi and Lucija Medojevic

Abstract: This study investigates lexical and morphological development in English in two bilingual children and one monolingual child over their first year of schooling in Australia. For the bilingual children, Serbian is their heritage language and Australian English the mainstream language including the school language. The first year of school attendance is a time when a dramatic reversal occurred in the rate of exposure to these two languages. Oral production data were collected from these children at three-month intervals over the year. The bilingual children's lexical and morphological development was compared with the Australian monolingual peer's. Processability Theory was used to measure morphological development. Results reveal that before school attendance the bilingual children show some inaccuracy in morphological markings involving past-tense-*ed* and 3rd person singular -*s* on verbs. However, after the first few months of school attendance, these inaccuracies disappeared and the bilingual children's English grammatical accuracy became indistinguishable from their monolingual peer. One area of English verbal morphology that seems to be challenging for all three informants, bilingual or monolingual, was the past tense marker -*ed*. This suggests that acquisition of this so-called "regular" verb past tense morphology in English raises a broad developmental question. The data analysis shows that bilingual children's language development does not lag behind once they start schooling in an exclusively English environment and may even show a lexical advantage in English by comparison with their monolingual peers.

Key words: bilingual children, English acquisition, first year of schooling, lexical and morphological development

Introduction

This study aims to trace the lexical and morphological development of English in two Serbian-English bilingual children during their first year of mandatory schooling in Australia. The first year of schooling is an important event in a child's life that causes a dramatic change in exposure to English and the home/heritage language alike (e.g., Clyne 1982; Cummins 1979; Di Biase & Dyson 1988). A wide range of new activities, new learning, new friends and new adults interacting with the child will

107

operate through English. The exclusively English-speaking environment at school will dramatically impact on the child's social network and his or her linguistic development. Although the development of both languages in bilingual acquisition is important, in this paper we focus on development of English.

The informants in this study are two 5-year-old Serbian-Australian children and one monolingual Australian English child. One of the Serbian Australian children is a second-generation female child, code named Dana, and the other is a third-generation male child, code named Tomas. Language development in English in these children will be compared to one monolingual Australian English child, code named Adam. Both bilingual acquirers were born in Australia and received linguistic input from two typologically different languages from birth: Serbian, the heritage language predominantly spoken at home, and English, the mainstream language of the school and other social environments. In the home environment the children were exposed not only to Serbian, a home language, but also to English every day at certain times, especially through English language television, English speaking visitors and friends. The type of bilingual children in the present study represents the most common case in immigrant families, in which situation-bound language input and use in a "one language-one environment" setting are the

norm (Qi 2011, p.6). Following Qi (2004, 2011) the type of language acquisition in this study is referred to as Bilingual First Language Acquisition (BFLA), which is defined as the development of language in young children who hear two languages spoken to them from birth (De Houwer 1990, 2009).

It has been reported that children who grow up with "situation-bound" language exposure (cf.Vihman & McLaughlin 1982; Qi, Di Biase & Campbell 2006) develop their two languages separately (De Houwer 1990, 2005; Meisel 1989). This is not to suggest that their two languages are learnt in the same fashion as in monolinguals (see Paradis & Genesee 1996). One language may be more weakly developed than the other (Qi 2004). In fact, such uneven development appears to be quite common (De Houwer 2009), although statistical information on this is lacking (De Houwer 2013).

In today's increasingly globalised world, growing number of families find themselves in such bilingual settings. Many worry whether early bilingualism will be a positive or a negative experience for their children (De Houwer 2013). Some bilingual preschool children are often reported to have smaller vocabulary sizes in either of their languages than monolingual children of the same age (e. g., Nicoladis 2003, 2006; Pearson, Fernandez, & Oller 1993). Furthermore, in some aspects of morphology, such as compound produc-tion, bilingual children produce fewer target constructions relative to monolingual children of the same age. However, lan-guage lags in development do not occur in all domain of language use (Nicoladis, Song, & Marentette 2012). In some cases, bilingual children seem to catch up, sug-gesting that maturational or developmental factors also play a role.

When children who are raised with two languages appear slow in developing lan-guage, grandparents, speech therapists and educators will be quick to put the blame on the bilingual situation (e. g. De Houwer 2009a), especially when monolingual chil-dren are treated by the wider society in which they live as the norm. Many teach-ers, parents and health care professionals believe that these bilingual children have a "double burden" and consequently go through the stages of language development more slowly than monolingual children (Genesee, Paradis & Crago 2004, p. 77). However, very little is known about bilingual children's language deve-lopment at the commencement and over the first year of schooling. Further, research-ers within the field of BFLA know little about children's lexical and morphosyntac-tic development beyond age five as studies of bilinguals' later language development, for this age group, are scarce (De Houwer 2009, p. 296).

The lack of general understanding of what these children know and do not know in the language of the school, English in this case, at the beginning of their school experience and how they would do over their first year of schooling is an issue of concern for parents and teachers alike. Thus this study aims to investigate how these bilingual children use and further de-velop their English during the first year of mandatory schooling. With this aim in mind, we present two research questions to guide the investigation:

(Q1) *What is the level of develop-ment of the English lexicon and morphology in Serbian-English bilingual children before school attendance?*

(Q2) *Does the first year of school help Serbian-English bilingual children to develop spoken English to the level of other native speaking children?*

It is expected that, with a dramatic in-crease in exposure to English-only do-mains, the first year of formal schooling would positively affect the development of English language skills in bilingual chil-dren. The analysis undertaken in this study includes the analysis of child's lexicon (lexical production size and cumulative growth of lexicon), followed by the analy-sis of the morphology within the frame-work of the Processability Theory (Piene-mann 1998; Bettoni & Di Biase, in press).

Processability Theory: theoretical framework

Processability Theory (PT) (Pienemann

1998; Pienemann, Di Biase & Kawaguchi 2005; Bettoni & Di Biase, in press) is chosen for our framework to measure language development due to its typological and psychological plausibility. PT incorporates Levelt's (1989) speech production model and Lexical Functional Grammar (LFG) (Bresnan, 2001) for the formal description of linguistic structures. The theory hypothesises developmental sequences, originally, in second language acquisition and it has been widely tested on typologically different languages: Arabic (e. g., Mansouri 2005), Chinese (e.g., Zhang 2004), English (e. g., Yamaguchi & Kawaguchi 2014), German (Pienemann 1998), Italian (e. g, Di Biase 2002), Japanese (e. g., Kawaguchi 2010), and Swedish (Pienemann & Håkansson 1999). Moreover, the theory has been expanded to, and tested on, language acquisition in atypical situations: Bilingual First Language Acquisition with English-Japanese (Itani-Adams 2007, 2011; Pienemann, Keßler & Itani-Adams 2011) and children with Specific Language Impairment (e. g., Håkansson 2001; Håkansson, Salameh & Nettelbladt 2003; Agostini & Best, in press).

PT claims that there is a universal developmental sequence in second language (L2) acquisition which is aligned in the sequence of grammatical encoding activation in the speech formulator (Kempen & Hoenkamp 1987). This sequence is implicationally arranged which means that each lower level procedure in the sequence is a necessary prerequisite for the next procedure. Based on this hierarchy, Pienemann (1998) hypothesises that L2 morphology develops in the following order:

(1) invariant form > lexical morphemes > phrasal procedure > inter-phrasal procedure

PT assumes that L2 learners process exchanges of grammatical information to produce morphological structures at different levels such as phrasal, clausal and so on. The notion of "feature unification" in LFG clearly captures this process. The *well-formedness condition* in LFG states that the value attributes of a constituent must not conflict (Kaplan and Bresnan 1982). When all the required information is compatible, then the features are "unified". PT stages in morphology are defined according to the type of "feature unification" which the speaker needs to handle. Table 1 summarises the PT stages of acquisition of English morphology after Di Biase et. al. (in press). This schedule is based on Pienemann (1998) except for the structural characterization of the VP procedure.

The first stage in morphological development is **lemma access**. Possible outcomes of this stage are single words or formulas of invariant form that do not require any morphological procedure or information exchange. The acquisition of language-specific **category procedure** characterises the lexical morphology stage, which does not require information exchange in the encoding process. For instance, insertion of the affix -s to mark PLURAL on a noun (e.g., *my friends*) can be achieved directly from conceptualisation as long as the speaker can identify the category of the word (noun in this case). In the third stage, the speaker acquires **phrasal procedure.** Structural outcomes of this procedure are phrases whose morphology requires information unification between the head and a modifier within a phrase. Plural agreement is an example involving phrasal procedure (e.g., *many*-PL *dogs*-PL) with NP. Recent PT literature added VP agreement in the morphological stage of phrasal procedure. Di Biase, Kawaguchi & Yamaguchi (in press) hypothesise that VP agreement involving auxiliary and lexical verbs (e.g. *be + eating, have + eaten*) will appear at this stage. Strictly speaking, English VP agreement is across two phrases (i.e., the auxiliary and the lexical verb) and thus is acquired after NP agreement. The next stage requires sentence procedure and now interphasal morphology will be possible. SV agreement in English involves interphasal procedure. In the sentence *Mary goes to school*, the morpheme -s on the verb indicates the subject's information of "NUM = SG" and "PERSON = 3" in the sentence. In this case, the subject of the sentence is *Mary* and the lexical entry states that "NUM = SG" and "PERSON = 3". Information coming from NP_{SUBJ} *Mary* and the verb *goes* is compatible in terms of NUM and PERSON values, and therefore unification is possible. This requires an interphasal procedure because the two elements *Mary* and *goes* belong to different phrases. The feature information for the NP_{SUBJ} has to be held in memory until the VP is produced and the values of the respective phrase are checked for compatibility. If compatible, unification happens (across phrase boundary) at the S-node. PT predicts that this type of morphology appears after phrasal morphology.

Table 1 Developmental stages for English morphology

Procedure	Morphological outcome/stage	English structure	Example
S-procedure	Interphasal morphology	3rd person singular-*s*	*Peter loves* rice
Phrasal procedure	*VP morphology*	AUX V: have V-ed MOD V be V-ing	*they **have studied*** *you **can go*** *I **am going***
	NP morphology	phrasal plural marking	***these** girls* ***many** dogs* ***three** black cats*

Continued

Procedure	Morphological outcome/stage	English structure	Example
Category procedure	Lexical morphology	past-*ed* V-*ing* plural-*s*	*Mary jumped* *he eating* *my brothers working*
Lemma access	Invariant forms	single words; formulas	*station, here* *my name is Pim*

Following Processability Theory, the notion of *emergence criteria* for morphological structures is adopted to determine the stages of the informants' language acquisition. The emergence criterion regards the first appearance of a grammatical feature in the learner's language as the acquisition point (e. g., Meisel, Clahsen & Pienemann 1981). In this criterion, the learner is considered to have entered a new stage of grammatical development at the point of "emergence", even though the rules from the previous stage may not yet have been mastered in all possible contexts. To satisfy the emergence criterion, the analysis needs to contain contrastive lexical and morphological variation. For example, only when the interlanguage sample contains the morphological structure in question with different verbs (lexical variation), and when any of these verbs can be found in contrastive morphological forms in the sample (morphological variation), can we rule out a formulaic use of a structure and consider the emergence criterion to be met (Di Biase & Kawaguchi 2002, p. 287 – 288). For example, if these verbs occur with different morphological suffixes (e.g. *-ing*, *-ed*) can we assume that the structure has emerged. (2) contains examples of the rule application of the morpheme *-s* with lexical variation (i. e., *drinks* versus *plays*) and formal variation (i.e., *drink* versus *drinks*).

(2) I *drink* coffee.

She *drinks* tea.

He *plays* basketball.

A significant aspect of this study is the application of PT as a theoretical framework in the field of Bilingual First Language Acquisition (BFLA). So far only one bilingual longitudinal study of a Japanese-English (Itani-Adams 2007) has shown that the bilingual child's language acquisition follows the sequence in the language-specific way which PT predicted. The study by Itani-Adams (2007) used PT for comparing the development of two languages in one-parent, one-language environment in Australia. The key question addressed was whether bilingual children differentiate between two linguistic systems from birth in the development of morphosyntax. Using PT as a standard of measurement enables one to compare the acquisition process directly between the two languages. However, there is no study assessing the bilinguals' development after 5 years of age or assessing the effects of the first year of school on the two languages where the majority language is English. This study in particular focuses on the development of English.

The longitudinal study

In order to investigate language development over the first year of schooling, parallel longitudinal case studies involving two Serbian-English bilingual children were conducted with observations at regular quarterly intervals. These bilingual children's English development was compared with the development of a monolingual English-speaking child also attending his first year of school.

1. Participants

The informants in this study are two Serbian-English bilingual children recruited through the Serbian Orthodox Community in Sydney. One is a second generation female child, code named Dana. The other is a third generation male child, code named Tomas. The monolingual Australian-English child, as control, code named Adam, attended the same class in the same public school as Tomas. All of the participants in this study were growing up in Sydney, where English is the majority language as well as the language of the School. The bilingual informants represent, respectively, the second and third generation of Serbian-Australians fitting into the so-called "typical" profile of endogamous Serbian family in an Australian setting.

Dana : She is a second-generation Serbian-Australian, born in Sydney. Dana's family consists of five members. She was 5;5 at the first interview. Her parents are native speakers of Serbian who migrated to Australia as adults and speak the Serbian Ekavic dialect at home. Dana has a 3-year-old sister. Her maternal grandmother also lives with the family and looks after the two granddaughters while the parents work full-time. The family lives in Sydney's Inner West. The children have never visited Serbia or travelled outside of Australia. Dana's parents use Serbian and English according to the interlocutor, in specific domains and for specific purposes. They self-reported that they only occasionally code-switch with acquaintances, children of relatives and friends, and friends of children who code-switch themselves.

Dana's parents were asked to estimate her exposure to the two languages from birth. From age 0 to 4 they estimate that Dana used 90% of Serbian with parents and grandmother in daily routines, while she was exposed to English only 10% of the time through TV English programs, activities outside home and English visiting friends and neighbours. Between ages 4 and 5;5, Dana started attending preschool classes in English three times a week as well as English reading classes organised in the local library. It was estimated that the exposure to English now increased to 30%. She was exposed to English through her teachers and English speaking peers. The mother also used English with the child with homework exercises. Serbian, however, remains the predominantly used language of communication for all other purposes. When Dana commenced school, the language exposure shifted in the opposite direction. According to the parents, she was now exposed to English 70% of the time. Serbian was still the only language of communication at home, except when doing homework exercises.

Tomas: He is a third generation Serbian-Australian. His family consists of 7 members: paternal grandparents who migrated to Australia in the 1960s, parents, an auntie (father's sister) and Tomas' twin brother Bob. This is a three generation family of Serbian migrants living in one large household in a relatively wealthy suburb in Sydney's West. The family speaks the Serbian Ekavic dialect. Tomas and his brother are non-identical twins. This study focuses only on Tomas who happens to attend the same class as our monolingual informant Adam. From the interviews conducted with each parent separately, it can be gathered that the mother's Serbian language skills are much stronger than her husband's. Tomas' parents often code-switch when communicating with each other and use English predominantly. They do not keep a clear separation of the use of the two languages at home. Parents were also asked to provide an estimate of Tomas' exposure to Serbian and English from birth.

From age 0 to 4;11 parents estimated that Tomas was exposed to Serbian 80% of the time. Tomas and his brother Bob never attended preschool and they were always cared for by the family members. Additionally, family never travelled outside Australia. English, they claimed, was present only 20% of the time through TV, activities outside the home as well as through English speaking visitors of the family. With the beginning of the first school year, the exposure to the two languages reversed. He was now exposed to English 80% of the time through English-speaking teachers, peers and at home with the father who helped with homework exercises. Parents still claimed that Serbian was used in the household after school.

Adam: He is a 5-year-old Australian English monolingual speaker, who attended the same class as Tomas during the first year of schooling. He lives with his parents and an older sister in a relatively wealthy suburb in Sydney's West. Adam's and Tomas' family live in close proximity and the parents of both boys are of very similar educational level. Adam and Tomas are, therefore, ideally matched for the purposes of comparison of their development of English during the first year of schooling. The boys have a similar socioeconomic background and experienced similar treatment from teachers and peers at school.

2. Data collection

The data were collected through four times over the first year of schooling. The two bilingual children's English spoken data baseline was obtained just before commencing school (Time 0) after which data were again collected at regular three month intervals until the end of the school year (Time 1 – 3) roughly coinciding with the New South Wales school terms for primary schools. The monolingual child's speech data were collected in parallel Time 1 – 3 sessions. Note that his data was not obtained in Time 0 because there was no way of finding out which child(ren) would be placed at the same class with our bilingual participants prior to the commencement of school.

All data collection sessions were conducted in the informants' homes. Participation involved face-to-face verbal interaction between the child informant and a researcher who was an adult native speaker of Australian English who does not speak or understand Serbian. The spoken language elicited from the three children includes naturalistic conversation and some controlled tasks such as story telling (e.g., "Goldilocks"; "Little Red Riding Hood"). After the recordings, each session was transcribed and processed for data analysis. All transcriptions were checked by trained native speakers of English. Discrepancies were checked and resolved in consultation with the researcher. The following three tables, Table 2a-2c summarise English corpus collected from Dana, Tomas and Adam respectively, which contains of 693 minutes of speech production.

Table 2　English corpus

a. Dana

Age	Session	Duration	Types	Tokens	Turns	Utterances
5; 05	T0	69 min	443	2270	383	468
5; 08	T1	45 min	495	2730	358	495
6; 01	T2	71 min	480	2560	367	472
6; 04	T3	46 min	390	1787	242	320
	Total	231 min	1808	9347	1350	1755

b. Tomas

Age	Session	Duration	Types	Tokens	Turns	Utterances
4; 11	T0	41 min	333	1166	228	249
5; 02	T1	63 min	441	2019	396	464
5; 05	T2	71 min	445	1976	372	470
5; 08	T3	68 min	409	2027	380	400
	Total	243 min	1628	7188	1376	1583

c. Adam

Age	Session	Duration	Types	Tokens	Turns	Utterances
/	T0	/	/	/	/	/
5; 03	T1	63 min	336	1650	466	474
5; 06	T2	66 min	347	1596	458	477
5; 09	T3	90 min	385	1757	537	490
	Total	219 min	1068	5003	1461	1441

Each child in the study showed their own personalities during data collection. Dana happily responded to all tasks from T0 which is reflected in the length of her first recording session (69 minutes) in Table 2a and the overall size of the data compared to other informants. The two boys, Tomas and Adam, on the other hand, were easily distracted during the data collection session. The investigator implemented different techniques to engage the children in the tasks including small rewards for each task completed: stickers of cartoons, small gift toys, and similar small rewards (with the parents' permission). At T0, for instance, investigator had to stop recording Tomas' sessions a few times as he would often run out of the recording room to get a toy. In the sessions at T1, T2, and T3 Tomas was much calmer and more cooperative. Adam, the monolingual English speaker, preferred to play silently by himself, especially in tasks that involved toys. Adam usually responded to investigator's questions with short utterances, which confirmed or negated investigators' statements. Finally, the difference between informants is also evident in the number of word types at T1; Dana produced almost double the amount of types compared to Adam.

Results and discussion

This section presents the results of the lexical and morphological development in English in two bilingual children, Dana and Tomas, which will be compared with an English monolingual child, Adam, over the first year of schooling. This section is organised as follows. Firstly we outline the development of lexicon: Dana's and Tomas' distribution of utterances and their ability to use the appropriate language with the English-speaking investigator and; the comparison of cumulative growth of lexicon in all three children during the first year of schooling. This is followed by the presentation of the development of morphology in Dana, Tomas and Adam individually and the comparison of morphological development between bilingual and monolingual children.

1. Development of lexicon

Dana's corpus was firstly checked for the distribution of utterances in all four recording session with the English-speaking investigator. All utterances in her corpus were classified as English unilingual. In other words, Dana used no Serbian nor did she use mixed utterances in her English recording sessions. She used English with the investigator prior to and throughout the first year of schooling.

Unlike Dana, at T0 Tomas used some mixed Serbian-English utterances and on one occasion a Serbian unilingual utterance with the English-speaking investigator. Out of 249 utterances at T0, Tomas used 93.3% (233 utterances) English unilingual utterances, 6.02% mixed utterances (15 utterances) and 0.4% of Serbian unilingual utterances (1 Serbian utterance). The examples in (3) present three types of mixed utterances that occurred spontaneously in Tomas' speech.

(3) Tomas' mixed utterances (MU) at T0

a. *jump-a*

jump-3.SG.PRES

[(he) is jumping]

b. *the bees* **pancš**

behind and want to eat the dog tale

the bees <u>fall-</u>2.SG.PAST behind

[the bees fall behind]

c. *one baby pig who* **jadi**

this oink oink

one baby pig who do-3.SG.PRES this...
oink oink

[one baby pig who does this... oink
oink]

In (3a) Tomas used the verb *jump* in
response to the investigator's question
about what a dog in a picture was doing and
added a verb suffix -*a*, that in Serbian
marks a present continuous action in 3rd
person singular (referring to the dog).
Next, in (3b) Tomas used the Serbian le
xical verb *paneš* (fall) in an otherwise English utterance where the Serbian verb suffix
did not agree in person with the subject in
the sentence (bees). Further, in (3c), the
informant used a Serbian verb *jadi* (do) in
3rd person present tense. In this example,
however, Tomas showed number and person agreement between the English SUBJ
and the Serbian lexical verb.

As Tomas started attending school
both mixed utterances and Serbian utterances disappeared altogether (from T1 on-
wards) when talking to the English-speaking investigator. This indicates that Tomas
became able to make a clear distinction between the two languages, English and
Serbian.

Figure 1 presents three children's
cumulative growth of word types used at
each interview session over the year. All
three children rapidly and extensively
expanded their lexicon. Dana, in particular, shows the largest lexicon size and the
highest lexical growth.

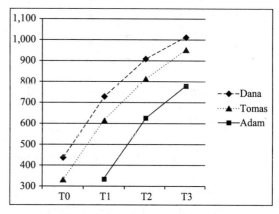

Figure 1 Cumulative growth of word types

Of crucial importance is the dramatic
lexical expansion found within both the
verbal and the noun word types. Figure 2
below compares the informants' cumulative
development of lexical verbs (left) and
nouns (right) over the year.

A surprising finding was that the two
bilingual children's cumulative lexical size
in nouns, verbs and total word types, in
sharp contrast to what several researches
report (e.g., Nicoladis 2003, 2006; Pearson, Fernandez & Oller 1993), not only
did not lag behind but were actually larger
than the English monolingual child,
Adam, at any point over the first year of
schooling. In fact, Dana's lexical development was the most advanced among the
three children. This may be partly attribut-
able to the fact that Dana is a few months
older than Tomas and Adam; Dana was 5;

08 while Tomas 5;02 and Adam 5;03 at T1. Previous literature, also, seems to agree that girls develop language skills earlier than boys (e. g., Karmiloff & Karmiloff-Smith 2002). Nevertheless also the other bilingual child, Tomas, who is one year younger than the monolingual child, Adam, has a greater lexical increase.

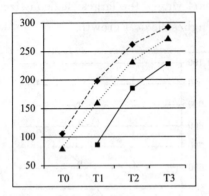 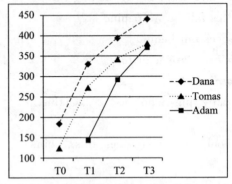

Figure 2   Cumulative growth of English lexical verbs (left) and nouns (right)

2. Development of morphology

A distributional analysis of Dana's data is presented below in Table 3. The total number of contexts in which a particular feature or structure has been supplied is marked by (+) if used in an obligatory context, by (−) if not supplied in an obligatory context, and by (>) if the feature or structure is oversupplied. PT's *emergence* criteria, presented earlier, are used to establish whether a feature has been acquired at each stage in the developmental hierarchy. As for lemma access, simply " + " is inserted as there are abundant instances.

Table 3   Dana's development of English morphology within PT

Procedures	Stages	English morphology	T0	T1	T2	T3
Sentence procedure	Interphasal morphology	3rd person singular -*s*	+9, −3	+22	+14	+4
Phrasal procedure	VP morphology	*have* + V-*ed*	+2	+1	+2	0
		MOD + V	+19	+27	+25	+22
		be + V-*ing*	+18	+17	+15	+5
	NP morphology	Phrasal plural marking	+11	+17	+13	+16
Category procedure	Lexical morphology	verb-*ing*	+5	+4	+3	+1
		past-*ed*	+6;>2	+16;>4	+15	+13
		plural-*s*	+42	+59,>1	+36	+28
Lemma access	Invariant forms	Single words; formulas	+	+	+	+

Category procedure

V-ing (*without Aux*): In T0, Dana produced five examples of lexical V-*ing*, exemplified in (4a). Dana sometimes omitted obligatory AUXs. The example in (4b) illustrates one of the four occasions in which Dana omitted an obligatory AUX.

(4) Dana T0 (E=English investigator, D=Dana)

a. E: *what do you think he's doing?*

D: *swishing it around*

b. D: *a dog looking there*

At T1, T2 and T3 Dana continued to use lexical-*ing* in short utterances as in (5). In sum, before school attendance Dana occasionally used lexical V-*ing* without AUX. During the school year omissions of AUX did not occur.

(5) Dana T2

E: *what's that butterfly doing there?*

D: *flying*

Past -ed: Dana provided six examples of lexical -*ed* on verbs at T0, including regular verbs such as *loved*, *looked*, *used*, *shouted*, *cleaned* and *finished*. Two examples were counted as over-supplied instances of -*ed* (>) on the base form of irregular verbs (6a-6b). Dana did, however, produce a variety of irregular verbs in past tense in 23 contexts, without -*ed* generalization, as exemplified in (6c-6d).

(6) Dana T0

a. *and he taked his one home*

b. *but when he waked up he saw no frog*

c. *the dog fell*

d. *the bees all went out*

After three months of school attendance, Dana produced 16 contexts for regular past tense, as in (7a). Instances of oversuppliance were found in four contexts with two lexical verbs (*cut* and *break*) as in (7b-7c), which indicates that she was still mastering the past tense morphology at this point in the study. Dana also used a greater variety of irregular verbs in appropriate past tense forms (18 types) at T1, some examples of which are presented in (7d-7e).

(7) Dana T1

a. *she followed the footprints in his house*

b. E: *what happened to the tomato ? it was ?*

D: *cuts cutsed*

c. D: *and someone's broked my chair said baby bear*

d. *then he ran and he ran*

e. *and then that woke Goldilocks up*

At T2 and T3 Dana no longer overgeneralised -*ed* with past tense. After one year of schooling Dana showed accurate use of the morpheme -*ed* in marking past tense on regular verbs.

Phrasal procedure

NP morphology: Dana used plural -*s* in contexts with quantifiers productively over the first year of schooling. The examples in (8) illustrate the different agreement contexts for plural -*s* on noun occur, i.e., with numeral quantifiers (8a) as well as with non-numeral quantifiers (8b).

(8) Dana T0

a. *three pigs*

b. *well when they go to the big park I see some birds*

VP morphology: Dana produced two structures of VP, MOD + V and *be* + V-*ing*, regularly through T0 to T3. The auxiliary *have* did not appear in its full form in Dana's or Tomas' English corpus. The contracted form of this auxiliary verb was used by Dana in three recording sessions, T0, T1 and T2, as in (9). However, it did not appear at T3. Over the first year of schooling she continuously added new forms of auxiliary verbs to her repertoire.

(9) Dana T0

I've got black and a pink one

Interphasal procedure

3rd person singular *-s*: at T0 Dana provided nine examples of 3rd person singular *-s* on different lexical verbs as in (10a-10b). This fully satisfies PT's emergence criteria. Yet, Dana also produced three contexts where the inflection *-s* on lexical verbs (*take*, *think* and *eat*) was not supplied as in (11a-11b). These were produced in a narrative task where Dana was asked to tell a story of a missing frog with the help of a picture book (Mayer 1969). At T0 Dana, like other informants, used the present tense forms of the verb for storytelling.

(10) Dana T0

a. *owl comes just in the night time*

b. *and she writes all the things lovely*

(11) Dana T0

a. D: *he looked at the window... no frog*

E: *really?*

D: *naughty frog... it's a naughty frog... the dog take the frog*

b. E: *oh...and this picture?*

D: *and the boy is grumpy because he think the the dog eat the frog*

After three months of schooling, Dana used SV agreement accurately in all contexts (100%). Some examples are presented in (12a-12b).

(12) Dana T1

a. *because he always goes to the shop*

b. *and he opens the gate*

Dana continued to use SV agreement productively and accurately over the remainder of the school year. In summary, the attendance of first year of schooling positively affected the development of Dana's English morphology.

As for Tomas, Table 4 shows that all structures in the PT hierarchy considered in this analysis have emerged as early as T0. However, inaccurate use of some morphemes was detected in T0 and T1, which was quickly rectified within the first few months of schooling.

Table 4   Distributional analysis of Tomas' English morphological structures

Procedures	Stages	English morphology	T0	T1	T2	T3
Sentence procedure	Interphasal morphology	3rd person singular *-s*	+5, −2 (9*)	+13, −1	+7	0
Phrasal procedure	VP morphology	*have* + V-*ed* MOD + V *be* + V-*ing*	0 +6 +5	0 +6 +52	0 +9 +47	+2* +15 +36
	NP morphology	Phrasal plural marking	+6	+16	+15	+14

Continued

Procedures	Stages	English morphology	T0	T1	T2	T3
Category procedure	Lexical morphology	plural-*s*	+41	+47	+45	+18
		past *ed*	+4,>2	+11, >4	+9	+6
		verb-*ing*	+18	+2	+3	+2
Lemma access	Invariant forms	Single words; formulas	+	+	+	+

Notes: * marks the ambiguous instances of inflection.

Category procedure

V-*ing* (*without AUX*): Like Dana, also Tomas omitted the auxiliary at T0, though he did so to a much greater extent. In T0, Tomas produced V-*ing* without AUX 18 times as exemplified in (13). After three months of school attendance, the pattern of use of lexical V-*ing* changed. At T1, Tomas used lexical -*ing* only in contexts in which the subject was dropped in short utterances as a brief response to the researcher's question as in (14).

(13) Tomas T0

the boy looking in the hole

(14) Tomas T1

(E=English investigator, T=Tomas)

E: mhm what are they doing now?

T: *drinking the milk*

Tomas showed further progress with the use of V-*ing*. At T1, T2 and T3 when lexical V-*ing* occurred it was either accompanied by auxiliaries or it occurred in nonfinite form as in (15).

(15) Tomas T3

I see three dogs chasing the bone

Past -*ed*: At T0 Tomas was able to supply this morpheme correctly on regular verbs as in (16a) but he also overgeneralised the use and supplied this morpheme even on verbs which do not require it as in

(16b-16c).

(16) Tomas T0

a. *a one big dog scared the little dogs*

b. *the owl flied. and the boy get down*

c. *boy... uh... falled and the dog*

He used five types of irregular verbs in past tense accurately after the commencement of schooling in T1, as in (17a-17b). But he also continued overusing of -*ed* as in (17c-17d).

(17) Tomas T1

a. *because Goldilocks ate all of the baby one*

b. *Goldilocks slept in the baby bed*

c. *he eated the ice cream*

d. *he drinked some soup*

Tomas' use of past tense further improved in T2 and T3, where no instances of non-supplied or oversupplied -*ed* were found. It is worth noting that the accurate use of irregular verbs also increased by T3 as in (18a-18b). Tomas had previously overgeneralised -*ed* with some verbs presented in (cf. 17c-17d).

(18) Tomas T3

a. *the boy woke up*

b. *and then the dog fell and the glass broke*

In summary, during the first year of schooling Tomas progressed from oversuppliance of *-ed* on irregular verbs at T0 and T1 to an accurate use of *all* the past tense forms of verbs.

Phrasal procedure

NP morphology: Tomas showed a number of instances of phrasal *-s* already at T0. No examples of non-suppliance or over-suppliance at phrasal level were found. Tomas continued to productively use the phrasal plural marking throughout the first year of schooling.

VP morphology: Tomas provided sufficient evidence for this VP morphology stage to be considered acquired at T0. Tomas was also shown to drop many AUXs at T0 (see Category procedure stage *V-ing*). The extensive exposure to English-only environments over the school year positively influenced Tomas' development of a variety of auxiliaries; he added new forms of the *be* auxiliary and modals especially between T0 and T1. Tomas did not produce "*have + V-ed*" structure until T3 as in (19a-19b).

(19) Tomas T3

a. *I've done it.*

b. *and I've got a game for Wii*

In summary, Tomas' data demonstrate that the school environment provided opportunities for more intensive and extensive language use resulting in a greater range of VP structures and greater accuracy.

Interphasal morphology

3rd person singular -s: Before school attendance at T0, Tomas provided five instances (tokens) of SV agreement. They appeared with only two different lexical verbs, as in (20a-20b). As there were 16

contexts of SV agreement in total, i.e., only 31.3% positive suppliance of third person *-s*. Out of the remaining 11 contexts, there were two clear instances of non-suppliance of *-s* on the verb as in (20c). The remaining nine instances were considered ambiguous because the examples occur in the storytelling task.

(20) Tomas T0

a. *the mole get out his hole and the boy thinks is that stinky*

b. *the boy dresses like*

c. *just Ben turn different aliens*

After three months of schooling Tomas produced 13 contexts of SV agreement in the present tense with six different lexical verbs (*carry*, *start*, *go*, *love*, *look* and *equal*) as in (21a-21b). This demonstrates his dramatic improvement in the use of SV agreement. Only one example of non-suppliance was found in this session as in (21c).

(21) Tomas T1

a. *and my brother loves Leo*

b. *two plus one equals three*

c. *E: what does a horse do?*

T: *eat some food*

As there were 14 contexts of SV agreement in total at T1, the positive suppliance of third person *-s* stands at 92.8%. This result is very different from T0. Three months later, at T2, Tomas continued to use SV agreement accurately in all contexts; he provided seven examples of SV agreement. In the last recording session at T3 he provided no context for SV agreement in present tense as his preference switched to the use of the past tense in narratives.[1]

Turning now to Adam, the monolingual child, his production of English morphology is presented in Table 5. The analysis shows his production of English at the age of 5 and the level of accuracy of these structures in use.

Table 5 Distributional analysis of Adam's English morphological structures

Procedures	Stages	English morphology	T1	T2	T3
Sentence procedure	Interphasal morphology	3rd person singular -s	+9	+13	+7
Phrasal procedure	VP morphology	have + V-ed MOD + V he + V-ing	+2* +9 +18	+1 +11 +35	+1 +7 +23
	NP morphology	Phrasal plural marking	+16	+25	+22
Category procedure	Lexical morphology	plural-s past-ed verb-ing	+29 +6, >6 +11	+45 +9 +3	+31 +8 +9
Lemma access	Invariant forms	Single words; formulas	+	+	+

Notes: * marks the contracted forms of AUX *have* that occured at T1.

Category procedure

V-*ing*: At T1, one word utterances that Adam provided to the investigator's questions and prompts as in (22), were counted as instances of lexical V-*ing* without AUX. Adam also used V-*ing* in nonfinite form at T2 and T3. Unlike Tomas and Dana, Adam, as a monolingual native speaker of English, did not produce the structure of "subject + V-*ing*" without Aux in his recordings.

(22) Adam T1

(E=English investigator, A=Adam)

E: so what do you see in that picture?

A: *a man reading a book*

However, in terms of V-*ed* Adam displayed a similar pattern of use as the bilingual informants at T1. Four instances were found with regular verbs occurring with -*ed* (*moved*, *screamed*, *finished*, and *jumped*) as in (19a). Past -*ed* was also used on base forms of irregular verbs *runned*, *catched*, and *breaked* as in (23b-23c). They were counted as over-supplied even though they show positive rule application of the -*ed* to indicate past tense. Adam successfully used correct past tense forms with 12 types of irregular verbs (*ate*, *had*, *found*, *saw*, *got*, *told*, *fell*, *woke up*, *won*, *went*, *broke* and *said*).

(23) Adam T1

a. *he already jumped in there*

b. *he accidently catched the dog*

c. *she breaked that one first*

Adam's marking of past tense at T2 and T3 had become fully accurate. It can be

---

[1] Each of the informants in this study switched to a predominant use of past tense at T3 to tell stories.

concluded that at T1 all informants, bilingual and monolingual, showed a similar linguistic behaviour regarding *-ed*; they oversupplied *-ed* on verbs that did not require it, and gradually attained accurate use of *-ed*.

Phrasal procedure

NP morphology: Adam produces four occurrences of *-s* on nouns with other quantifiers as in (24). He had no difficulties with the use of phrasal plural *-s*. The pattern seems to be the same in all informants at this point in time.

(24) Adam T1

some stars

VP morphology: Adam showed abundant variety of AUX *be* in use at T1. For instance, AUX *am* occured in three contexts in its contracted form with two types of lexical verbs, as in (25a). AUX *is* occurred in ten contexts with six types of lexical verbs (*opening*, *eating*, *drinking*, *coming*, *going* and *looking*). *Are* appeared in four contexts in its contracted form, as in (21b). AUX *was* frequently occurred in Adam's corpus and was illustrated in (25c). Adam provided the whole variety of AUX *be* in use at T2 and T3. The pattern is similar to Tomas'.

(25) Adam T1

a. *I'm whacking them*

b. *they're playing*

c. *he was trying*

Modal AUX + V: Adam used many examples of modal auxiliary verbs at T1: five examples with auxiliary *can*; AUX *will* was used in two instances; AUX *should* and *won't* also occurred at T1.

Examples are presented in (26a-26d). The variety of modal AUXs remains rather constant in Adam's language corpus between T1 and T3.

(26) Adam T1

a. *it can drive*

b. *I'll show you the game*

c. *because she won't eat. because she won't eat it*

d. *he should go that way*

AUX have + V-ed: Auxiliary *have* rarely occurs as an AUX in the speech of Adam except in contracted form at T1, as in (27). At T3 a negative form of *have* in its full form is also found, as in (28).

(27) Adam T1

you've got one point

(28) Adam T3

we haven't done the belt

In summary, Adam uses a wide variety of auxiliary verbs during the first year of schooling much as would be expected from native speakers' of his age.

Interphasal procedure

3rd person singular -s: Adam produces a total of nine contexts for positive SV agreement with five different verbs (*break*, *like*, *go*, *see* and *jump*) as in (29a-29b) at T1. As other 5 year olds he is at the interphasal stage in the PT morphological hierarchy and uses it productively at T2 and T3.

(29) Adam T1

a. *because it breaks*

b. *he jumps*

Overall, Adam's use of English morphology at T1 was target-like except in the use of lexical morpheme *-ed* in past tense formation, as reported for all informants in the study. Attendance at school allowed him to learn past tense forms for verbs he may not have encountered before.

Now we compare morphological development between bilingual children and the monolingual control. The two bilingual children, Tomas and Dana, were at the interphrasal stages in PT's morphological hierarchy before school began (i.e., T0). However, their use of verbal morphology was not always accurate. This was also true at T1, three months after the commencement of schooling. Adam, the English monolingual peer, was also at the interphasal stage in PT at T1, but his use of morphological structure was accurate except for past tense -ed. So the difference between the bilingual and the monolingual children at T1 was the accuracy in morphology. In particular, Tomas showed the occurrence of lexical verbs with -ing without AUX (as in *the boy looking in the hole*), the high rate of non-suppliance of SV agreement and the unstable suppliance of tense marking (-ed) in past tense contexts. The second generation bilingual child, Dana, produced fewer inaccuracies in these areas than Tomas. On the other hand, Adam was error free with all morphological structures with the exception of the regular past -ed where he behaved like the bilingual children. The use of the past tense morphology -ed was still in the process of mastery for all three informants. Only after six months into the school attendance (i.e., T2) Dana, Tomas and Adam became able to use the past tense

marker-*ed* accurately without overextending the marker on irregular verbs. This raises questions about the status of -*ed* in development.

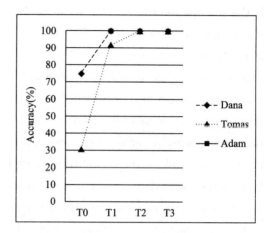

Figure 3   Change in accuracy rate of
3rd person singular -*s*

Our results suggest that verbal morphology is likely to be the focal point in morphological development in the first year of schooling. Tomas, in particular, improved his English enormously, especially in the first three months of school attendance (between T0 and T1). Both Tomas and Dana added a variety of AUXs which were no longer omitted in obligatory context within the first three months of school attendance. Both bilingual informants also mastered the use of the SV agreement quickly. This is evident from Figure 3 showing the change in accuracy rate of 3rd person singular -*s* on verb. At this point in T2 our bilingual informants were not distinguishable from Adam in terms of the use of these morphological structures.

As a final point in the discussion it may be worth commenting on the role of

PT in examining bilingual and heritage speakers. It seems that, apart from acting as a shorthand developmental checkpoint, it has very little role to play if we apply only the emergence criteria. Had we done that we would have found that the bilinguals were already at the top of the PT scale at time zero, so there would have been nothing to add, unless one also looked at accuracy. This allowed us to see that in a handful of morphological areas there was something to be said in differentiating second from third generation and bilingual from monolingual. So it seems useful both to look at accuracy and to explore more advanced syntax (as in Bettoni and Di Biase, in press).

Conclusion

This study investigated lexical and morphological development in two Serbian-English bilingual children and an English monolingual child over their first year of schooling. First we checked the level of development in English lexicon and morphology in the two Serbian-Australian bilingual children before school attendance (i.e., research question 1). We found some differences between the two bilingual children in their use of lexicon and morphology. In terms of lexical choices, Dana, a second generation bilingual, addressed the English-speaking investigator entirely in English without language mixing or code-switching. On the other hand, Tomas, a third generation bilingual, used some mixed Serbian-English utterances with the

same E-interlocutor at T0. This includes the use of Serbian words in English utterances and also insertion of Serbian morphology on English nouns and verbs. Which probably means he was uncertain about the boundaries of the two languages. But this phenomenon completely disappeared soon after the commencement of schooling. In terms of morphological development, both children attained the highest stage in PT, i.e., interphasal stage. However, both of them showed some inaccurate use in morphology and especially Tomas' English at T0, evident in his use of verbal morphology described above. Dana's English language seemed to be marginally ahead of Tomas'. She, however, also showed some inaccurate use in verbal morphology with past -ed where she overextended the morpheme on irregular verbs. She also occasionally failed to use -s on the verb to mark subject information of 3rd person singular at T0. Thus, we identified some similarities and differences among the two bilingual children in their English level before school attendance.

The study also investigated whether the first year of schooling helped bilingual children develop English to the level of other native speaking children (i.e., research question 2). In order to answer this question, we compared, longitudinally, the two bilingual children's lexical and morphological development with those of an English monolingual child who attended the same class with one of them, Tomas. The first year of schooling, an eventful episode in children's life, helped both bilingual children and the monolingual child, Adam. Tomas, the third-generation Serbian-Australian, developed the skill to use English without mixing elements of the two languages when speaking to monolingual English interlocutors. So he became quickly able to differentiate the two languages clearly over the first term of schooling. Also, Tomas and Dana rapidly developed their English morphological ability, especially in accuracy, to the point of being indistinguishable from the monolingual peer, Adam, after only three months of school attendance. English morphology continued to develop in all three children in a similar fashion over the remainder of the first year of schooling. The use of the regularizing -ed marker on verbs that did not require it appears to be common among both bilingual and monolingual children. Thus, the study confirmed that the overgeneralisation of -ed is a developmental phenomenon (e.g., O'Grady 2005). The occasional omission of 3rd person singular -s on verbs, on the other hand, was found to be specific to the bilingual children before the commencement of schooling but this was also quickly rectified after the first three months of school attendance in Dana and after 6 months for Tomas.

As for the lexicon however, bilingual children's production of vocabulary turned out to be much richer than their monolingual peer as the bilingual children produce almost double the number of types at time 1. What is more, they maintained their lexical advantage by the end of the school year. This is contrary to previous research that reported bilingual preschool children having smaller vocabulary in either of their languages than monolingual children of the same age (e.g., Nicoladis 2003, 2006; Pearson, Fernandez, & Oller 1993). As Figure 1 shows, Dana shows the highest vocabulary size, followed by Tomas and then monolingual Adam. These results show that bilinguals may have a lexical advantage in English by comparison with their monolingual peer and that children's language development does not lag behind monolinguals: it may more simply and realistically display great similarities and some differences in the shared language. Needless to say the bilinguals will have the advantage of knowing a whole other language by the time they get to School.

Acknowledgment

An earlier version of this paper was presented at the Symposium on the Bilingualism and Intercultural Communication, August, 2013, School of Humanities & Communication Arts, UWS. We thank the audience at the Symposium for their invaluable comments and advice to improve this paper. We are also thankful to Bruno Di Biase and two anonymous reviewers for their helpful comments.

References

Agostini, T., & Best, C. T. (in press). Exploring Processability Theory-based Hypotheses with a High Functioning Autistic Child Acquiring Italian as a Second Language. In: *Grammatical Development in Second Languages: Exploring the Boundaries of Processability Theory*, C. Bettoni & B. Di Biase eds. EUROSLA Monographs. http://eurosla.org/monographs/EMhome.html.

Bettoni, C., & Di Biase, B. (in press). Processability Theory: Theoretical Bases and Universal Schedules. In: *Grammatical Development in Second Languages: Exploring the Boundaries of Processability Theory*, C. Bettoni & B.Di Biase eds. EUROSLA Monographs. http://eurosla.org/monographs/EMhome.html.

Clyne, M. 1982. *Multilingual Australia*. Melbourne: River Seine.

Cummins, J. 1979. Linguistic Interdependence and the Educational Development of Bilingual Children. *Review of Educational Research* 49(2), 222 – 251.

De Houwer, A. 1990. *The Acquisition of Two Languages from Birth: A Case Study*. Cambridge: Cambridge University Press.

De Houwer, A. 2005. Early Bilingual Acquisition. In: *Handbook of Bilingualism: Psycholinguistic Approaches*, J. F. Kroll & A. M. B. de Groot eds. Oxford: Oxford University Press.

De Houwer, A. 2009. *Bilingual First Language Acquisition*. Clevedon: Multilingual Matters.

De Houwer, A. 2013. Harmonious Bilingual Development: Young Families' Well-being in Language Contact Situations. *International Journal of Bilingualism*.

Di Biase, B. 2002. Focusing Strategies in Second Language Development: A Classroom-based Study of Italian in Primary School. In: *Developing a Second Language: Acquisition, Processing and Pedagogy of Arabic, Chinese, English, Italian, Japanese, Swedish* (pp. 95 – 120), B. Di Biase ed. Melbourne: Language Australia.

Di Biase, B., & Dyson, B. 1988. *Language Rights and the School: Community Language Programs in Primary Schools in Australia*. Leichhardt, N.S.W: FILEF Italo-Australian Publishers.

Di Biase, B., & Kawaguchi, S. 2002. Exploring the Typological Plausibility of Processability Theory: Language Development in Italian Second Language and Japanese Second Language. *Second language research* 18(3), 274 – 302.

Di Biase, B., Kawaguchi, S., & Yamaguchi, Y. (in press). The Development of English as a Second Language. In: *Grammatical Development in Second Languages: Exploring the Boundaries of Processability Theory*, C. Bettoni & B. Di Biase eds. European Second Language Association.

Genesee, F., Paradis, J., & Crago, M. B. 2004. *Dual Language Development & Disorders: A Handbook on Bilingualism & Second Language Learning*, vol 11. Paul H Brookes Publishing.

Håkansson, G. 2001. Tense Morphology and Verb-second in Swedish L1 Children, L2 Children and Children with SLI. *Bilingualism: Language and Cognition* 4(1), 85-99.

Håkansson, G., Salameh, E., & Nettelbladt, U. 2003. Measuring Language Development in Bilingual Children: Swedish-Arabic Children with and Without Language Impairment. *Linguistics* 41(2), 255 – 288.

Itani-Adams, Y. 2007. *One Child, Two Languages: Bilingual First Language Acquisition in Japanese and English*. Doctoral dissertation, University of Western Sydney.

Kaplan, R. M., & Bresnan, J. 1982. Lexical-Functional Grammar: A Formal System for Grammatical Representation. In: *The Mental Representation of Grammatical Relations* (pp. 173 – 281), J. Bresnan ed. Cambridge, MA: MIT Press.

Karmiloff, K., & Karmiloff-Smith, A. 2002. *Pathways to Languag*. Harverd University Press.

Kawaguchi, S. 2010. *Learning Japanese as a Second Language: A Processability Perspective*. New York: Cambria Press.

Kempen, G., & Hoenkamp, E. 1987. An Incremental Procedural Grammar for Sentence Formulation. *Cognitive Science* 11(2), 201 – 258.

Levelt, W. J. M. 1989. *Speaking: From Intention to Articulation*. Cambridge, MA: MIT Press.

Mansouri, F. 2005. Agreement Morphology in Arabic as a Second Language: Typological Features and Their Processing Implications. In: *Cross-linguistic Aspects of Processability Theory* (pp. 117 – 153), M. Pienemann ed. Amsterdam: John Benjamins.

Mayer, M. 1969. *Frog, Where Are You*? New York: Dial Books for Young Readers.

Meisel, J. 1989. Early Differentiation of Languages. In: *Bilingualism Across Lifespan: Aspect of Acquisition, Maturity and Loss* (pp. 13 – 40), K. H. L. Odle ed.

Cambridge: Cambridge University Press.

Meisel, J. M., Clahsen, H., & Pienemann, M. 1981.Determining Developmental Stages in Natural Second Language Acquisition. *Studies in Second Language Acquisition* 3(2), 109–135.

Nicoladis, E. 2003. Cross-linguistic Transfer in Deverbal Compounds of Preschool Bilingual Children. *Bilingualism Language and Cognition* 6(1), 17–32.

Nicoladis, E. 2006. Cross-linguistic Transfer in Adjective-noun Strings by Preschool Bilingual Children. *Bilingualism Language and Cognition* 9(1), 15–32.

Nicoladis, F., Song, J., & Marentette, P. 2012. Do Young Bilinguals Acquire Past Tense Morphology Like Monolinguals, Only Later? Evidence from French-English and Chinese-English Bilinguals. *Applied Psycholinguistics* 33(3), 457–479.

O'Grady, W. 2005.*How Children Learn Language*. Cambridge, UK: Cambridge University Press.

Pearson, B. Z., Fernández, S. C., & Oller, D. K. 1993. Lexical Development in Bilingual Infants and Toddlers: Comparison to Monolingual Norms. *Language Learning* 43, 93–120.

Pienemann, M. 1998. *Language Processing and Second Language Development: Processability Theory*. Amsterdam: John Benjamins.

Pienemann, M., & Håkansson, G. 1999. A Unified Approach Towards the Development of Swedish as L2: A Processability Account. *Studies in Second Language Acquisition* 21(3), 383–420.

Pienemann, M., Di Biase, B., & Kawaguchi, S. 2005. Extending Processability Theory. In: *Cross-linguistic Aspects of Processability Theory* (pp. 199–252), M. Pienemann ed. Amsterdam: John Benjamins.

Pienemann, M., Keßler, J. U., & Itani-Adams, Y. 2011. Comparing Levels of Processability Across Languages. *International Journal of Bilingualism* 15(2), 128–146.

Qi, R. 2004.*From Nominal Reference to the Acquisition of Personal Pronouns in a Mandarin-English Bilingual Child*. Doctoral Dissertation, University of Western Sydney.

Qi, R. 2011. *The Bilingual Acquisition of English and Mandarin: Chinese Children in Australia*. New York: Cambria Press.

Qi, R., Di Biase, B., & Campbell, S. 2006.The Transition from Nominal to Pronominal Person Reference in the Early Language of a Mandarin-English Bilingual Child. *International Journal of Bilingualism* 10(3), 301–329.

Vihman, M. M., & McLaughling, B. 1982. Bilingual and Second Language Acquisition in Pre-school Children. In: *Progress in Cognitive Development Research. Verbal Processes in Children*, C. J. Brainerd & M. Pressley eds. Berlin: Springer Verlag.

Yamaguchi, Y., & Kawaguchi, S. (in press in 2014). Acquisition of English Morphology by a Japanese School-aged Child: A Longitudinal Study. *Asian EFL (English as a Foreign Language) Journal*.

Zhang, Y. 2004. Categorial Analysis, Processing Demands, and the L2 Aquisition for the Chinese Adjective Suffix-de (ADJ). *Language Learning* 54(3), 437–468.

Notes on contributors

Satomi Kawaguchi, PhD, Senior Lecturer in School of Humanities and Communication Arts, University of Western Sydney (Email: s.kawaguchi@uws.edu.au). Her research interests are first and second language acquisition in Japanese and English, bilingual language acquisition, technological intervention in language learning and teaching.

Lucija Medojevic, PhD, School of Humanities and Communication Arts, University of Western Sydney (Email: l.medojevic@uws.edu.au). Her research interests are bilingualism, second language acquisition.

129

澳洲塞尔维亚语—英语双语儿童入学 第一年英语词汇和形态发展

Satomi Kawaguchi

Humanities and Communication Arts & MARCS Institute,

Bilingualism Research Lab, University of Western Sydney, Australia

Lucija Medojevic

Humanities and Communication Arts, University of Western Sydney, Australia

提　要:本研究探讨两名塞尔维亚语-澳大利亚英语双语儿童和一名澳大利亚英语单语儿童在澳大利亚入学第一年的英语词汇和形态发展。对于这两名双语儿童,塞尔维亚语是他们的传承语,而澳大利亚英语是学校和其他社会环境中的主流语言。入学的第一年会使他们的两种语言输入比率产生巨大的逆转。本研究历时一年每间隔三个月收集这三名儿童的口语语料,并比较双语儿童与同龄的澳大利亚英语单语儿童的词汇和形态发展。可加工性理论被用来测量形态发展。结果表明,入学前双语儿童在动词过去式-ed和第三人称单数-s形态标记方面不准确。然而,入学几个月后,这些不准确现象消失,双语儿童的英语语法的准确性与同龄的单语儿童难以区分。英语动词过去式形态-ed似乎对三名受试者,无论是双语儿童还是单语儿童,都具有挑战性。这表明儿童获得英语中所谓"规则"动词的过去式形态方面的问题具有普遍发展特征。数据分析表明,一旦双语儿童开始在全英文环境下学习,他们的语言发展并不落后于单语儿童,甚至可能在英语词汇方面比英语单语儿童更显优势。

关键词:双语儿童　英语　入学第一年　词汇和形态发展

Motivational Changes during Study Abroad in China: A Study of Australian L2 Learners of Chinese Language

Linda Tsung and Penny Wang Hooper

Abstract: This study investigates Australian students' experiences and perceptions of acquiring Chinese as a second language (CSL) while engaging in a full-year study abroad (SA) in China: (a) whether they identified any motivational changes within themselves over time, and (b) what they perceive as the causes of these changes. A small group of 11 students from an Australian university participated in the study. All of them studied at one of its two partner universities in the mainland China. The study was governed by the survey-based research method, involving 3 questionnaire surveys throughout the year of 2012, that is, prior to, during, and upon the completion of SA, and a face-to-face interview which was conducted at the end of their yearlong study abroad. The findings indicated that overall the students' motivation for learning Chinese was increased despite a few students reported otherwise. Their motivational changes could be influenced by their learning experiences in classes, their need to participate in daily activities and to socialize with native friends, and their newly established goals while in China. In light of these findings, the study suggests that teachers of Chinese at home universities must endeavour to improve the delivery of their curriculum in order to better satisfy their students' motivational needs and in particular to better facilitate future students in their journey towards learning Chinese as a second language in a SA context.

Key words: learning motivation, study abroad, Chinese language, second language acquisition

Introduction

One of the approaches of investigations into how second languages are acquired is influenced by the field of psychology, examining differences between learners' characteristics and learners' language learning success. Such studies partially derive from the humanistic framework within psychology that "calls for consideration of emotional involvement in learning such as affective factors of aptitude, motivation and anxiety level".

(Saville-Troike 2006, p. 17). The present study deals with one of these domains: motivation, exploring learners' perceptions of how motivation affects their acquisition of Chinese and whether their perceptions change over time when study abroad (SA) in China.

The aspect of motivation in second language (L2) learning is important in determining learners' L2 acquisition and proficiency. A large body of studies has revealed that learners with strong motivation toward L2 learning are more likely to enhance their language acquisition than those whose motivation is less strong (e.g. Gardner et al. 2004). Learners' L2 motivation can be inspired by a number of factors: (a) having an interest in L2 (Allen 2010) and the desire to integrate with people in the target community (Isabelli-Garcia 2006); (b) determination to satisfy course requirements or boost future career prospects (Allen 2010; Isabelli-Garcia 2006; Hernandez 2006); (c) class learning situations that involve the course and the teacher (Gardner 1985; Gardner et al. 2004; Campbell & Storch 2011); (d) effort towards learning (Gardner 1985), learners' academic achievements can bolster their motivation to learn (Bavendiek 2008); (e) other considerations such as the yearning to understand TV shows or films in L2 (Allen 2010). Research studies have also found that SA exerts a profound influence on learners' motivation (Allen 2010; Isabelli-Garcia 2006), which in turn can affect their second language acquisition (SLA). Changes in learning environments can lead to changes in motivation depending on the SA experiences. SA learners' motivation in L2 learning may either increase (Allen 2010) or decrease (Allen 2010; Wikinson 2002).

Foreign learners of Chinese studying abroad in China can be traced back to as early as the East Han Dynasty (25 – 220 AD). Throughout Chinese history, there have been a few noticeable influxes of foreigners studying Chinese in China due to China's economic prosperity and cultural advancement. For example, during the Tang Dynasty (618 – 907 AD) which was regarded as one of the most vibrant dynasties in Chinese history, a group comprised of envoys and scholars from Japan, known as "Qian Tang Shi" arrived in China. Along with learning Chinese political and military systems, they also learned Chinese language and culture (Shao 2005). In the past 30 years, there has been an increasing number of foreign learners embarking to China, studying Chinese language in various educational institutions right across China (Lu & Zhao 2011), and it is believed that this positive trend will continue in the foreseeable future (Liao et al. 2014, Tsung & Cruickshank 2011). However, to date, very few research efforts have been made to investigate learners' learning experiences in China, in particular their motivational aspect of Chinese language acquisition. This study attempts to fill this gap by looking at the issues from the learners' perspective.

Motivation and L2 learning

Amongst all research in the relationship between individual variables and L2 learning success, motivation has been the most active topic to be discussed and explored. Gardener and MacIntyre (1993) define motivation as: "[a] desire to achieve a goal, [b] effort extended in this direction and [c] satisfaction with the task" (p.2). As a pioneer in the study of motivation and attitudes in SLA, Gardner (1985) proposed a socio-educational model, which is constituted of three central components: integrativeness (comprising integrative orientation, interest in foreign languages and attitudes toward the L2 community), attitudes toward the learning situation (including attitudes toward the L2 course and the teacher), and motivation (involving effort, desire and attitude toward learning) and which "is seen as important in determining how actively the individual works to acquire language material" (Gardner 1985, p.147). According to Gardner, all these elements of motivation are in part responsible for individual differences in L2 learning and language achievement. Gardner and MacIntyre (1992) gave further explanation for the model. They pointed out that individual differences can arise in both formal (inside the classroom) and informal (outside the classroom) language acquisition contexts. Within these contexts, learners' use of L2 can be either motivated or demotivated. Therefore, the socio-education model is dynamic and a learner's attitudes and motivation in language learning are subject to change as he/she progresses through the learning process (MacIntyre 2002).

In an early study, Gardner and Lambert (1959) introduced two kinds of motivation in the language field: integrative and instrumental motivation. The former refers to language study which aims "to learn more about the language group, or to meet more and different people". And the latter is associated with reasons for learning a language that "reflect the more utilitarian value of linguistic achievement" (p.267).

Which motivational type is more likely to promote learners engaging in L2 study? Some studies found that learners prioritised instrumental motivation ahead of integrative motivation. Hernandez's (2006) investigation with students of Spanish in America revealed that instrumental motivation such as "increase job opportunities" was the reason to drive them to study the language. The integrative motivation like "using it with Spanish-speaking friends" was not regarded as important in their study. However, in his other study, Hernandez (2010) found when students SA in Spain, integrative motivation was more predominate.

Some researchers do not see these two types of motivation as separate entities, but rather as simply an integral part of the learning motivation. Dornyei (2005) developed a concept of "the ideal self" which refers to "the representation of the attributes that someone would ideally like to possess (i.e., a representation of personal hopes, aspirations or wishes)". He postulated that "the proficiency in the target language is part and parcel of one's ideal" and concluded that "this will serve as a powerful motivator to learn the language" (Dornyei & Ushioda 2009, p.4).

Drawing on this construct, Yashima (2009) developed a concept of "international posture" which "tries to capture a tendency to relate oneself to the international community" (p.145). It could be characterised as the following:

(a) *An interest in foreign or international affairs*;

(b) *A willingness to go overseas to stay or work*;

(c) *A readiness to interact with intercultural partners*;

(d) *An openness or a non-ethnocentric attitude toward different cultures.*

(Yashima 2002, p.57)

Changes in L2 motivation

Is learners' motivation subject to change? Gardner's (1985) study of L2 motivation suggests that motivation is not static, but changing under the influence of a variety of factors over time. This notion was tested by Bavendiek (2008) in a small scale qualitative research project, conducted with students in a modern language degree course in England. Each student was interviewed and asked to fill out a questionnaire twice: at the beginning and during the second semester of their university study. By comparing the students' self-reported questionnaire data, the researcher found that among 12 students, only 1 student's motivation had increased; 7 students' motivation had decreased and 4 remained the same. The analysis of interviews revealed that students' academic outcomes could either build up or weaken their confidence in learning, as they remarked:

"*When I get a good mark it does make me want to work that hard again, but when I get bad mark…it makes me lose motivation…*"

"*I always get back bad marks…I suppose…if you don't put effort in anyway and you get a bad mark and you do feel 'oh well, I deserved it'. But [if]… you are just more disheartened by it and you feel that there is less of possibility that you are being able to do it in the end.*"

(Bavendiek 2008, para. 72 & 75)

The change of motivation in a class learning situation was also reflected in Campbell and Storch's (2011) study with eight learners of Chinese in Australia. By using a questionnaire and three interviews within one semester, the study found over the semester, all learners' motivation changed, three increased but five decreased. The changes were caused by factors such as teachers, and enjoyment and satisfaction of the coursework.

Gardner et al. (2004) invited 197 Canadian university students of French to self-rate their attitudes and motivation against a number of motivational variables on six different occasions during a one year period. Through close inspection, they found:

(a) There was a greater change for measures that involved the classroom environment (the course and the teacher);

(b) There was relatively little change for measures of integrativeness (interest in foreign languages, attitudes toward French Canadians) and instrumental orientation (learning French is useful in getting a good job);

(c) There was a strong positive link between students' level of proficiency and their attitudes and motivation toward the target language (TL) learning.

Changes in L2 motivation and study abroad

The findings from SA research have gone hand in hand with those above. When students study abroad, changes in their learning motivation may or may not occur. Isabelli-Garcia (2006) conducted a thorough and comprehensive investigation with four US students undertaking five months SA program in Argentina. A close examination of the data collected from the sources of interviews, students' diary entries and their social network logs found that, while SA, learners' initial high motivation might or might not change. One student was integratively motivated at the beginning of the program and maintained the same motivation throughout the entire program. The other was initially instrumentally motivated, i. e., fulfilling home university's requirements, but changed to integrative motivation as he formed more and more friendships with native speakers (NSs). The remaining two's motivation decreased due to negative perceptions of the host culture or unpleasant personal experience during the stay.

Allen (2010) carried out a case study, comparing the experiences of two US students of French during a 6-week SA in France. By analysing principally the students' blogs, she found that both students were very much motivated to study French before SA although they had different motivational orientations. Student M had a linguistically oriented motivation, aiming at developing her conversational skills and oral confidence while student R had an instrumentally related motivation, that is, to satisfy her course requirement and for future career opportunities. During the time in France, student M conversed daily with host family. She also watched films and game shows on TV, as a result, her motivation in pursuing French was strengthened, and this further motivated her to study French even when the SA program was completed.

Student R, on the other hand, had a rather dissatisfying experience in France, particularly with her host family. As a result, she spent little time interacting with them to improve her oral proficiency, and her initial motivation in learning French was not enhanced but diminished instead. She discontinued learning French when the requirement for her minor was completed.

The situation with student R was not an isolated one. Another study on SA in France arrived at the same conclusion. Wilkinson (2002) found that her American students' initial enthusiasm and high motivation in learning French changed due to negative perceptions of their native interlocutors while in the country, and this could lead to disengagement and avoidance to interact and communicate with their NSs. One of the students interviewed indicated that after a while, she preferred to spend more time with her American friends rather than take the advantage of conversing with her host to improve her oral skills.

As can be seen, due to varied SA conditions and experiences, learners' motivation in studying the TL differs, and this can affect their language acquisition and its proficiency. Hence, SA immersion programs may or may not necessarily foster acquisition.

The findings of these studies have

demonstrated there is a considerable variation among learners in relation to motivation and learning achievements. Changes of learners' motivation and attitudes toward language learning do take place, but with various degrees. Moreover, the changes are not uniform across all the learners; while some maintain a stable level of motivation throughout their learning, others' motivation could be decreased considerably due to unsatisfactory learning experiences they have had, in particular when SA.

The study aims to investigate learners' perceptions of motivational aspect of their Chinese language learning. In particular it attempts to gain insights into the following questions:

• What changes in motivation do learners identify in the course of a one year SA in China?

• What are the main causes of learners' motivational changes?

Methodology

Participants

The participants in the study were 11 undergraduate students from an Australia university who were engaging in the SA program at its Chinese partner universities in the entire year of 2012. There were 2 males and 9 females from an age group between 18 and 25. They were from various academic backgrounds, majoring in law, tourism, and many other disciplines. Based on their linguistic and cultural backgrounds, they could be categorised into two types: ones with native Chinese background and ones with non-native Chinese background. Regardless their levels in Chinese, all of them had studied Chinese at the home university for two years prior to their departure to China. The detailed profile of these students can be seen in Table 1.

Table 1 Demographic features of the participants

Student	Gender	Age group	Second major	Place of birth	Language spoken at home	Speaking to Chinese community	Level of Chinese at UTS	SA prior to UTS ICS program
S1	Female	18—25	Industrial design	Australia	English	No	Level 4	No
S2	Male	18—25	Communications	Australia	English	No	Level 4	No
S3	Male	18—25	IT	Australia	English or Cantonese with mother	No	Level 4	No
S4	Female	18—25	Science	Australia	English	No	Level 4	No
S5	Female	18—25	Education	Australia	Korean and English	No	Level 4	No
S6	Female	18—25	Law	Australia	English	Sometimes	Level 4	No
S7	Female	18—25	Business	Australia	English or Cantonese with father	Yes	Level 4	No

Continued

Student	Gender	Age group	Second major	Place of birth	Language spoken at home	Speaking to Chinese community	Level of Chinese at UTS	SA prior to UTS ICS program
S8	Female	18—25	Law	Australia	English	Sometimes	Level 6	No
S9	Female	18—25	Law	Australia	Mandarin with parents	Sometimes	Level 6	No
S10	Female	18—25	Tourism	Hong Kong 18 years	Cantonese with parents, grandma	Sometimes	Level 6	Yes
S11	Female	18—25	Tourism	Macau 18 years	Cantonese with parents, grandma, brother	Sometimes	Level 6	Yes

Research instruments

Survey-based research was employed to conduct this study, involving two main instruments: computerised online questionnaire surveys and face-to-face interviews.

Questionnaires

To elicit data from the students, closed-ended questions were used in our design of the questionnaire. The survey questions consisted of two parts, which were written in English.

Part A: Student Background Information which contained three segments.

(a) General information about the students;

(b) Students' language information (e.g. language/s spoken at home);

(c) Information about students' Chinese language study prior to their SA.

Part B: Individual students' orientations regarding learning motivation. There were 10 items used to measure students' learning motivation, which was adapted from the scales developed by Schimidt and Watanabe (2001). Using a 5-point Likert-type scale, the students were required to indicate the extent to which they agreed with statements listed by selecting among "strongly agree, agree, neutral, disagree and strongly disagree".

Interviews

The interviews were conducted on a face-to-face basis in English and were arranged to take place at the completion of the final survey. The interview questions can compensate for any inadequacy of the largely closed-ended questions in the questionnaire, which not only allowed our students to recount their experiences of Chinese language learning in China and to give more detailed opinions and concerns over the issues under investigation, but also enabled us to clarify any unclear aspects of the data obtained in the previous questionnaires and to gain more accurate reflection and more insightful thoughts and beliefs from the students. The interviews were audio-recorded and all responses were noted down for later references and analysis.

Procedures

The questionnaire surveys were delivered via an Online survey forum which was anonymous. Part A (Students' background information) of the survey was only sent once in the first survey of the series. Part B (Students' perception of learning motivation) was sent three times, that is, prior to, during and upon completion of students' SA. The interviews were conducted only once for each student, which took place at the end of their SA in China.

The survey 1 was conducted between January and February, 2012. An email was sent to the participants in early January to ask them to fill out the first questionnaire-survey of the series online; noting it should be completed before the commencement of the new semester in China. The surveys 2 and 3 were carried out between May and July, 2012, and between December 2012 and January 2013 respectively. In both times, emails were also sent to remind them to do the survey on the same site. Finally, face to face interviews were conducted for a period of 4 weeks when they completed their study in China.

Data analysis

The demographic characteristics of the participants in Part A of the questionnaire were summarized and presented in table form (See Table 1).

Descriptive statistical analysis was applied to the data collected from Part B of the questionnaire. The means and standard deviations of individual variables investigated in learning motivation were calculated. The figures were analysed in or-der to determine whether there were any changes in the participants' views on the motivational variables prior to, during and upon completion of their SA.

The qualitative data generated from the interviews were analysed using the research instrument of content analysis. The texts in this study were transcripts from the open-ended interviews which were coded into categories. This allowed us to achieve a more thorough and accurate analysis, and to identify the commonalities of the participants' responses regarding their experiences and thoughts in relation to the acquisition of Chinese.

Findings

A close examination of the 3 surveys found that items 1, 9 and 5 were largely unchanged among 10 measured items as the key motivational factors that inspired them to learn Chinese. As illustrated in Table 2, items 1 and 9 gained the high rankings. This showed that these students highly valued the importance of Chinese language, and their desire to learn the language was primarily motivated to integrate with Chinese people they know. In the meantime, however, they were proud of being Australians. This was particularly so when they were in China as shown in item 10. Its ranking was positioned last amongst all the measured items in survey 3. Item 5 also received a higher ranking which indicated movies and music were the favoured forms of entertainment for the students, they thus had an urge to understand the dialogue or narrative while watching Chinese TV programs and films and the lyrics while listening to Chinese music. The next two ranked items were items 3 and 8 that showed the students held a positive attitude towards Chinese language learning, and for some, their Chinese heritage motivated them to pursue the study. Items 6 and 7 consistently remained in a relatively low ranking in all 3 surveys as some students were uncertain about whether being able to speak Chinese would bring them more money, as well as ensure them gaining more respect from other people. The most dramatic change was in item 4. In survey 1, it obtained the lowest ranking; many students did not perceive that gaining good grades in speaking assessments was the reason for them to learn Chinese. In survey 2 and 3, however, it jumped up which indicated their learning achievements gained in China played an important role in motivating them to learn the language (see Table 2).

Table 2 Descriptive statistics of the 10 items on motivation

Item	Statement	Survey 1:M	Survey 1:SD	Survey 2:M	Survey 2:SD	Survey 3:M	Survey 3:SD
1	I feel that Chinese is an important language in the world.	4.73	0.45	4.64	0.48	4.91	0.29
2	My parents encourage me to learn Chinese.	3.82	1.19	4.0	0.95	4.09	1.31
3	I really enjoy learning Chinese.	4.0	0.60	4.18	0.39	4.09	0.51
4	I have received excellent grades in speaking.	3.36	1.23	4.27	0.45	4.36	0.77
5	I would like to understand Chinese films, TV or music.	4.45	0.50	4.27	0.75	4.73	0.62
6	Increasing my proficiency in Chinese will have financial benefits for me.	4.0	0.74	3.82	0.72	3.91	0.79
7	Being able to speak Chinese will add my social status.	3.55	0.99	3.73	0.75	3.82	1.03
8	Chinese is important to me because it is part of my identity.	4.0	1.28	4.0	1.13	4.09	1.5
9	I want to be able to communicate with Chinese friends/ acquaintances.	4.73	0.45	4.64	0.48	4.64	0.64
10	I want to be more a part of Chinese community.	3.91	1.0	3.82	0.72	3.82	1.10
	Overall	4.06	0.84	4.14	0.68	4.25	0.86

Notes: Items were rated on a 5-point scale. 5 = strongly agree; 4 = agree, 3 = neutral, 2 = disagree; 1 = strongly disagree.

Overall the survey showed that the students had a very strong motivation towards learning Chinese and there was a positive trend over the year. As indicated in Table 2, in survey 1, the overall mean score of motivation was 4.06. In survey 2, this figure increased up to 4.14, and it went even further to 4.25 in survey 3, which means the longer they stayed in China, the more motivated they became.

While there was an overall increase in students' motivation, particularly when the transition took place from Australia to China, for some, their motivation decreased over time. The causes of the motivational changes were identified in the interviews, and pertained to the following factors:

• In class learning experience

According to the students, their motivation in class learning was linked to the approaches of teachers and their teaching methods which could either strengthen, as interviewee 1 stated below or weaken their learning motivation, as reported by interviewee 10:

Learning Chinese in China increased my motivation. The teachers are strict there, so you strive hard. They make you feel bad if you don't do your homework. (Interviewee 1)

Mine has gone down. In the first semester, I burnt out. There was so much to learn. The teacher demanded a lot. Every day there was "tingxie" (Dictation). There was too much Chinese in one go. (Interviewee 10)

• Participating in daily activities

Students reported in the interview that their motivation for speaking Chinese increased resulting from their needs to participate in daily activities, in particular in the initial stage of their SA. There was a practical use for the language which motivated them as the following students reported:

It (motivation) has increased, because you are surrounded by the people who don't speak English, like the shop keepers, so you speak Chinese to them every day. In Australia, even I have Chinese friends, I don't speak Chinese with them. (Interviewee 11)

I am much more motivated to learn Chinese, because when you go over there, you realise how important it is to communicate in the same language with someone... It's embarrassing to try to order something in MacDonald's, and not be able to say things properly. You feel like you need to learn more about the language, so they won't look down on you. (Interviewee 1)

• Socialising with native friends

The practical use of everyday language also occurred when students tried to better socialise and integrate with Chinese friends, and that could lead to their increased motivation, as one student cited:

My motivation to learning Chinese became more practical in China, because I could use the language to make friends. Once I knew people understood me with little trouble, the more I wanted to learn in order to get to know them. (Interviewee 11)

Likewise, interviewee 9 is a dance

enthusiast. She joined a local dance club and found friends there.

I think it is so interesting, because the teacher teaches dancing in Chinese, and that motivated me to learn Chinese harder.

• Changing of career goals

Three students revealed that their initial motivation for learning Chinese was more linguistically oriented, that is, to have a better communication and integration with people who speak the Chinese language whether they are the parents, community members or retail employees. Their SA experience led to a shift in motivation which became more career focused. They perceived that their abilities in Chinese would bring greater chances of future employment. The following students articulated:

I think motivation is linked with goals. Before going to China, my goal [for learning Chinese] was to be able to order things. But now I want to link that to my future career... If I work in relation to Australia and China economic relations, I need to know Mandarin. There are many Chinese wanting to work in Australia, so the competition gets higher. That means to study hard. I am more motivated in that sense. (Interviewee 5)

Before I went to China, my main motivation was to improve my fluency, my communication with other people in my Chinese community, but now I find one of my main motivations is that I actually want to go back to China to work. (Interviewee 8)

Originally, I just wanted to better

communicate with my family, but went there and saw so many international businesses based in Shanghai, just to be able to speak Chinese fluently is an asset. So it (study Chinese) is not just for social purposes, but for career as well. (Interviewee 6)

Unlike the above students, for interviewee 3, however, his SA experience undermined his initial career oriented motivation, as he explained:

My original motivation when I started in Australia was professional... I thought in order to diversify my skills, make myself more employable, Chinese is something good to have. Since going to China, I can't say I am fully in love with the life style there... So I think as a result, my motivation has dimmed a lot. I can't see myself using Chinese professionally. (Interviewee 3)

The data suggest that though initial impetus for learning Chinese was lost with interviewees 3 and 10 during SA, the majority of the students increased their learning motivation both inside and outside the classroom. They were motivated by their real needs to integrate with NSs and to gain a desirable job, by their in-class learning experiences and academic achievements as well as by other considerations such as the need for personal entertainment.

Discussion

Findings show that on the whole students always maintained a high level of motivation for learning Chinese. And it got stronger and stronger over the year. It

141

seems that overall SA experience motivated them to learn Chinese. This was realized by many obvious reasons, for example, the need to survive, to form friendships, to travel and so on. A large body of research has demonstrated that learners' motivational levels have a potent impact on their linguistic attainment in L2. Learners who have high motivational levels tend to foster high levels of proficiency in the language they undertake as they invest more time and energy into learning (Gardner et al. 2004). Thus, it is reasonable to assert that the high motivation the students reported in the present study has helped them improve their Chinese language proficiency.

The dynamic nature of motivation proposed by Gradner and MacIntyre (1992) was attested to by many research studies either in At Home① (Bavendiek 2008; Campbell & Storch 2011; Gardner et al. 2004) or SA contexts (Allen 2010; Isabelli-Garcia 2006; Wilkinson 2002). Despite the overall positive change of students' motivation, no significant changes were found amongst all measured variables except one item which pertained to the grades they were rewarded. Prior to SA, students did not perceive that the grades would greatly affect their motivation to learn the language, but this view shifted markedly in the next two surveys. It appeared that the students paid more attention to learning grades in China than in Australia. There were two likely explanations for this. One is that when they were in Australia,

Chinese was one of the subjects they chose to study. Though having good marks that would encourage them to learn the language, this might be overridden by other motivational factors such as having a desirable career or making it easy for them to communicate with their Chinese relatives or friends. In China, however, all their efforts were made towards learning Chinese. A satisfying academic performance would be an endorsement of their efforts and therefore would stimulate them to sustain the learning. Moreover, it is also possible that the grades that students gained in China were higher than those in Australia. Unlike in China where Chinese is exclusively set up to cater for foreign learners of Chinese, in Australia, Chinese is an integral part of courses offered by the university. Thereby, as expected, the benchmark for grading students' academic performance is high, which might affect the students' perceptions towards grades and their impact on motivation for learning the language. The study confirmed the reports made by the participants in Bavendiek's (2008) investigation that the marks played a critical role in their learning motivation, which could either strengthen or weaken their eagerness to learn. The finding complied with one of the dimensions of Gardner's (1985) socio-educational model in motivation that involves effort, desire and attitude toward learning.

Another dimension of the model is

---

① The term "At Home" here refers to learning in the home country as opposed to the abroad. It has been used by many researchers (e.g. Freed 1995).

that learners' motivation is influenced by their attitudes toward the learning situation. Since language learning largely takes place in the classroom environment, "evaluative reactions to the language teacher, toward the language course, and toward the materials, etc. will influence the student's level of motivation to learn the language". (Gardner & Lalonde 1985, p.8) The present study concurred with this notion. The survey data showed that there was little change in students' perceptions of in-class learning. By and large, they enjoyed the learning process at both home and host universities despite differences in the characters of individual teachers and their teaching styles. For instance, teachers in China are generally more stringent than those in Australia. The materials that teachers use in China are basically textbooks, whereas in Australia teacher-generated materials are more inclined to be used to assist learning. These differences did not change the positive attitudes students held towards their class learning experiences, and their motivation to learn Chinese. However, such situations did not always suit everyone. For example, in the interview, while one student found the teacher being strict motivated her to learn, the other student thought the teacher being too demanding actually demotivated her. Such a contrast in reaction towards challenging teachers could be caused by the different chemistry between class teachers and students. Students' personalities, their learning styles as well as a different rapport they had with their teachers could also

affect their learning motivation. The students' different attitudes toward the same learning situation demonstrate the complex nature of human psychology.

The third dimension which is the most central part of the model is integrativeness. It involves integrative motivation as opposed to instrumental motivation, and their attitudes toward the L2 community and its language. The present research found that integrativeness was the most prominent motivation for this population of students. In all three surveys, the students indicated strongly that they believed that "Chinese is an important language in the world", and a good grasp of the language would empower them to "communicate with Chinese friends/acquaintances". There could be several explanations for this. First, the realisation of China's rising economic power in the world and Mandarin Chinese gradually becoming a lingua franca amongst Chinese people in various parts of the world might have led them to think of the importance of the language. Second, as more migrants and international students have been coming from mainland China to Australia in recent years, there was a desire to be able to integrate and communicate with Chinese people living in Australia. Third, many of them were Chinese background students. Being able to communicate in Chinese would enhance their integration with people in their community more satisfactorily and successfully, just as Peng (2007) puts it: "Learners who are attitudinally affiliated with the L2 community will be more motivated to persevere in learning the L2 in both formal and informal situations" (p. 38). Fourth, while in China, it was imperative for them to integrate with Chinese people. The finding of the study was aligned with an earlier work done by Hernandez (2010) that integrative motivation was a key motivational determinant for L2 learners.

Just like Gardner et al.'s (2004) finding in their longitudinal study, the current investigation also reached the same conclusion that overall a minimal change had taken place in students' integrative motivation. However, for some students, the positive experiences of carrying out daily activities such as shopping, ordering food and socialising with Chinese friends in China boosted their integrative motivation. This was in contrast to other research findings that SA could generate negative motivational change because of dissatisfying experiences learners had with NSs (Allen 2010; Wilkinson 2002).

The questionnaire surveys also revealed that in general students did not entirely believe that their Chinese proficiency would land them a good job in the future, and in turn bring financial benefits for them. Though this fluctuated, there was no significant change in this view over the course of the year. Notwithstanding, for some students, experience in China changed their learning motivation to be more instrumentally orientated. In the interview, they expressed their aspirations to work in China or in China related fields in the future. The finding offered some support to the concept of " international

posture" developed by Yashima (2009), in which a language learner perceives him/herself a future participant of the international community and is willing to go overseas to stay or work. For these students, I think their SA experiences helped to form, even strengthen, their identity as global citizens as these experiences equipped them with language skills and cultural knowledge which paved the way to an international career.

On the other hand, one student's original motivation to learn Chinese was driven by his desire to use Chinese professionally. It is not surprising since career orientated motivation has been found in many studies as the strongest determinant to inspire learners to learn a new language (Hernandez 2006). However, such motivation somehow diminished due to his attitudinal change towards Chinese society while in China. The key deterrent here was his disagreement with the Chinese life style. It seems that despite living in China for a year, this student still had an issue with cultural adjustment. His difficulty in the acceptance of differences between Chinese and western cultures was not resolved. These findings further underscored the notion that "motivation is diverse, complex, and undergoes many fluctuations" (Campbell & Storch 2011, p. 166). And there are no uniform changes across all learners (Gardner et al. 2004).

Additionally, the students indicated firmly that understanding aural media was a strong motivational factor for them, suggesting that not only were they interested in the aural media for personal entertainment, but also they had an urge to understand and integrate with the Chinese community around them. The finding was in accordance with a research finding that using L2 for personal purposes was one of learners' primary motivational factors for learning the L2 (Allen 2010).

To sum up, based on Gardener's (1985) motivational framework, the discussion mainly examined the students' motivational changes in Chinese language acquisition. The instrumental motivation relating to learning a language for job opportunities was also included in the discussion. There were two conclusions that could be drawn from this. From the motivational factor point of view, a significant change took place in the impact of grades on students' learning motivation. Other motivational factors such as "Integrativeness" and "attitude towards learning situation" experienced little change. From the learners' point of view, some students were more susceptible to motivational change than others due to their SA experiences. With these students, changes occurred in terms of their attitudes towards the class learning situation, integrating with NSs of Chinese and their future career identity. The conclusions demonstrated the dynamic, diverse and complex nature of motivation. There are a multitude of reasons for learners to begin, sustain and suspend the learning of a language. The reasons could be associated with the learning environment, as well as the individual learners' goals and desirability of learning the language. A deep understanding of learners' motivation would enable educators to help learners maintain, even elevate their motivation in their journey towards SLA.

Conclusions

The research findings confirmed that the students' motivation for learning Chinese increased over the year. The most significant change was the growing interest in academic learning outcomes. Compared to the time of learning at their home university, they paid more attention to the grades being awarded and were more motivated by them. Though not a large number, a few students' motivations changed to be more instrumentally orientated, that is, learning Chinese for the purpose of enhancing future career prospects. There was a minimal change in the motivation for integrativeness. Consistently, the students regarded integrativeness as their major motivational determinant for learning Chinese. They held a positive attitude towards Chinese language and considered learning Chinese was valuable, and their desire to integrate with Chinese people always remained very strong. In addition, their inclination to understand the aural media of films and TV programs also motivated them to learn Chinese and learn it well.

There are a number of implications that can be drawn from the findings of this study, which could be noted by Chinese language teachers. First of all, the motivational factor of integrativeness was consistently and overwhelmingly perceived as the key element in inspiring students to learn

145

Chinese. Teachers should incorporate aspects relating to this into their curriculum. Combined with strategy practice, assignments that require students to interview NSs outside the class can be used to support and strengthen such motivation. Second, some students indicated that SA motivated them to study Chinese for the purpose of a future career. For this reason, during pre-departure briefings, teachers should encourage students to seek part-time employment or internships in China to meet their professional interests. For example, students who are majoring in education can seek a job as an English language teacher there. This not only would enable them to gain work experience, but more importantly, allow them to integrate into the Chinese community and in turn improve their Chinese proficiency. Additionally, teachers should strongly advise students to participate in various extracurricular activities, for instance, becoming a member of the Australia China Youth Association (if in Australia) to build social networks in an aim to gain more access to communicative practice in Chinese. Finally, teachers should integrate media-based programs into their teaching by showing segments of selected films and TV shows in class to lift students' confidence and, more precisely, their receptive skills for the Chinese language.

It has to be noted though that most participants of the study were ethnic Chinese, therefore the findings of the study may apply more to them than other learners of Chinese. However, that is not to say that the implications of the findings are totally irrelevant to the latter, in particular in relation to encouraging them to build social networks with people in the Chinese community in an Australian context, e.g. Chinese migrants and Chinese international students. Actively immersing themselves into the Chinese community can enhance their opportunity for learning, both linguistically and culturally. This also helps them to be better prepared for their future in-country experience whether it is for the purposes of study or travels.

A follow-up study could be done to examine if any perception change occurs in returning students. It would be interesting and insightful to discover whether their learning motivation in Chinese continues to soar or simply spirals downwards as they are back to the environment in which the target language is no longer the mainstream language being spoken in the general community.

References

Allen, H. W. 2010. What Shapes Short-term Study Abroad Experiences? A Comparative Case Study of Students' Motives and Goals. *Journal of Studies in International Education* 14(5), 452 – 470.

Bavendiek, U. 2008. *Investigating Changes in the Motivational Profiles of First Year Students on a Modern Languages Degree Programme*. Retrieved from www.llas.ac.uk/resourcedownloads/ 2631/bavendiek.pdf.

Cambell, E., & Storch, N. 2011. The Changing Face of Motivation: A Study of Second Language Learners' Motivation over Time. *Australian Review of Applied Linguistics* 34(2), 166 – 192.

Dornyei, Z. 2005. *The Psychology of the Language Learner: Individual Differences in Second Language Acquisition*. Kahwah, NJ: Lawrence Erlbaum.

Dornyei, Z., & Ushioda, E. 2009. Motivation, Language

Identities and the L2 Self: A Theoretical Overview. In:
Motivation, Language Identity and the L2 Self
(pp. 1 – 8), Z. Dornyei & E. Ushioda eds. Bristol: Multilingual Matters.

Free, B. F. 1995. What Makes Us Think That Students
Who Study Abroad Become Fluent? In: *Second Language Acquisition in a Study Abroad Context* (pp.123 –
148), B. F. Freed ed. Amsterdam: Benjammins.

Gardner, R. C. 1985. *Social Psychology and Second Language Learning: The Role of Attitudes and Motivation*. London: Edward Arnold Publishers.

Gardner, R. C., Masgoret, A. M., Tennant, J., & Mi-
hic, L. 2004. Integrative Motivation: Changes During a
Year-long Intermediate-level Language Course. *Language Learning* 54(1), 1 – 34.

Gardner, R. C., & Lalonde, R. N. 1985. *Second Language Acquisition: A Social Psychological Perspective*. A paper presented at the Annual Convention of the
American Psychological Association (93rd, Los Angeles, CA, August 23 – 27).

Gardner, R. C., & Lambert, W. E. 1959. Motivational
Variables in Second Language Acquisition. *Canadian
Journal of Psychology* 13, 266 – 272.

Gardener, R. C., & MacIntyre, P. D. 1992. A Student's
Contributions to Second Language Learning. Part I :
Cognitive Variables. *Language Teaching* 25, 211 – 220.

Gardener, R. C., & MacIntyre, P. D. 1993. A Student's
Contributions to Second Language Learning. Part II :
Cognitive Variables. *Language Teaching* 26, 1 – 11.

Hernandez, T. 2006. Integrative Motivation as a Predictor
of Success in the Intermediate Foreign Language Classroom. *Foreign Language Annals* 39(4), 605 – 617.

Hernandez, T. A. 2010. The Relationship Among Motivation, Interaction, and the Development of Second Language Oral Proficiency in a Study-abroad Context. *The
Modern Language Journal* 94(4), 600 – 617.

Isabelli-Garcia, C. 2006. Study Abroad Social Networks,
Motivation and Attitudes: Implications for Second Lan-
guage Acquisition. In: *Language Learners in Study
Abroad Contexts* (pp. 231 – 258), M. A. DuFon & E.
Churchill eds. UK: Multilingual Matters Ltd.

Liao, Z. J., Yan, H., Yuan, J. R., Wan, Y., & Yu, Y.
C. 2014. Yue laiyue duo waiguoxue sheng laihuashenzao
(More and More Foreign Students Study in China).
People's Daily. Retrieved from http://world. people.
com.cn/n/2014/0228/c1002 – 24487726.html.

Lu, J. J., & Zhao, Y. X. 2011. Teaching Chinese as a
Foreign Language in China: A Profile. In: *Teaching and
Learning Chinese in Global Contexts: Multimodality
and Literacy in the New Media Age* (pp.117 – 130), L.
Tsung & K. Cruickshank eds. London: Continuum In-
ternational Publishing Group.

MacIntyre, P. D. 2002. Motivation, Anxiety and Emotion
in Second Language Acquisition. In: *Individual Differences in SLA* (pp. 45 – 69), P. Robinson ed. Amsterdam: John Benjamins.

Peng, J. E. 2007. Willingness to Communicate in an L2
and Integrative Motivation Among College Students in
an Intensive English Language Program in China. *University of Sydney Paper in TESOL* 2, 33 59.

Saville-Troike, M. 2006. *Introducing Second Language
Acquisition*. Cambridge: Cambridge University Press.

Schmidt, R., & Watanabe, Y. 2001. Motivation, Strategy Use, and Pedagogical Preferences in Foreign Language Learning. In: *Motivation and Second Language
Acquisition* (pp. 312 – 357), Z. Dornyei & R. Schmidt
eds. Honolulu: University of Hawaii, Second Language
Teaching and Curriculum Centre.

Shao, H. L. 2005. Duiwai Hanyujiaoxue de fazhan li shi
(Development History of Teaching Chinese as a Foreign
Language). In: *Duiwai Hanyujiaoxuegailun (An Introduction to Teaching Chinese as a Foreign Language)*
(pp.20 – 35), C. L. Chen ed. Shanghai: Fudan University Press.

Tsung, L., Cruickshank, K. 2011. Emerging Trends and
Issues in Teaching and Learning Chinese. In: *Teaching
and Learning Chinese in Global Contexts:
Multimodality and Literacy in the New Media Age*
(pp. 1 – 10), Linda Tsung & Ken Cruickshank eds. London: Continuum.

Wilkinson, S. 2002. The Omnipresent Classroom During
Summer Study Abroad: American Students in Conver-
sation with Their French Hosts. *The Modern Language
Journal* 86(2), 157 – 173.

Yashima, T. 2009. International Posture and the Ideal L2
Self in the Japanese EFL Context. In: *Motivation, Lan-
guage Identity and the L2 Self* (pp. 144 – 163), Z.
Dornyei & E. Ushioda eds. Bristol: Multilingual
Matters.

Notes on contributors

Linda Tsung（Email：linda. tsung @ sydney. edu. au），PhD, Associate Professor in Department of Chinese Studies, School of Languages and Cultures, the University of Sydney. Her research interests：Chinese linguistics, Chinese pedagogy, Second language acquisition, social and political changes in China, multi-culturalism and multi-lingualism in China, minority education.

Penny Wang Hooper（Email：Penny. Hooper-1@ uts. edu.au）, Faculty of Arts and Social Sciences in University of Technology, Sydney. Her research interests：foreign / second language teaching methodologies, culture, cross-cultural communication and understanding.

来华留学生汉语学习动机变化研究：以澳大利亚学生为例

Linda Tsung

Department of Chinese Studies, the University of Sydney，Australia

Penny Wang Hooper

School of Arts and Social Sciences, University of Technology, Sydney，Australia

提　要：本研究调查澳大利亚学生在中国留学期间学习中文作为第二语言（CSL）的经历和看法,尤其是探讨他们的学习动机是否有所变化,以及造成学习动机变化的原因。研究对象是澳大利亚某大学的11名学生。这些学生在2012年一年间就读于该母校两个有合作关系的中国大学。研究方法采用三次网络问卷调查：分别为出发之前,留学中期和留学结束后。学生返回母校后又进行了每个学生的深入访谈。研究结果表明：所有参与本研究学生的学习动机在不同时期有所增强。他们的学习动机变化受到各种原因的影响。有的学生是受到在课堂上学习经历的影响,使他们增强了很少的学习动机；有的学生是由于参加课外日常社交活动,并与当地人交朋友,使他们树立了新的学习目标,从而增强了他们的学习动机。该研究说明在中国留学并不能使所有的学生获得中文学习的成功。母校的教师应该在留学前给予学生充分的训练,以便更好地满足学生留学期间的需求,特别是引导学生更好地利用中国目的语的语境,促进学生在留学期间更大的学习动机和中文习得成效。

关键词：学习动机　留学　学习中文　第二语言习得

CDA-based EFL Listening Diagnostic Modelling: Towards Personalized Online Diagnoses *

Ma Xiaomei and Meng Yaru

Abstract: How to identify learners' latent individual differences in language assessment so as to provide them with "tailored" instruction is a challenging question that language researchers and teachers are endeavouring to answer. This study aims at constructing an EFL listening diagnostic model based on the theory of Cognitive Diagnostic Assessment (CDA). The ultimate goal is to make it ready to be used in a personalized online EFL learning diagnostic system. Compared with the traditional classical assessment, CDA can offer fine-grained feedbacks on the learner's knowledge structure and cognitive process. The diagnostic test modelling starts with the identification of EFL attributes relevant to listening comprehension, followed by the hypothetic Q-matrix model and diagnostic test design, and finally, a psychometric G-DINA model analysis. Through both qualitative and quantitative validation, the hypothetic diagnostic model proves to be good enough to offer reliable preliminary diagnostic feedbacks, where individual learners' potential strengths and weaknesses in listening comprehension can be easily identified, and is therefore qualified for personalized online diagnostic purposes.

Key words: Cognitive Diagnostic Assessment, personalized learning, EFL listening comprehension, diagnostic model

Introduction

The rapid development of information and communication technology has allowed students to have quick access to abundant e-learning resources. This, to the delight of many language educators, makes it possible to accommodate each individual's learning needs and interests. In other words, "personalized" and "self-directed" learning are achievable with the help of technologically-mediated tools.

Personalized EFL learning is a learner centered modern education approach emphasizing "tailored EFL instruction". It affords the learner a degree of choice with respect to what is learned, when it is learned and how it is learned (Hargreaves 2009). It

* The research project is funded by China National Social Science Fund (Project No.12BYY055) and China Ministry of Education of Humanities and Social Science (Project No.12YJA740057).

provides learners the opportunity to learn in ways that suit their individual learning styles and multiple intelligences. However, how to precisely identify learners' individual differences, and their gaps in language learning, so as to provide them with "tailored" instruction is a challenging question that language researchers and teachers are endeavouring to answer. For many years, suggestions have been made that intelligent tutoring technology should be used to model learners' knowledge structure (Chapelle 2010) or intelligent assessment be constructed for analysis of learners' constructed responses (Alderson 1988; Corbel 1993). However, these aims seem far from being achieved since the research becomes extremely complex, crossing the boundaries between assessment, language and technology (Chapelle 2010).

Cognitive Diagnostic Assessment (CDA) is a newly developed psychometric approach. Once empowered by Internet technology, it is possible to create an intelligent response model that provides learners with "personalized" or "tailored" EFL learning anytime and anywhere. Unlike traditional assessment, CDA aims to measure fine-grained information of individual learners' knowledge states and cognitive processing skills well beyond an overall score. With CDA, learners' latent knowledge structures and cognitive learning skills could be diagnosed through their item response patterns, and thus individual strengths and weaknesses could be assessed, and more importantly, this assessment is followed by detailed diagnostic feedback from different perspectives (Leighton & Gierl 2007; Rupp, Templin & Henson 2010).

Compared with other skills, EFL listening is the most difficult skill (Graham 2006) and merits more analysis and support (Vandergrift 1999; Liao 2009). Assessment experts such as Alderson (2005) as well as Buck (2011) articulate the acute need for the creation of new diagnostic listening assessments that will identify specific areas where learners need improvement, and in so doing they will better inform the instructional process regarding learners' listening abilities.

In this study we integrate theories of CDA with cognitive theories of EFL listening to construct a diagnostic test model (DTM). The constructed DTM is then employed in the web system, Personalized English Learning: Diagnosis and Guidance (PELDiaG) as an assessing instrument for the learners to identify their latent deficiencies in listening and for teachers to work out remedial instruction as well. Specifically, this paper aims to present how the listening diagnostic test model is designed and verified using cognitive diagnostic approaches.

An overview of related theories and concepts

Cognitive theories in listening comprehension

Listening comprehension is a highly complex process of information encoding and decoding. Though it may seem effortless for native listeners, successful comprehension in foreign language is actually the result of a myriad of complex cognitive processes because of its transient nature and the limited degree of control by the listener on the stream of speech. According to Buck (2011), listening assessments should be designed so that they can be used diagnostically to evaluate and monitor learners on particular aspects of their language skills. Measuring how the listening process works involves interdisciplinary knowledge in linguistics, cognitive psychology and psychometrics. Buck (2011) points out that listening requires both linguistic and non-linguistic knowledge. Among linguistic knowledge are phonology, lexis, syntax, semantics and discourse structure and non-linguistic knowledge includes topics, the context and general knowledge about the world and how it works. Apart from these, complex mental processes are also highly involved.

From the cognitive perspective of the Three-phase Language Comprehension Model (Anderson 2000), language comprehension goes through three levels of processing: perception, parsing and utilization. The model provides information on how aural texts are processed and comprehended in human brains. The perceptual process is the first stage by which the acoustic message is originally encoded. In listening, this process involves segmenting phonemes from the continuous speech stream. In the parsing stage, the segmented words are transferred into a mental representation of the combined meaning of the words. In the utilization stage, listeners relate a mental representation of the text to existing knowledge which is stored in long-term memory to get a meaningful understanding of the whole message. These three phases are interrelated and recursive in language comprehension. The construction of a diagnostic test model must take into account the complex cognitive processes underlying listening comprehension.

Cognitive Diagnostic Assessment (CDA)

As a newly developed psychometric theory, Cognitive Diagnostic Assessment is developed from the combination of cognitive psychology and measurement theory. It aims to measure the specific knowledge states and cognitive processing skills a test taker has acquired (Leighton & Gierl 2007). Unlike a traditional test, which merely provides an overall score without indicating in which specific areas the test takers are weak, CDA tests can specify the student's latent proficiency, or potential knowledge structure underlying the overall test score. Such specification allows for possible intervention to address individual and group needs and improve instruction for effective learning and progress (Lee 2009). CDA models generally follow four major steps: (a) definition of attributes, (b) Q-matrix construction, (c) data analysis and validation, and (d) score reporting and feedback. Basic CDA concepts such as Attributes, Q-matrix, Attributes Master Pattern will be explained in what follows.

(1) *Attributes*

In CDA, attributes refer to cognitive processes, strategies, skills, and any knowledge components of the test item (Birenbaum & Tatsuoka 2005; Lee & Sawaki 2009; Rupp, Templin & Henson 2010). For example, sound discrimination, word recognition or gist understanding can be taken as cognitive or linguistic attributes in listening comprehension. On the other hand, selective attention, short-term memory and note taking can serve as cognitive or strategic attributes. However, the number of attributes should be kept within a manageable degree, say, no more than 15 for the language diagnosis (Lee & Sawaki 2009). Too many attributes would require more complex statistical processing.

(2) *Q-matrix*

A Q-matrixis is a two-dimensional incidence matrix used to reveal the relationship between attributes and a particular set of test items (Rupp, Templin & Henson 2010). To be specific, it is about whether mastery of an attribute is required by an item. A Q-matrix then is constructed with items in the row and attributes in the column, as Table 1 illustrates. Its entries can be expressed with 0 or 1 indicating whether or not a particular attribute is involved in the cognitive process when students respond to an item. For instance, the Q-matrix below (Table 1) exemplifies a listening test with five items (in five rows) and three attributes (in three columns). Item 1 involves only attribute one (A1 sound discrimination) whereas Item 2 is supposed to test attribute two and three (A2 word recognition and A3 main idea understanding) and Item 5 all the three attributes (A1, A2 and A3). So, in order to answer Item 5 correctly, the student has to master all three attributes.

On surface, a Q-matrix embodies the design of the assessment instrument in use and in essence determines the quality of the diagnostic information obtained through the assessment instrument (Rupp & Templin 2008). It goes beyond the item scores, and probes into the underlying knowledge structure and cognitive process of both the test items and the respondents. So it is crucial to evaluate whether the Q-matrix is reasonably constructed. Otherwise an unreasonable Q-matrix may lead to a wrong diagnosis (Zhang 2006; Tu, Qi & Dai 2008).

(3) *Attribute mastery pattern*

Attribute mastery patterns, also referred to as knowledge state, consist of various combinations of all attributes involved in the test items. CDA model analysis of the test takers' responses will classify them into different mastery groups. Each group represents a different set of attributes. Table 2 illustrates the expected attribute mastery patterns of a test with 3 attributes. Test takers falling into Pattern 1 have not mastered any attributes (3 "0"s) while test takers with Pattern 4 mastered only A3 (Attribute 3). In contrast, test takers with Pattern 8 have mastered all the three attributes (3 "1"s).

Table 1　Example of a Q-matrix

	A1 (Sound discrimination)	A2 (Word recognition)	A3 (Main idea understanding)
Item 1	1	0	0
Item 2	0	1	1
Item 3	0	0	1
Item 4	0	1	0
Item 5	1	1	1

Table 2　Example of attribute mastery patterns

Pattern number	Representation of pattern
Pattern 1	0,0,0
Pattern 2	1,0,0
Pattern 3	0,1,0
Pattern 4	0,0,1
Pattern 5	1,1,0
Pattern 6	1,0,1
Pattern 7	0,1,1
Pattern 8	1,1,1

This classification of test takers into latent groups based on attribute mastery patterns contributes immensely to better understanding of learners benefiting both learning and teaching.

Previous studies on CDA

Studies on CDA arose in late 20th century and, in recent years, have been growing rapidly in psychometrics. Most of them focus on theoretical issues of psychometric models and model justification (Tatsuoka 1983; de la Torre 2008a; Rupp et al. 2010; De Carlo 2011). To date, over 120 models have been developed which demonstrates the fast progress in CDA theory (Fu & Li 2007, cited in Lee & Sawaki 2009). Among these, G-DINA model, the general version of DINA (Deterministic Input, Noisy and Gate) has been widely accepted for its simplicity of computation and estimation in identifying the role an individual attribute plays in completing a task. The concept of Q-matrix (Tatsuoka 1983) has also driven the CDA theory into a new phase, including validation of Q-matrix specification (Rupp & Templin 2008; DeCarlo 2011), analysis of model goodness of fit (Sinharay & Almond 2007; de la Torre 2011), and estimation algorithm (de la Torre 2008a). However, the theoretical research on CDA models seems far removed from the reach of language researchers.

CDA based language assessment is still in its infancy and it is expected to become an emerging research orientation. Kasai (1997) applied one major CDA model to the reading comprehension section of the TOEFL, identifying 16 primary attributes and another 11 interaction attributes based on the primary attributes. Buck et al. (1997) also analyzed the cognitive attributes of a multiple-choice test of L2 reading comprehension from TOFEL based on CDA and Buck and Tatsuoka (1998) examined attributes of a free response listening test. In the past decade, various CDA models have been used in language assessment. Lee and Sawaki (2009) applied three cognitive diagnosis models to ESL reading and listening assessment. Wang, Pearson, and Gierl (2011) used the AHM (Attribute Hierarchical Model, another CDA model) to make diagnostic inferences about examinee's cognitive skills in critical reading. Jang (2005, 2009a, 2009b) did studies on reading in the context of NG TOEFL (Next Generation Test of English as a Foreign Language). She argued that the construction of a Q-matrix requires multiple sources of evidence supporting the representation of the construct with well-defined cognitive skills and their explicit links to item characteristics. In China, very few studies could be found in CDA-based language assessment. Cai (2010) conducted a study based on CDA to assess the group-level EFL reading problems of middle

school students. Another study is the application of diagnostic reading attributes to evaluate reading abilities for hundreds of middle school students (Cai, Ding, Tu 2011).

Previous CDA-based studies in language indicate that most of the diagnostic tests focus on L2 reading from large scale tests like TOFEL or SAT, mainly from the perspective of psychometrics. Very few attempts were made to study EFL listening cognitive diagnosis from the linguistic perspective, let alone in developing Internet-based diagnostic tests.

Research design

The current paper, as a pilot study, represents an attempt to construct a cognitive diagnostic test model in EFL listening and verify the model in order to produce accurate and reliable diagnoses. The specific research questions are as follows:

(1) How is an EFL listening hypothetic diagnostic test model (DTM) constructed?

(2) Does the constructed DTM fit with learners' item response data?

(3) What diagnostic feedbacks can the DTM produce?

The study was conducted in two parts: (a) Hypothetic DTM Construction, (b) Hypothetic DTM Validation. As mentioned above, the Hypothetic DTM Construction starts with attribute identification, followed by Diagnostic Q-matrix Model Construction and test development; Hypothetic

Model Validation, then, follows the procedure of test item analysis and Q-matrix model verification. Three versions of Q-matrix were verified: one from test developers (M1), another from the domain experts (M2) and the third one was the synthesized one (M3) from M1 and M2, and G-DINA model analysis was carried out for each of them (see Figure 1).

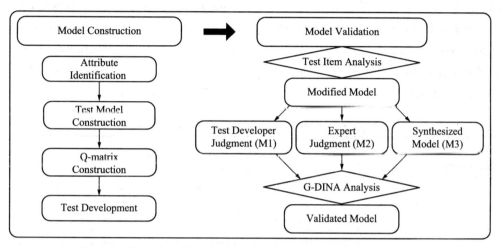

Figure 1   Procedure of Hypothetic Diagnostic Test Model Construction

Hypothetic Model Construction

Attribute identification

Listening involves physiological and cognitive processes at different levels as well as attention to contextual and "socially coded acoustic clues" (Swaffar & Bacon 1993) apart from its linguistic nature. Thus the major attributes of EFL listening comprehension can be divided into four basic categories: ① Basic EFL linguistic knowledge including segmenting phonemes from speech stream continua, lexical and syntactical meaning; ② Understanding content, form and function in sentence level; ③ Understanding content, form and function above sentence level; ④ Inferring the implied meaning in sentence level or above sentence level (Wang, Mark & Gierl 2011).

Out of the above 4 basic categories, more specific candidate attributes (over 30) were sorted out. Twenty-five teachers were invited as expert panel to rank the candidate attributes (A) from the most important to the least important. Eventually, 9 attributes were chosen as factors that affect listening comprehension. They are A1 phonology, A2 lexis (vocabulary & phrases), A3 syntax (key structures and functions), A4 details & facts, A5 main idea, A6 inference, A7 background knowledge, A8 selective attention, and A9 short term memory and note taking (See Table 3).

In addition, based mainly on Jack Richard's (1983) framework on listening skills and Buck's (2011) construct definitions on listening test, Zou's (2005) three dimensions in listening design principles were believed to be the most applicable to the Chinese learners' context. As a consequence, a theoretical framework of EFL listening attributes was developed, as shown in Table 3, including four dimensions into which the nine chosen attributes fall. These are: ① micro-linguistic meaning comprehension, including basic language knowledge such A1, A2, and A3; ② direct meaning comprehension such as understanding content, form and function as surface level comprehension in which A4 and A5 are included; ③ indirect meaning comprehension, i.e., implied meanings belonging to deep level comprehension, such as A6 and A7; ④ major strategies used, such as selective attention, short term memory and note taking (A8 and A9) (Zou 2005; Ma et al. 2012).

Table 3 Attributes in EFL listening comprehension

Major dimensions	Attribute	Definition of attributes
Micro-linguistic meaning	A 1	Phonology: Understanding information through phonological knowledge and prosodic features such as discriminating phonemes of liaison and assimilation, stress and weak syllable, and sentence intonation.
	A 2	Lexis: Understanding word meaning of low frequency, recognizing idiomatic oral expressions and chunks and guessing unfamiliar words from context.
	A 3	Syntax: Understanding grammatical functions, esp. subordination, emphatic construction, recognizing numbers and relevant calculation.
Direct meaning	A 4	Details & facts: Understanding details such as time, place and the relationship between speakers.
	A 5	Main idea: Understanding the author's purposes, goals and strategies.
Indirect meaning	A 6	Inference: Inferring Implied meaning or guessing from context.
	A 7	Background knowledge: Understanding implied meanings through activating background, esp. cultural knowledge.
Major strategies	A 8	Selective attention: Knowing how and when to give selective attention.
	A 9	Short term memory & note taking: Knowing how to memorize key information through effective note-taking.

Diagnostic Test Model (Q-matrix)

With the above framework and diagnostic attributes as a guideline, the details of the test model were established reflecting the nature of listening comprehension, listening strategies and skills as well as the requirements of college English syllabus (Band 4). The test model becomes the essence of the blueprint according to which the test items were developed (see Table 4). This blueprint not only demonstrates the test Q-matrix by specifying the relationship between attributes and test items, but also the relationship between task types and phases in the cognition process. It provides useful information for the test writers to develop tests.

Table 4   The blueprint for DTM

Section	Item No.	Attributes & testing tasks for different purposes	Task types	Cognitive phase
I	1	(A1) Phonology: discriminating phonemes of liaison and assimilation	Statement with MCQ	Perception
	2	(A1) Prosody: stress and weak form, intonations		
	3	(A2) Recognition of words		
	4	(A2) Recognition of idiomatic oral expressions and chunks		Perception + Parsing
	5	(A2) Guessing of new words from the context		
	6	(A3) Grammatical functions, subjunctive mood and inverted	Short conversation with MCQ	
	7	(A3) Recognition and calculation of numbers		
	8	(A5) Understanding of main idea, comprehension of main idea of short conversation		Parsing + Utilization
	9	(A6) Making inference		
	10	(A7) Making inferences based on cultural knowledge		
II	11	(A7) Making inferences based on background knowledge	Short passage with MCQ	Utilization
	12	(A5) Comprehension of main idea of short passages		
	13	(A4) Comprehension of details and facts in short passages		
	14	(A6) Making inference in short passages		
III	15	(A9) Note-taking, working memory, choosing the exact missing sentence	Dictation with MCQ	attention
	16	(A8) Note-taking, working memory, choosing main idea of the miss sentence		memory
IV	17	(A5) Understanding of main idea of a video clip	Video clips with MCQ	Utilization
	18	(A4) Facts and details in video clips		
V	19	Self-report question of difficulty	Self-report MCQ	Emotion
	20	Self-report question of affect & anxiety		

Notes: A=attribute; A1=attribute 1; MCQ=multiple choice question.

From the above blueprint derives the Q-matrix model as an ideal response model (See Table 5). Whether this test is reasonably designed needs further verification from other evidence such as domain experts.

Table 5　Hypothetic DTM Q-matrix M1 (Test Developers' Model)

Item	A1	A2	A3	A4	A5	A6	A7	A8	A9
1	1	0	0	0	0	0	0	0	0
2	1	0	0	0	0	0	0	0	0
3	0	1	0	0	0	0	0	0	0
4	0	1	0	0	0	0	0	0	0
5	0	1	0	0	0	0	0	0	0
6	0	0	1	0	0	0	0	0	0
7	0	0	1	0	0	0	0	0	0
8	0	0	0	0	1	0	0	0	0
9	0	0	0	0	0	1	0	0	0
10	0	0	0	0	0	0	1	0	0
11	0	0	0	0	0	0	1	0	0
12	0	0	0	0	1	0	0	0	0
13	0	0	0	1	0	0	0	0	0
14	0	0	0	0	0	1	0	0	0
15	0	0	0	0	0	0	0	0	1
16	0	0	0	0	0	0	0	1	0
17	0	0	0	0	1	0	0	0	0
18	0	0	0	1	0	0	0	0	0

Notes: A=attribute required for answering each item; 1=presence of a certain attribute; 0= absence of a certain one.

Test item development

Based on the above attributes and Q-matrix, 4 test developers began to write test items. As indicated above, the model test is composed of 5 parts, with 18 items in the first 4 parts and 2 self-report ones in the last complementary part. All the test items take the form of multiple choice questions. Except for the two short video clips (item 17 and 18), all the listening materials were recorded by two native speakers, one male from America and the other female from Britain. Vocabulary is controlled at the level of College English Test Band 4 according to the glossary of College English Curriculum Requirements (2007). The test types include short conversation, short passage, long passage, dictation and video clip, of genres typical of CET tests such as lectures, campus life, and so on (See Table 4). Eventually, 180 items in 10 tests were produced strictly following the definition of nine attributes and the test blueprint.

Hypothetic DTM (Q-matrix) Validation

In order to verify whether the test model was good enough to serve as a diagnostic test instrument, the analysis of item parameters (based on item response theory) was made first and then followed by the G-DINA model-data fit analysis.

Data collection

The data were learner's pilot responses of the first test. The piloting was administered in order to check the assessment dimensions involved and to uncover the diagnostic information embedded in examinees' item response data so that inferences about their strengths and weakness can be made. The piloting sample included 87 paper-based participants and 254 online-based participants, totalling 341. They were all first year college students in a Northwest China "985" university.

Item analysis

Item analysis aims to identify poorly written items to improve the quality of items on a test. The data were processed using BILOG-MG. Interpretation of the results were made to screen out the unqualified items and choose the ones with the best statistical indexes. In item analysis, item parameters such as discrimination (a), difficulty (b) and guessing probability (c) may be obtained (but only the first two parameters can be obtained at the first attempt). It is noted that the mean discrimination (a = 0.40) and difficulty (b = −0.85) all fall into the acceptable value ranges 0 to 3 and −3 to 3 respectively (Luo 2012) and discrimination is often better between 0.30 and 2. However, statistical analysis showed that discrimination of item 2 is exceptionally low (a = 0.25) and the difficulty of item 15 is over 3 (b = 4.08). The two items (shaded in Table 6) interfere with the reliability of the test as a whole (See Table 6).

Table 6 Item parameters of the DST Model (18 items for 2 parameters)

Item	a	b	Item	a	b
No.01	0.41	−2.21	No.10	0.46	−1.19
No.02	0.25	1.07	No.11	0.44	−0.88
No.03	0.50	−1.77	No.12	0.37	0.23
No.04	0.40	−1.47	No.13	0.35	−1.55
No.05	0.35	−1.58	No.14	0.32	−0.02
No.06	0.50	−2.14	No.15	0.18	4.08
No.07	0.37	−2.27	No.16	0.33	1.02
No.08	0.59	−0.78	No.17	0.32	−2.85
No.09	0.64	−1.42	No.18	0.35	−1.63

Notes: a=discrimination; b=difficulty.

After item 2 and 15 were removed, the item analysis results improvement was statistically significant. Table 7 contrastively shows the mean and standard deviation between the 18 items test on the left side of Table 7 and the 16 items test on the right side.

Table 7 Contrastive parameters of the 2 DTM of 18 items and 16 items

18 items(2 parameters)			16 items(3 parameters)		
Parameter	Mean	S. D.	Parameter	Mean.	S. D.
a	0.40	0.11	a	0.81	0.37
b	−0.85	1.64	b	0.41	0.95
c	—	—	c	0.47	0.05

Through item parameter analysis, the adjusted test model with 16 items proved to be good enough to make the further G-DINA Model analysis.

Q-matrix model verification

The original Q-matrix (M1) was built by the 4 test developers (See the left column of Table 8). Their EFL teaching experience is 17, 18, 20 and 33 and two of them have received professional training in test development. The constructed M1 was then verified by domain experts consisting of 8 senior English teachers, all of whom hold MA degrees in Applied Linguistics. Their teaching experience ranges from 13 to 21 years (see the right column of Table 8).

Table 8 Teaching experience of 4 test developers and 8 domain experts

4 test developers		8 domain experts			
Name	TE (year)	Name	TE (year)	Name	TE (year)
1 TD No. 1	33	1 DE No. 5	20	5 DE No. 9	21
2 TD No. 2	17	2 DE No. 6	19	6 DE No. 10	17
3 TD No. 3	18	3 DE No. 7	19	7 DE No. 11	13
4 TD No. 4	20	4 DE No. 8	19	8 DE No. 12	13

Notes: TD=Test Developer; DE=Domain Expert.

Again, take Test 1 as a pilot study. The domain experts were required to judge the test items developed by the 4 test developers respectively and code what attributes are necessary to successfully complete each item. One attribute was determined when 4 or more experts agreed upon. It was then assigned/coded 1, otherwise it would be 0. Their coding result becomes the second Q-matrix model (M2). It was compared with the test developers' Q-matrix model (M1). Then, M1 and M2 were synthesized into Q-matrix model 3 (M3), the one decided by 12 teachers (4 test developers and 8 domain experts). See Table 9 and 10 for M2 and M3.

Table 9   Q-matrix Model 2 (by 8 experts)

Item	A1	A2	A3	A4	A5	A6	A7	A8	A9
1	1	0	0	0	0	0	0	0	0
2	0	1	0	0	0	0	0	0	0
3	0	1	0	0	0	1	0	0	0
4	0	0	0	0	0	1	0	0	0
5	0	0	1	0	0	1	0	0	0
6	0	0	0	1	0	0	0	0	0
7	0	1	0	1	0	0	0	0	0
8	0	0	0	1	0	1	0	0	0
9	0	0	0	0	0	0	1	0	0
10	0	0	0	1	0	0	1	0	0
11	0	0	0	0	1	0	0	0	0
12	0	0	0	1	0	0	0	1	0
13	0	0	0	0	0	1	0	0	0
14	0	0	0	0	0	0	0	1	1
15	0	0	0	1	0	0	0	1	1
16	0	0	0	1	0	0	0	0	0

Table 10   Q-matrix Model 3 (by 12 teachers)

Item	A1	A2	A3	A4	A5	A6	A7	A8	A9
1	1	0	0	0	0	0	0	0	0
2	0	1	0	0	0	0	0	0	0
3	0	1	0	0	0	1	0	0	0
4	0	1	0	0	0	1	0	0	0
5	0	0	1	0	0	1	0	0	0
6	0	0	1	1	0	0	0	0	0
7	0	1	0	1	1	0	0	0	0
8	0	0	1	0	1	0	0	0	0
9	0	0	0	0	0	0	1	0	0
10	0	0	0	1	0	0	1	0	0
11	0	0	0	1	0	0	0	0	0
12	0	0	0	1	0	0	0	1	0
13	0	0	0	0	0	1	0	0	0
14	0	0	0	0	0	0	0	1	1
15	0	0	0	1	0	0	0	1	1
16	0	0	0	1	0	0	0	0	0

Notes: The test has 16 items. The boxed and shaded "1"s are the identified attributes for each item.

Each Q-matrix represents different relationship between attributes and the test items. Which of the 3 hypothetic models, is the most reasonable and valid to produce reliable diagnostic results will be determined through psychometric approach, G-DINA model analysis in this case, to see the model-data fit.

G-DINA model analysis

After item analysis, the original 18-item hypothetic model was rejected and the modified 16-item model was adopted. The collected data for the 16 items were used for G-DINA model analysis with the 3 hypothetic Q-matrixes (M1, M2 and M3) separately.

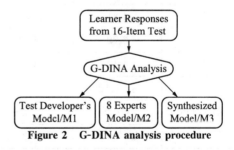

Figure 2   G-DINA analysis procedure

G-DINA Model, one of many current CDA models (de la Torre 2008b), is employed in this study because of its easy recognition of the effects an individual attribute plays in completing a task. Mastery of one attribute will increase the probability of a test takers responding correctly to an item (de la Torre 2008b). The more attributes are mastered, the higher the possibility for testees to provide correct responses to items. For G-DINA model analysis, the software, Ox 6.21 (Doornik 2002—2011)[①] was used to check model-data fit. The data analysis can be generally divided into two parts: one is the model-data fit statistics which includes absolute fit statistics and relative fit statistics. The other is inference of diagnostic outcomes, which involves item parameter estimates and standard errors, latent class and their posterior probabilities, and person classification (psychometric concepts). The former aims at verifying whether the results are statistically sound in diagnostic model construction, i.e., Q-matrix, whereas the latter offers detailed parameters of test and learners. If the model-data fit fails, the attributes of the Q-matrix have to go through multiple rounds of adjustment and trial (for example, one attribute was decided with 4 or 5 experts/teachers' agreement) until a good fit is obtained. The purpose was to have every possible attribute considered and tried.

In the following analysis, the absolute and relative fit evaluation is integrated to judge the model-data fit. The absolute fit statistics Max.z (r) and Max.z (l) are used for determining if the Q-matrix model fits the data adequately. If the Max Z scores of both Z (r) and Z (l) are smaller than the Zc Score (BC), the Q-matrix model is retained; otherwise it is rejected. The relative fit statistics (e.g., AIC and BIC) are only for comparing different Q-matrix models; the lesser the values the better, especially with BIC value (Chen, Torre, & Zhang 2013)(See Table 11).

Table 11 Absolute and relative fit statistics

Fit statistics	Absolute fit statistics		Relative fit statistics		
	Max.z(r)	Max.z (l)	-2LL	AIC	BIC
M1	4.81	4.52	6,042.76	6,616.76	7,716.51
M2	3.72	3.53	6,033.15	7,159.15	9,316.50
M3	4.40	3.79	5,827.77	6,961.77	9,134.44
Zc Score (BC)	$\alpha=0.10$	2.73 3.34 3.34			
	$\alpha=0.05$	2.96 3.53 3.53			
	$\alpha=0.01$	3.42 3.93 3.93			

Notes: M1= test developer's Matrix; M2= experts panel's Matrix; M3= the synthesized Matrix of the former two. Max. z(r) = maximum z score for r; Max. z(l) = maximum z score for l. -2LL$=-2$ log likelihood; AIC= Akaike' information criterion; BIC= Bayesian information criterion.

As indicated in the above table, both maximum z score for *corr*, z(r) and maximum z score for *log*, z(l) of M2 are smaller than Zc Score (BC) at $\alpha=0.01$ level, meaning the 8 domain expert-model M2 fits the data best and is accepted as the estimation and classification model. At the same time, M1 and M3 are rejected.

---

① Ox and all its components are owned by Jurgen A Doornik (JAD) and protected by United Kingdom and international copyright laws.

From the (above) G-DINA analysis, we can say that M2 has a good fit with learners response data and therefore the results of DTM M2 can be used for further diagnostic inferences. It can be concluded that the diagnostic Q-matrix model (M2) by the domain experts is proved to be reliable and valid for further online application.

DTM diagnostic results

By applying G-DINA model, we can find that the statistic output presents not only the results of the model-data fit, but also the very comprehensive estimation outcomes. Among all the parameters and statistic results, person classification is the attribute classification of learners both on group level and individual learner and attribute level.

On group level

Person classification offers an overall picture of the 9 attributes mastery patterns both in frequency and percentage. 341 samples are classified into 122 patterns, with 50% learners falling within the top 20 patterns (as shown in Table 12). It can be seen that the 19 test takers who had mastered all the attributes account for the top 5.56% of the 341 students, followed by 4.97% of the learners who mastered all but attribute 9 (note taking and memory). 4.39% (15 students) fall into the third pattern, mastering 6 attributes. It is possible that with the accurate information of learners' different attribute mastery levels, the teacher will know what the students' gaps are, and what remedial measures should be taken to bridge them. The G-DINA Model analysis on person classification is evidently significant for pedagogical improvement.

Table 12 Attribute mastery patterns for top 20 (50% of the sample)

Person classification	Frequency	Percent(%)	Person classification	Frequency	Percent (%)
(1) 1 1 1 1 1 1 1 1 1	19	5.56	(11) 1 1 1 1 0 1 1 1 0	7	2.05
(2) 1 1 1 1 1 1 1 1 0	17	4.97	(12) 1 0 1 1 1 0 1 1 0	7	2.05
(3) 1 0 1 0 0 1 1 1 1	15	4.39	(13) 1 0 1 0 0 0 1 0 0	6	1.75
(4) 1 1 1 1 0 0 0 1 0	12	3.51	(14) 0 0 1 0 1 0 1 0 0	6	1.75
(5) 1 1 1 1 1 0 1 1 0	10	2.92	(15) 1 1 1 1 0 0 1 0 0	5	1.46
(6) 1 1 1 1 0 0 1 1 0	10	2.92	(16) 0 0 1 0 0 1 1 1 1	5	1.46
(7) 1 0 1 1 0 0 1 1 0	10	2.92	(17) 1 1 1 0 1 0 0 0 0	4	1.17
(8) 1 1 1 1 1 0 0 1 0	9	2.63	(18) 1 1 0 1 1 1 1 1 0	4	1.17
(9) 1 1 1 1 0 1 1 1 1	9	2.63	(19) 1 1 0 0 0 1 0 0 1	4	1.17
(10) 1 1 1 0 0 0 1 1 0	8	2.34	(20) 1 0 1 1 1 1 1 1 1	4	1.17

Notes: 1=mastery of a certain attribute; 0=non-mastery of a certain one.

However there is still room for improvement. Although the 9 attributes are proven to work, to process 122 attribute mastery patterns will take quite a while to work out online. Therefore, 9 attributes will be modified if the model is uploaded onto the system.

On individual attribute level

Examining the mastery of knowledge states in listening comprehension, we can see learners' various mastery levels of individual attribute. Table 13 shows that Attribute 1 (sound discrimination) and Attribute 3 (functional sentence structures) are the skills best mastered, with A1 included in 18 mastery patterns, into which 46.8% of the test takers fall, and A3 in 16 patterns covering 47.7% of the sample. This result suggests that A1 and A3 are the most basic attributes and should be mastered before other attributes. It is interesting to find that Attribute 8 (selective attention) and Attribute 7 (cultural background) are the 3rd and 4th better mastered skills with 42.7% and 41.5% of the sample respectively, meaning these students are better prepared in test-taking techniques, and their target cultural knowledge is fairly good for listening comprehension purpose. Attribute 4 (understanding of facts and details) and Attribute 2 (less frequent vocabulary and oral expressions) are both in 13 mastery patterns with respectively 36% and 34.5% of the sample. Attribute 9 (short term memory and note-taking skill) in 9 mastery patterns with 33.6% of the sample needs some instruction and practice. In sharp contrast, Attribute 5 (main ideas) with 23.5% of the sample, and attribute 6 (inferring implied meaning) with 24.6%, are the least mastered skills (See Table 13).

Table 13 Mastery state of each attribute

Attribute	A1	A2	A3	A4	A5	A6	A7	A8	A9
Mastery order	1	6	2	5	9	8	4	3	7
Mastery sample (%)	46.8	34.5	47.7	36.0	23.5	24.6	41.5	42.7	33.6
Mastery pattern No.	18	13	16	13	9	9	16	15	14

We note that A1 (phonology) and A3 (sentence structures) are surface level skills and constitute basic linguistic knowledge based on which other skills can be acquired. However, the last two attributes, A5 (main idea) and A6 (inference), are deeper level or contextualized skills not to be mastered easily. With this information, teaching and learning can be tailored to specific needs. This is the typical characteristic feature of CDA results.

On individual learner level

With CDA analysis, each learner is offered an individual knowledge state report aside from the traditional score. Students can have a clear idea of their strengths and weaknesses. Even with the same score, the learners' mastery patterns can be totally different. Table 14 shows, for instance, that the 67 students in Example 1 had the same score, i.e., 62.5, but they fell into 37 different attribute mastery patterns. In

Example 3, 39 students with the score of 81.3 fell into 23 different patterns. The implication is that it is quite possible for a number of students to have the same score but to have mastery patterns that are quite different. This may seem strange on surface. However, since each attribute is tested in no less than 3 items, it is reasonable if those who got the majority of items right but these items happened to test only one or two attributes. In this case, the test scores might be high but the attribute mastery pattern can be pretty poor, just as ID 243 illustrates. The reverse may also be true. Take ID 115 for instance, this learner may score low but got most items testing 7 attributes (the "1"s) right. In contrast, student with ID 79 may score low and got most items testing the rest 6 attributes (the "0"s) wrong.

Table 14　Examples of different mastery patterns with the same scores

Example	Test score	No. of respondents	No. of patterns	Sample mastery patterns
1	62.5	67	37	ID 79: 1 0 1 1 0 0 0 0 0 ID 87: 1 1 1 1 0 0 0 1 0 ID 100: 0 1 1 0 1 0 0 0 1 ID 115: 1 1 1 0 1 1 0 1 1
2	75	45	26	ID 187: 0 0 1 0 1 0 1 0 0 ID 190: 1 1 1 1 0 0 1 1 0 ID 215: 1 1 1 1 1 0 0 1 1 ID 203: 1 0 1 0 0 1 1 1 1
3	81.3	39	23	ID 243: 0 1 1 1 0 0 0 1 1 ID 276: 1 0 0 0 1 1 1 0 1 ID 277: 1 1 1 1 1 1 1 1 0 ID 305: 1 1 1 1 1 1 1 0 1

Notes: ID=a student ID number in the current sample.

It is clear from the above that the CDA-based diagnostic model can go beyond the overall scores and offer fine grain-sized estimates and classifications of the learners, so that detailed inference about their knowledge states and skill mastery profiles can be obtained. This individualized and fine-grain sized diagnosis fulfils the purpose of personalized assessment of listening comprehension that the traditional tests can never achieve. They can be used either by instructors, for future tailored teaching, or by learners themselves to embark on their personalized and autonomous learning journey.

Conclusion

This paper presents a pilot study in constructing the listening diagnostic model for PELDiaG system using Cognitive Diagnostic Assessment. The answers to the three research questions are as follows:

(1) A listening hypothetic DTM is constructed in 3 steps. It begins with the identification of 9 attributes in listening comprehension. Then the diagnostic Q-matrix model was built, the pivotal step in constructing the diagnostic test model. On

the basis of this model, the test items are developed.

(2) The hypothetic model is validated through item analysis, Q-matrix verification and G-DINA analysis. In the item analysis, Item 2 and 15 proved to be unqualified in the parameter of difficulty and discrimination and therefore removed from the subsequent G-DINA analysis. For Q-matrix verification, comparative psychometric analysis of test developers' Q-matrix (M1) and domain experts' judgment Q-matrix model (M2) and the synthesized Q-matrix (M3) was conducted by using G-DINA. Hypothetic Q-matrix M2 turned out to be the best model-data fit. It can serve as the preliminary online diagnostic assessment instrument.

(3) The validated diagnostic model produces different diagnostic results apart from an overall score. They include classification of learners into groups according to their attribute mastery patterns, individual learner' knowledge state and individual and group attribute mastery profiles. These detailed feedbacks make it possible for learners to be informed of their strengths and weaknesses in listening comprehension so that they know clearly what to focus on in the future, while the teacher will know what to do in teaching based on learners' attribute mastery both on individual and group levels. Thus, with the aid of the CDA models, aspects of tailored instruction and learning may be achieved.

The constructed CDA test model is effective in providing formative diagnostic feedback through a fine-grained reporting to individual learners which the traditional assessment can never do. The availability of such diagnostic feedbacks also allows the teacher to identify the learner's specific deficiencies and to plan instruction to meet the needs of a particular learner. This may also facilitate learners on their own journey to autonomy (Meng 2013).

This study is significant because it is among the first very few to introduce CDA into foreign language teaching and learning. Integrated with Internet technology, the produced CDA-based diagnostic model will make it possible to fulfil the aim of intelligent assessment and tutoring. This, to a certain extent, signifies a great progress toward a more personalized, self-directed and easy-accessible EFL learning and assessment. The significance also lies in the fact that it not only enriches the theory of language assessment, but also demonstrates great potentials for large-scale applications in future personalized English e-learning and e-assessment. What's more, it broadens language assessment research.

Without exception, limitations in the current study cannot be ignored. First and foremost, in the Q-matrix model construction, we didn't consider test takers' opinions on what kind of attributes they would think are needed in the test-taking process though we have the domain experts' judgment. It is desirable to have test takers' verbal reports in Q-matrix construction for future research. As Jang (2005) argued, the construction of a Q-matrix requires multiple sources of evidence supporting the representation of the construct with well-defined cognitive skills and their explicit links to item characteristics. Second, the number of test items in this pilot test was not big enough to represent all the 9 attributes, each of which is supposed to be in no less than three items according to CDA theory. In view of CDA, the more attributes are involved, the more calculating time it may take to produce attribute mastery patterns online. Therefore, the 9 attributes will be reduced or more test items should be generated if the model is uploaded onto the system. We believe these limitations can be addressed in future research when the formal CDA EFL listening diagnostic model is constructed. We hope our efforts in this cross-disciplinary area can inspire other in-depth exploration of the CDA-based online language assessment from researchers and teaching practitioners in L2 research field.

Acknowledgment

This study belongs to the research project funded by China National Social Science Fund (Project No. 12BYY055), China Ministry of Education of Humanities and Social Science (Project No.12YJA740057) and National Project "985 Phase Ⅲ". The current paper was presented at the Asian-Pacific SLA Symposium in Sydney, Nov. 2013. We thank the audience at the Symposium for their valuable advice on the paper.

We'd like to extend our sincere thanks to Professor Bruno Di Biase and Dr. Satomi Kawaguchi for their invaluable suggestions and comments on the paper revision. We are also thankful to He Huiqing and Liu Rui for their contributions to the listening test development.

References

Alderson, J. C. 2005. *Diagnosing Foreign Language Proficiency—The Interface Between Learning and Assessment*. Britain: Continuum.

Anderson, J. R. 2000. *Cognitive Psychology and Its Implications*. New York: Worth Publishers.

Buck, G., Tatsuoka, K., & Kostin, I. 1997. The Subskills of Reading: Rule-space Analysis of a Multiple-choice Test of Second Language Reading Comprehension. *Language Learning* 47(3), 423 – 466.

Buck, G., & Tatsuoka, K. 1998. Application of the Rule-space Procedure to Language Testing: Examining Attributes of a Free Response Listening Test. *Language Testing* 15(2), 119 – 157.

Birenbaum, M., Nasser, F., & Tatsuoka, C. 2005. Large-scale Diagnostic Assessment: Mathematics Performance in Two Educational Systems. *Educational Research and Evaluation* 11(5), 487 – 507.

Buck, G. 2011. *Assessing Listening*. Beijing: Foreign Language Teaching an Research Press.

Cai, Y. 2010. 群体水平的英语阅读问题解决能力评估及认知诊断 [*Group-level Ability Assessment and Cognitive Diagnosis on English Reading Problem Solving*]. Unpublished doctorate dissertation, Jiangxi Normal University.

Cai, Y., Tu, D. B., & Ding, S. L. 2010. 认知诊断测验编制的理论及方法 [Theory and Method on Compilation of Cognitive Diagnosis Test]. *Examination Research* (3), 79 – 92.

Cai Y., Ding, S. L., & Tu, D. B. 2011. The Cognitive Diagnosis of English Reading Problem Solving. *Journal of Psychological Science* 34(2), 272 – 277.

Chapelle, C. A., & Douglas. 2010. *Assessing Language Through Computer Technology*. Beijing: Foreign Language Teaching and Research Press.

Chen, J., Torre, J. D. L., & Zhang, Z. 2013. Relative and Absolute Fit Evaluation in Cognitive Diagnosis Modeling. *Journal of Educational Measurement* 50 (2), 123 – 140.

De Carlo, L. T. 2011. On the Analysis of Fraction Subtraction Data: The DINA Model, Classification, Latent Class Sizes, and the Q-matrix. *Applied Psychological Measurement* 35(1), 8 – 26.

De la Torre, J. 2008a. An Empirically Based Method of Q-matrix Validation for the DINA Model: Development and Applications. *Journal of Educational Measurement* 45(4), 343 – 362.

De la Torre, J. 2008b. The Generalized DINA Model. The International Meeting of the Psychometric Society,

Durham, NH.

De La Torre, J. 2011. The Generalized DINA Model Framework. *Psychometrika* 76(2), 179 – 199.

De la Torre, J. 2010 Estimation Code for the G-DINA Model. In: *Software for Calibrating Diagnostic Classification Models: An Overview of the Current State of the Art*, A.A. Rupp ed. Maryland: University of Maryland.

Graham, S. 2006. Listening Comprehension: The Learners' Perspective. *System* 34(2), 165 – 182.

Hargreaves, A., & Shirley, D. 2009. *The Fourth Way: The Inspiring Future for Educational Change*. Corwin: London.

Jang, E. E. 2005. *A Validity Narrative Effects of Reading Skills Diagnosis on Teaching and Learning in the Context of NG TOEFL*. University of Illinois at Urbana-Champaign.

Jang, E. E. 2009a. Cognitive Diagnostic Assessment of L2 Reading Comprehension Ability: Validity Arguments for Fusion Model Application to Language Assessment. *Language Testing* 26(1), 31 – 73.

Jang, Eunice Eunhee. 2009b. Demystifying a Q-Matrix for Making Diagnostic Inferences About L2 Reading Skills. *Language Assessment Quarterly* 6, 210 – 238.

Kasai, M. 1997. Application of the Rule Space Model to the Reading Comprehension Section of the Test of English as a Foreign Language. Urbana: University of Illinois at Urbana-Champaign.

Lee, Y. W., & Sawaki, Y. 2009. Cognitive Diagnosis Approaches to Language Assessment: An Overview. *Language Assessment Quarterly* 6(3), 172 – 189.

Leighton, J. P., & Gierl, M. J. 2007. *Cognitive Diagnostic Assessment for Education—Theory and Application*. Cambridge University Press.

Liao, Y. F. 2009. *A Construct Validation Study of the GEPT Reading and Listening Sections: Re-examining the Models of L2 Reading and Listening Abilities and Their Relations to Lexico-grammatical Knowledge*. Teachers College, Columbia University.

Luo, Z. S. 2012. 项目反应理论基础 [*Item Response Theory*]. Beijng: Beijing Normal University Publishing Group.

Ma, X., Meng, Y., He, H., & Liu, R. 2012. Personalized EFL. Audio-Visiondiagnostic Model Construction and System Development. *Foreign Language Education* (5), 59 – 63.

Meng, Y. R. 2013. 大学英语听力能力认知诊断评估模型的构建与验证 [*Developing a Model of Cognitive Diagnostic Assessment for College EFL Listening*]. Unpublished doctorate dissertation, Shanghai International Studies University.

Richards, J. C. 1983. Listening Comprehension: Approach, Design, Procedure. *TESOL Quarterly* 17(2), 219 – 240.

Rupp, A. A., & Templin, J. 2008. The Effects of Q-matrix Misspecification on Parameter Estimates and Classification Accuracy in the DINA Model. *Educational and Psychological Measurement* 68(1), 78 – 96.

Rupp, A., Templin, A. J., & Henson, R. 2010. *Diagnostic Measurement: Theory, Method, and Applications*. New York, London: The Guilford Press.

Sinharay, S., & Almond, R. G. 2007. Assessing Fit of Cognitive Diagnostic Models: A Case Study. *Educational and Psychological Measurement* 67(2), 239 – 257.

Swaffar, J., & Bacon, S. 1993. Reading and Listening Comprehension: Perspectives on Research and Implications for the Classroom. In A.O. Hadley Lincolnwood, ILL: National Textbook Co.

Tatsuoka, K. K. 1983. Rule Space: An Approach for Dealing with Misconceptions Based on Item Response Theory. *Journal of Educational Measurement* 20(4), 345 – 354.

Tu, D., Qi, S., & Dai, H. 2008. Cognitive Diagnostic Assessment in Educational Testing. *Testing Research* 4(4), 4 – 15.

Wang, C., Mark, P., & Gierl, J. 2011. Using the Attribute Hierarchy Method to Make Diagnostic Inferences About Examinees' Cognitive Skills in Critical Reading. *Journal of Educational Measurement* 48(2), 165 – 187.

Vandergrift, L. 1999. Facilitating Second Language Listening Comprehension: Acquiring Successful Strategies. *ELT Journal* 53(3), 168 – 176.

Zhang, W. M. 2006. *Detecting Differential Item Functioning Using the DINA Model*. Greensboro: The University of North Carolina.

Zou, S. 2005. *Language Assessment*. Shanghai: Shanghai Foreign Language Education Press.

Notes on contributors

Ma Xiaomei(马晓梅), Professor and PhD supervisor

of SLA in Language and Culture Systematics, at the Center for Graduate Studies of Foreign Languages in the School of Foreign Studies, Xi'an Jiaotong University. Hel research areas are Second Language Acquisition, Language Teaching & Technology. Email: xiaomei @ mail.xjtu.edu.cn.

Meng Yaru(孟亚茹), PhD, Associate professor of the Center for College English in the School of Foreign Studies, Xi'an Jiaotong University. Her research directions are L2 Teaching and Technology, L2 assessment. Email: maryann@mail.xjtu.edu.cn.

基于认知诊断的个性化英语在线听力诊断模型构建

马晓梅　孟亚茹

西安交通大学

提　要: 如何挖掘语言测评中学习者个人的潜在差别以便为他们提供"量身定制"的教学指导,这是语言研究者一直致力于回答的具有挑战性的问题。本文旨在探讨如何运用认知诊断方法构建英语听力诊断模型,为研发"个性化英语学习指导系统"的听力诊断评估做准备。与传统测试评估相比,认知诊断评估能提供颗粒度更细的被试的知识状态和认知加工过程,有助于解决以上问题。依据认知诊断的方法,该诊断模型的构建过程首先是确定听力理解的属性,然后构建假设诊断模型 Q 矩阵和诊断试题,最后通过认知诊断 G-DINA 模型专设软件验证假设 Q 矩阵模型的拟合度。通过定性和定量验证,假设的 Q 阵模型与被试作答拟合良好,可提供可靠的诊断反馈,由此获得学习者个体对听力理解掌握的潜在优势和不足,可用于初步的网络在线诊断。

关键词: 认知诊断评估　个性化学习　英语听力理解　诊断模型

Processability Theory, Question Constructions and Vocabulary Learning in English L2

Satomi Kawaguchi

Abstract: The paper introduces Processability Theory (PT) and a second language acquisition (SLA henceforth) cross-sectional investigation. It illustrates how PT may be used in studying the relationship between question constructions (both yes/no-and wh-questions) and vocabulary learning in English as a second language (ESL). The study involves nine adult Japanese L1-English L2 late bilinguals in Australia, selected out of a total of 22 who sat for a standardised vocabulary size test, three each from Top, Middle and Low vocabulary size groups. These nine informants performed, additionally, communicative oral production tasks for second language (L2) speech profiling. The linguistic production of each informant was analysed against PT syntactic schedule for English L2 question constructions. Results suggest that vocabulary and syntactic development are closely related. Low and Mid vocabulary size ESL learners have problems in specific areas of question constructions, such as the choice of auxiliary verbs. High vocabulary learners, on the other hand, were able to cope with the whole range of question constructions investigated in the study. Question constructions were confirmed to be a key indicator of ESL learners' syntactic development.

Key words: ESL, Processability Theory, question sentence

Introduction

Processability Theory (PT) received its first full formal publication in 1998 (Pienemann 1998). It is a theory explaining second language development. The theory is considered among the ten or so main approaches to SLA (García Mayo et. al. 2013; Jordan 2004; Van Patten & William 2007). Historically speaking, PT was predominately developed in Germany and Australia.[①] Due to this background, PT has been largely influential in Europe, Australia as well as in some US contexts. Therefore, scholars in other countries, especially those in Asian countries, may be unfamiliar with this theory. In recent years, interest in PT has been rapidly increasing in some countries, such as Japan, and thus several SLA books/textbooks started to include a section on PT (e.g., Shirahata et. al. 2010). However, the outreach of the theory remains insufficient in the region and few applied linguists are familiar with the theory well enough to use it in their research. Thus, this paper first provides a brief

---

① See Di Biase (2011, 5 – 10) for a quick historical sketch.

overview of the theory for the readers largely from Asian countries. Given the fact that English is the most widely taught foreign language in this region, this article focuses on the acquisition of English as a second language (ESL/EFL) using PT.

After introducing PT, I will present a cross-sectional study using PT as a theoretical framework to determine the learners' linguistic development. In particular, this study investigates the development of question constructions in conjunction with vocabulary learning. This aspect of English development is selected because it is central to the acquisition of syntax. For instance, word order in English depends on whether the sentence is either declarative or interrogative. Also, English requires a variety of auxiliaries and syntactic frames for the construction of *Yes/No* and content questions (also known as *Wh*-questions). This cross-sectional study presented below looks at adult speakers of Japanese L1 who have learned (or are beginning to learn) English as a L2 and are considered late bilinguals. The study examines, on the one hand, the relationship between learner's vocabulary size in English, measured according to Nation and Beglar's (2007) vocabulary size test and, the syntactic development measured according to the English L2 developmental stages hypothesised in PT. Thus the research question to be answered through the study is: Is there a relationship between the learner's vocabulary size and his/her syntactic ability, as measured through PT, when producing question sentences in English L2?

Processability Theory (PT)

The framework of this study, Processability Theory (PT), is a universal theory of second language acquisition based on general human cognition including speech processing architecture, lexical access and memory capacity. The theory accounts for the specific order in which the second language learner develops his/her language. PT's psychological and typological plausibility makes it a valuable instrument for describing, predicting and accounting for the development of L2 syntax and morphology in speech of very different second languages as demonstrated by fruitful work on Arabic L2 (Mansouri 2005), Chinese L2 (Zhang 2005), English L2 (Pienemann 1998; Sakai 2008), Italian L2 (Di Biase and Kawaguchi 2002; Bettoni & Di Biase 2011), Japanese L2 (Iwasaki 2008; Kawaguchi 2010) and Swedish L2 (Pienemann & Håkansson 1999) among others.

In terms of the processing perspective, PT is based on Levelt's (1989) speech generation model, which shares many basic notions with Kempen and Hoenkamp's (1987) Incremental Procedural Grammar (IPG), a performance production grammar, and Lexical Functional Grammar (LFG) (Kaplan & Bresnan 1982; Bresnan 2001 among others) as a psychologically and typologically plausible formal grammar. All three theories (i.e., Levelt's model, IPG and LFG) share the assumption that

171

grammar is lexically driven. Based on this lexical assumption, as well as on the incremental nature of speech processing, Kempen and Hoenkamp's (1987) propose that grammatical encoding activates the speech processing procedures sequentially in the following order:

(1) lemma;

(2) the category procedure (lexical category of the lemma);

(3) the phrasal procedure (instigated by the category of the head);

(4) the S-procedure and the target language word order rules;

(5) the subordinate clause procedure—if applicable.

Pienemann (1998) hypothesises that there is a hierarchical relationship for the acquisition of the processing resources by the L2 learner. This hierarchy follows the same sequence as the activation of the five speech processing procedures in the production process sketched above. Based on Levelt (1989), Pienemann (1998) claims that the acquisition of processing resources at the lower levels is a prerequisite for the higher level ones. The acquisition of these resources allows for staged developmental sequences in L2 syntax. Pienemann, Di Biase and Kawaguchi (2005) extended PT's scope by including discourse-pragmatic aspects in syntactic development accounting for, e. g., topic assignment and passive constructions. These additions were further refined by current work on prominence assignment (Bettoni & Di Biase, in press).

These newer developments were able to be captured by further advances in LFG (Bresnan 2001; Dalrymple 2001). Next, I summarise PT hypotheses for morphological and syntactic development in second language, which have been tested against empirical data in many studies on typologically different languages previously mentioned.

Morphology

Pienemann (1998) hypothesised that morphology is acquired according to the different types of information processing (or "unification" in LFG terms), in the following order: Word/Lemma access > Lexical morphology > Phrasal morphology > Inter-phrasal morphology. The next paragraphs illustrate each morphological type in English and Japanese, and its processing mechanism.

Word/Lemma access: This stage is non language-specific and requires no exchange of grammatical information with other words. In this first stage, everyone can normally learn a word or formula such as those used for greeting people in a language other than one's own. For example, the Japanese word *tsunami* has been learned and is now used in many other languages to denote some major, sudden and undesirable change. Assuming the learner is not Japanese, the form, the meaning of this word, once learned, i.e., mapped onto each other, and somewhat adapted to the pronunciation of the learner's language, is then listed in the mental lexicon as a whole item, without any of the other potential grammatical features or specifications that the word may have in the original Japanese language.

Lexical morphology: This second stage is language-specific. PT predicts that lexical morphemes emerge when the category procedure is acquired by the learner, e.g., where the L2 learner begins to make a difference between nouns and verbs in the new language in ways similar to that of the L2. In many languages this is done via diacritic features such as "tense" or "aspect" for verbs on the one hand or "number" or "classifier" for nouns on the other hand. When learning how any of these features are expressed (or marked), the learner lists them, gradually, in the lexical entry of words. So, for instance, insertion of the affix -s on the English noun for indicating a positive value for the feature "plural", as in *they have dogs* can be achieved directly from conceptualisation as long as the speaker knows the category of the word ("noun" in this case). Hence lexical morphology only requires category procedure where no information exchange with other words (*they*, *have*) in the phrase is required.

Phrasal morphology: An example of a phrasal morpheme in English is also the plural marker -s, as can be seen in the expression *many dogs*. PT predicts that the plural marker -s which requires exchange of grammatical information between the head noun and its modifier is acquired after lexical morphology. The lexical entries of the two lexical items *many* and *dogs* are

shown in Figure 1 with the (simplified) tree diagram for the phrase.

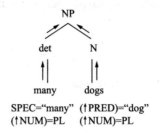

SPEC="many"   (↑PRED)="dog"
(↑NUM)=PL   (↑NUM)=PL

Figure 1   Phrase structure of *many dogs* with lexical entries.

In the phrase *many dogs*, information exchange must happen within the phrase. Both the determiner *many* and the head noun *dogs* contain the plural value of the number feature information of the head noun. The value of the feature NUM(ber) attributed to both the determiner and the noun flows up the tree node. Feature unification needs to happen at the NP node as shown in Figure 2 because the number information coming from two sources (i.e., NUM = PL) must be compatible for well-formedness. In PT, this type of unification is called "phrasal" because it occurs at the phrase level. So, in a phrase such as ** many dog*, the grammatical features fail to unify due to the conflicting information coming from *many* ("NUM = PL") and *dog* ("NUM = SG"), so the resulting phrase is filtered out as ungrammatical. The sequence lexical > phrasal is validated for plural -s in cross sectional and longitudinal studies (e.g., Yamaguchi 2008).

Inter-phrasal morphology: This next level is represented in the phrase structure of the sentence *Peter owns a dog*, with the corresponding lexical entries in Figure 2.

Up- and down-arrows (i.e., ↑ and ↓) indicate information flow. This illustrates the subject-verb agreement process in English, where the exchange of information occurs between different types of phrases (NP and VP).

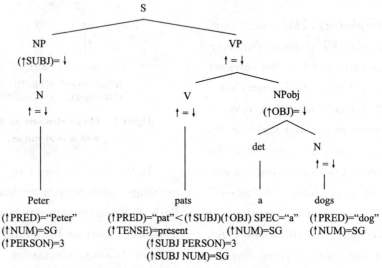

Figure 2   C-structure of *Peter pats a dog* with lexical entry.

The morpheme -*s* on the verb contains the sentence subject information "Number=singular" and "PERSON=3rd". Likewise, the subject of the sentence is *Peter* whose features are also "NUM=singular (SG)" and "PERSON=3rd". Therefore, information coming from NP$_{SUBJCT}$ *Peter* and the information flowing from the verb *owns* is compatible in terms of the value of the features NUM and PERSON of the two different phrasal constituents, and therefore unification is possible. Thus, placement of -*s* on the verb requires inter-phrasal information processing (so the features values for *Peter* need to be temporarily stored in working memory) because the two elements *Peter* and *owns* belong to different phrases and unification happens across phrase boundary at the S-node. PT predicts that this type of morphological agreement emerges after phrasal morphology. Table 1 below summarises PT's stages of morphological development with examples from English L2.

Table 1   Stages of development for English L2 Morphology

Stages	Processing procedures & English structural outcomes	English L2 examples
4	\<S-procedure\> Subject-Verb agreement	*Peter pats a dog.*
3	\<phrasal procedure\> Plural agreement	*many dogs*
2	\<Category procedure\> Form variation	*We like dogs*

Continued

Stages	Processing procedures & English structural outcomes	English L2 examples
1	\<Lemma access\> Single words, formula	*How are you?* *Dog*

Syntax

Two hypotheses account for developmental sequence in L2 syntax. They are the Prominence Hypothesis (Bettoni & Di Biase, in press) which deals with the discourse functions (Topic and Focus) interacting with syntax at sentence level, and the Lexical Mapping Hypothesis (Pienemann, Di Biase & Kawaguchi 2005). But only the former is relevant to this study and therefore, I will show only the Prominence Hypothesis in conjunction with development of Y/N and Wh-questions in English L2.

The Prominence Hypothesis and development of Y/N and Wh-questions

The Prominence Hypothesis states that:

In second language acquisition learners will initially not differentiate between grammatical functions (GFs) and discourse functions (DFs), e.g., between SUBJ and TOP. Differentiation begins when an XP is added to the canonical string in a position of prominence (e.g., the first in the sentence). This XP can be either TOP in declaratives or FOC in interrogatives leaving the canonical string unaltered. At the next stage, learners will be able to construct noncanonical strings assigning prominence to any constituent in an unequivocal way (Bettoni & Di Biase, in press).

This hypothesis predicts Y/N questions and Wh-questions in English to be acquired following the order as schematically presented in Table 2 and Table 3 respectively (beginning from lower to higher rows in the tables). These stages are attest-ed in a longitudinal study (Yamaguchi 2013; Di Biase, Kawaguchi & Yamaguchi, in press). As can be seen in Table 2, the first stage of interrogative is lemma access realised as single words and formula (e.g., *Coffee?*) with QUE^p where the superscript "p" indicates that the question modality is expressed only prosodically (with raising intonation). Exclusively prosodic marking [QUE^p] continues also at the second, i.e., Canonical Order, stage (*Tom is happy?*) where the question modality is still entrusted to the prosodic envelope of the Canonical Order expression, which would otherwise express a declarative. At the next stage some lexical material (beside the prosody) starts to distinguish questions. This lexical material is a kind of particle which is preposed (in topical position) hence outside of the Canonical Order block "QUE particle + Unmarked alignment" as in *do they have cat?* The highest stage (in single clauses) involves marked alignment as in *have you tried pizza?* where English canonical order SUBJ-VERB-OBJ is superseded by the auxiliary occupying the particle position. The auxiliary is different from the particle because it carries subject person marking or tense information similar to native English. In short, the learner progresses from single words to canonical order (unmarked alignment) then to particle and finally to marked alignment.

As for the developmental stage of content questions (see Table 3), a similar progression occurs but this time the Focus is expressed by Question words (Wh-). The first stage is also single words and unanalysed formulaic expressions involving question words, such as *what?*, *how much?* or *how are you?* The next stage may be realised as In-Situ WH-question constructions where the canonical, unmarked alignment is preserved, such as *John eat what?* common in languages such as Chinese or Japanese. Not all learners go through this stage which may turn out to be marginally grammatical (except in marked, specific discourse). The next stage is QUE (stion) word + unmarked alignment such as *what he eat?* which in English also exhibits ungrammatical construction. The highest stage (in single clause) in Wh-questions involves marked alignment as in *when are you going?* English indirect question sentence such as *I wonder where the station is* involves subordination and inter-clausal processing (cf. Pienemann & Kessler 2011), which I do not discuss in this paper.

Table 2　Developmental stages for English syntax: Y/N questions (after Bettoni & Di Biase, in press)

Stages	Structures	Examples
4. marked alignment	AUX$_{QUE}$ SUBJ V (O) MOD$_{QUE}$ SUBJ V (O) *have*$_{QUE}$ SUBJ OBJ copula$_{QUE}$ SUBJ predicate	*have you tried pizza?* *can Ann swim?* *have you a boyfriend?* *is Joan happy?* *are you there?*
3. QUE (stion) particle + unmarked alignment	QUE [canonical order]	*do they have cat?* *is your man have a red hat?* *is Mary is happy?*
2. unmarked alignment	[QUE^p canonical order]	*dog eating the doughnut?* *you like pizza?* *you are there?* *Tom is happy?*
1. lemma access	[QUE^p single words] [QUE^p formulas]	*Jim happy?* *coffee? going?*
QUE^p *feature is only prosodic*		

Table 3　Developmental stages for English syntax: constituent questions (after Bettoni & Di Biase, in press)

Stages	Structures	Examples
4. XP$_{FOC}$ marked alignment	WH$_{QUE}$ AUX SUBJ VO WH$_{QUE}$ MOD SUBJ V (O) WH$_{QUE}$ copula SUBJ	*what has Tom eaten?* *where did Joan go?* *when are you going?* *what can Mary do?* *where are they?* *what is this?*

Continued

Stages	Structures	Examples
3. XP$_{FOC}$	WH$_{QUE}$ canonical order	*what he eat?* *when you go?* *where Joan is?*
2. unmarked alignment	in-situ$_{QUE}$ [Canonical Order]	*Joan eat what?*
1. lemma access	single word formula	*what? what colour?* *how much is it?*

Vocabulary size and language acquisition

Previous studies on L2 lexicon and lexical acquisition (e. g., Nation 2001; Laufer & Hulstijn 2001; Kroll & Tokowicz 2001) offer insights into lexical acquisition in areas such as second language acquisition and language professions, e. g., translation and interpreting. However, a key issue with these studies is that they tend to treat all vocabulary items in a statistically uniform way. Yet, many modern theories of grammar (Bresnan 2001; Culicover & Jackendoff 2005; Van Valin & la Polla 1997; Van Valin 2005) assume that syntax is driven by the lexicon. Some researchers believe lexical size is one way of indicating L2 learner's proficiency level especially in reading and listening (Nation 2001). It can also be used as a reference point for phonological, morphological and syntactic development, such as mean length of utterance (MLU), which is used in first language acquisition. However, what lexical size seems to measure is the learner's semantic knowledge of a word but not necessarily its grammatical and combinatorial features and their values (i.e., the full *lemma* in Levelt, 1989; Bock & Levelt 1994 and Levelt, Roelofs & Meyer, 1999's terms), and therefore its actual use in connected oral and written production. In fact, many current cognitive approaches to SLA (e. g., DeKyser 2007; Pienemann 1998; VanPatten & Houston 1998) show that grammatical knowledge (i. e., declarative knowledge) is different from language procedural skills for speech production and comprehension. Then learner's lexical size based on word frequency lists may not be sufficient to predict learners' *productive ability* in L2 syntax. This study may be able to contribute to making lexical size instruments better connected to overall L2 development, and hence point towards additional instruments to resolve the limitations of the lexical size test.

Study

This section describes the study design including informants, procedure, tasks and data analysis methods to answer the research question presented earlier.

Informants

The informants in this study were 22 Japanese L1 speakers of English L2 (five male and 17 female) aged between 20 and 56 years (mean 31, SD 9.9) with length of stay in Australia ranging from 9 days to 27 years. They include working holiday participants, university students (all undergraduate, MA and PhD), business people and their wives and one professional translator. Adult informants of varying lengths of stay may provide a wide range of attainment in English L2.

Procedure

A vocabulary size test was first conducted with 22 Japanese L1-English L2 speakers in Australia. The vocabulary test results were then analysed and three informants from the Top, Mid(dle) and Low (i.e., bottom) vocabulary size groups, nine in total, were selected to proceed the next step. These three groups of informants enable us to compare syntactic abilities of the English L2 speakers of different vocabulary sizes[1]. The next step involved the interview with each of these nine informants using a profiling task to check their syntactic developmental stage, particularly with question sentences, based on Processability Theory. The data obtained through the profiling task was then analysed against PT predictions shown in Table 1 and 2. This involves full distributional analysis, followed by implicational scaling for measuring language development, thus providing the framework within which the relationship between vocabulary size and syntactic stage is examined.

Tasks

a. *Vocabulary size test*

The Nation and Beglar (2007) vocabulary size test which measures vocabulary knowledge (for comprehension) up to the 14,000 word families level was used in order to identify three informants from the top, mid and bottom vocabulary size range among the 22 informants. This vocabulary size test is well supported (e.g. Nation 2006) as a significant correlation between vocabulary size and receptive language abilities (i.e. reading and listening) has been established. It is interesting to test whether productive (as against receptive) language ability also shows a relationship with vocabulary size.

b. *Profiling task*

A profiling task was used to elicit production data to analyse the participant's PT stages. First, a short interview which gathered general information about the participant was conducted. This aims to elicit the participant's bio data (such as ESL instruction, length of stay in Australia, etc.) but also aims to elicit various syntactic structures. The interview is followed by a "spot the differences" task (see Appendix), that aims to elicit various English question sentences, which constitutes indicators for identifying ESL PT stage. In this task, the participant and the interviewer each take one of two fairly similar pictures which differ in some (around 10) details. For example, both pictures may depict a public garden but one picture has one dog while the other has two dogs in it. The task for the participant is to find differences between the two pictures by first describing their pictures and then by asking questions about the interviewer's picture. Neither

---

① This study looks at adult English L2 speakers in Australia who have completed compulsory English studies at least six years in Japan. Thus, High, Mid and Low may not correspond to general definitions of learners' lexical ability.

participant can see the other's picture. In this particular study the research assistant, a native speaker of Japanese with an advanced command in English, who has an MA in Applied Japanese Linguistics, acted as the interviewer.

Results

Vocabulary size test

Figure 3 lists the distribution of the vocabulary size for 22 informants. Minimum and maximum sizes are 3,000 and 12,700 word families respectively (mean 7,141, SD — 2,466). Nation and Beglar note that "undergraduate non-native speakers successfully coping with study at an English speaking university have a vocabulary around 5,000—6,000 word families. Non-native speaking PhD students have around a 9,000 word vocabulary" (2007, p. 9). Out of the 22 informants in the present study, who range from well below undergraduate university level to beyond PhD level, three informants each from Top, Middle and Low lexical size groups were selected for a focused investigation of their syntactic development in ESL. The three highest and three lowest vocabulary size informants were selected for the "Top" and "Low" lexical size groups respectively. As for the "Middle" group, I selected the two informants with the median (i.e., the middle value), which is 6,800, and one more informant with the closest value to the median (i.e., 6,900). Their vocabulary size and other relevant information are summarized in Table 4. These nine informants were asked to proceed to perform the profiling and translation tasks. The last column in the table lists the total number of turns each informant produced through the profiling task.

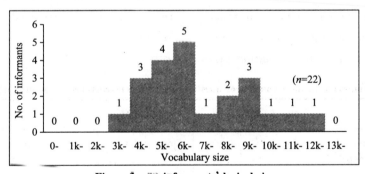

Figure 3 22 informants' lexical size

Table 4 Lexical size and background information of High, Mid and Low vocabulary size learners

Group	Code name (male or female)	Vocabulary size	Age	Length of stay in Australia (current occupation)	Total No. of turns produced via profiling task
High	JA 03 (F)	12,700	43	8 years (Translator)	120 turns
	JA 13 (F)	11,200	29	2yrs & 9 months (MA student)	96
	JA 02 (M)	10,100	27	2yrs & 6 months (PhD student)	150

Continued

Group	Code name (male or female)	Vocabulary size	Age	Length of stay in Australia (current occupation)	Total No. of turns produced via profiling task
Mid	JA 06 (F)	6,900	32	4 months (Wife of an engineer sent to Australia for business)	104
	JA21 (F)	6,800	32	9 months (Employee at a Japanese agency)	97
	JA 08 (F)	6,800	21	6 months (Working holiday participant)	119
Low	JA 19 (F)	4,600	24	8 weeks (Student of an English school)	146
	JA 20 (F)	4,100	34	4 weeks (Student of a short vocational course)	182
	JA 11 (F)	3,000	40	6 months (House wife)	130

Profiling task: Question sentence constructions

This section presents the analysis of the informant's production of question sentences produced through the profiling task. Table 5 summarises frequency count of their question sentences production according to the question type: ① yes/no questions and ② wh-questions while Table 6 shows the breakdown of the question sentence production against PT stages. A particular syntactic stage is considered to be acquired in PT when an informant produces any construction belonging to that stage more than once with lexical variation (this excludes formulaic or echoic production).

Applying this acquisition criterion, the nine informants' PT stages in question sentences are identified. In Table 6, the highest stage acquired by each informant is shaded: J11 and J19 are at Stage 1; J20 is at Stage 3; all the others J08, J21, J06, J02, J13 and J03 are at Stage 4. Note that "−" (minus) next to the number as in "−1" indicates negative evidence for acquisition. Notice that numbers are listed in the cell only if the informant produced a particular structure.

Table 5 Summary on the frequency of question sentence constructions by the nine informants

Group	Low			Mid			High		
Informants (lexical size: x 1,000)	J11 (3.0)	J20 (4.1)	J19 (4.6)	J08 (6.8)	J21 (6.8)	J06 (6.9)	J02 (10.1)	J13 (11.2)	J03 (12.7)
Y/N questions	6	7	2	16	9	7	7	5	6
Wh-questions	1	5	6	6	3	10	5	7	7
Total	7	12	8	22	12	17	12	12	13

Table 6 Breakdown of the question sentences against PT stages

Stage		Structure	Low			Mid			High		
			J11 3.0	J19 4.6	J20 4.1	J08 6.8	J21 6.8	J06 6.9	J02 10.1	J13 11.2	J3 12.7
4	Marked alignment	Y/N questions	1/−1		1		7	2	2	1	1
		Wh-questions	0	1/−1	−1	2	2	8	1	5	4
3	QUE particle + unmarked alignment	Y/N questions	1	1	5/−1	3		4	4		1
		Wh-questions			2						
2	Unmarked alignment	Y/N questions	1			2	1		1		
		Wh-questions									
1	Lemma access	Y/N questions	2	1		11	1	1	4		4
		Wh-questions	1	4	2	4	1	2	4	2	3

Low vocabulary size informants

Two of three Low vocabulary size informants (J11 and J19) are still at the lowest Stage 1 (i.e., lemma access) because they used only single words or formulaic questions as in (1) and (2). One Low vocabulary size informant, J20, showed substantial evidence for Stage 3 QUE + unmarked alignment as in (3).

(1) J11 Black cats?

(2) J19 when?

(3) J20 does girl have ball ball?

Also, the low vocabulary size group were often unable to complete the question sentences: they started with a particular question construction but changed the question sentence structure from Wh to Y/N or the other way around. In the example (4a), J20 started a "do-question" (Stage 3, QUE [Unmarked alignment]) but was unable to complete it. J20, instead, changed the pattern and attempted "wh-question" requiring Stage 4 operation (Marked alignment) but was unsuccessful. They also have problems selecting the appropriate auxiliary verb to form a question as in (4b).

(4) a. J20 do you have (X) do you.? hum hummm how many oh no no no no uhm how many people. there is. there the. bench in ? (laugh)

b. J19 how long how long uhm di do do you uh how long are you there?

One of those in the low vocabulary size group also attempted a higher stage structure which she has not reached and ended up ungrammatical, i.e., negative evidence of acquisition. The sentence (5) exemplifies an unsuccessful attempt of Stage 4 (Marked alignment) which lacks the subject.

(5) J11 *can see cats?

Further, two learners showed some problem with Wh questions involving SUBJ as in (6) and (7). These examples exhibit incorrect functional assignment of the WH-pronoun by providing extra SUBJ in the sentence. Functional assignment requires the procedural skill placed at Stage 4 according to PT but these informants have not attained that stage.

(6) J19 *how many birds are you here?

(7) J20 * how many people di did did did you ride your (X) ride a bicycle?

Mid vocabulary size informants

All of the mid vocabulary size informants have attained Stage 4 (Marked alignment). (8) and (9) are examples of Stage 4 WH and (10) Y/N question which requires marked alignment.

(8) J08 ok. ah. how long have you been?

(9) J06 umm ok. which language do you usually use?

(10) J21 can you see one spider in the middle of this?

Although these informants are at Stage 4, they also produced the lower, Stage 3, unmarked alignment Y/N question simply using raising intonation as in (11). J21 and J08 produced such question sentences once and twice respectively.

(11) J08 brother is ah special school . school?

Another observation among the mid vocabulary size informants is that J08 (lexical size 6.8) lacks production of Stage 4 Y/N questions.

High vocabulary size informants

All three high vocabulary size informants produced a variety of question sentences belonging to different stages. All of them are at Stage 4 and produced both Y/N and WH-questions at this stage. There was no ungrammatical production among these informants. Unlike Low vocabulary size informants, J02 was able to produce WH-question asking SUBJ information correctly as follows in (12). Superficially, this SUBJ

in-situ question sentence follows unmarked alignment. But without acquiring functional assignment of the event participants, production of this sentence pattern is not possible.

(12) J02 who is trying to feed duck?

In conclusion, two Low vocabulary size informants (size 3.0k and 4.6k) were at Question Stage 1 and one (size 4.1k) at Stage 3. All Mid and High vocabulary size informants are at Stage 4.

Relationship between vocabulary size and the acquisition of question construction

We now look at the relationship between vocabulary size and the acquisition of question construction based on the results gained through the study. Figure 4 shows that PT stages in question constructions, as achieved by the nine informants, are related to their vocabulary sizes. The two Low vocabulary size learners J11 and J19 are at the lowest PT stage and one Low, J20 at Stage 3. All Mid and High vocabulary size learners are at the highest PT stage. Recall that according to Nation and Beglar (2007), the overseas students who are able to cope with undergraduate study successfully at English medium universities possess around 5,000—6,000 vocabulary size. Mid and High vocabulary size learners in the current study are beyond this level and all achieve the highest PT stage. This indicates that ESL learners of Mid and High vocabulary size are able to produce both Y/N and WH questions including marked alignment without any problem, while Low vocabulary learners are unable to do so.

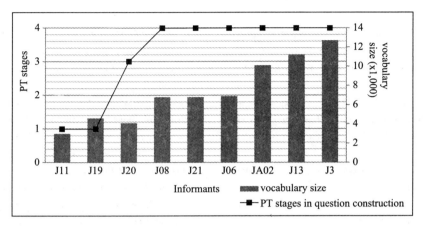

Figure 4   Informant's vocabulary size and their PT stages in question constructions

Conclusion

This paper introduced a current, major theory of second language acquisition, Processability Theory (Pienemann 1998 and further developments). PT adopts the principle of processing prerequisites that is, the learner builds up additional processing resources in order to process the L2 and gradually deploys these in an automatic way. Developmental sequences predicted by PT relate to the requirements of the specific procedural skills needed for the target language (any L2). In this way, predictions can be made for language development that can be tested empirically. The task for the learner, then, is to build, alongside the L2 lexicon, the language-specific procedures needed to handle the Target Language. These procedures will be different for different languages, but always ordered in the same sequence.

Also a cross-sectional study in ESL using PT was presented. The analysis of the data was conducted using the current proposal for ESL question constructions in Processability Theory (Bettoni & Di Biase,

in press). The study investigated, in particular, the relationship between vocabulary learning and syntactic development in English as a second language. Question sentences were at the centre of our syntactic analysis. The findings can be summarized as follows. Regarding question sentence constructions Mid and High vocabulary sizes (6,000 or over) can predict the highest L2 developmental stage as defined by PT (i.e., marked alignment). All Lower vocabulary size group learners had difficulties in constructing various English question sentences. The problems include marked alignment, selection of auxiliary verbs, and constructions of SUBJ WH-questions. From the learning and teaching point of view a clear awareness of the importance of vocabulary size and non-default mapping helps plan more focused interventions to promote higher levels of language development.

References

Bettoni, C., & Di Biase, B. (Eds.). (in press). *Grammatical Development in Second Languages: Exploring the Boundaries of Processability Theory.* Eurosla Monographs. http://eurosla.org/monographs/EMhome.html.

Bettoni, C., & Di Biase, B. 2011. Beyond Canonical Order: The Acquisition of Marked Word Orders in Italian as a Second Language. *EUROSLA Yearbook* 11, 244 - 272.

Bock, K., & Levelt, W. J. M. 1994. Language Production: Grammatical Encoding. In: *Handbook of Psycholinguistics*, M. A. Gernsbacher ed. San Diego: Academic Press.

Bresnan, J. 2001. *Lexical-functional Syntax*. Malden, MA: Blackwell Publishers.

Culicover, P., & Jackendoff, R. 2005. *Simpler Syntax*. Oxford: Oxford University Press.

DeKeyser, R. 2007. Skill Acquisition Theory. In: *Theories in Second Language Acquisition* (pp. 97 - 135), B. Van Patten & J. Williams eds. Mahwah: Laurence Erlbaum.

Di Biase, B. 2011. *A Processability Approach to the Acquisition of Italian as a Second Language: Theory and Applications*. PhD thesis, 2007 August 25. Australian National University, Digital Collections. April 2011 @ http://hdl.handle.net/1885/6982.

Di Biase, B., & Kawaguchi, S. 2002. Exploring the Typological Plausibility of Processability Theory: Language Development in Italian Second Language and Japanese Second Language. *Second Language Research* 18(3), 274 - 302.

García Mayo, M. D. P., Gutierrez Mangado, M. J., & Matínez Adrián, M. 2013. *Contemporary Approaches to Second Language Acquisition*. Amsterdam: Phiiladelphia: John Benjamins Publishing Company.

Jordan, G. 2004. *Theory Construction in Second Language Acquisition*. Amsterdam and Philadelphia: John Benjamins.

Kaplan, R. M., & Bresnan, J. 1982. Lexical-Functional Grammar: A Formal System for Grammatical Representation. In: *The Mental Representation of Grammatical Relations* (pp. 173 - 281), J. Bresnan ed. Cambridge, MA: MIT Press.

Kawaguchi, S. 2010. *Learning Japanese as a Second Language: A Processability Perspective*. New York: Cambria Press.

Kempen, G., & Hoenkamp, E. 1987. An Incremental Procedural Grammar for Sentence Formulation. *Cognitive Science* 11(2), 201 - 258.

Kroll, J. F., & Tokowicz, N. 2005. Models of Bilingual Representation and Processing. *Handbook of Bilingualism: Psycholinguistic Approaches*, 531 -

553.

Laufer, B., & Hulstijn, J. 2001. Incidental Vocabulary Acquisition in a Second Language: The Construct of Task-induced Involvement. *Applied Linguistics* 22(1), 1 - 26.

Levelt, W. J. M. 1989. *Speaking: From Intention to Articulation*. Cambridge, MA: MIT Press.

Levelt, W. J. M., Roelofs, A., & Meyer, A. S. 1999. A Theory of Lexical Access in Speech Production. *Behavioral and Brain Sciences* 22(1), 1 - 38.

Mansouri, F. 2005. Agreement Morphology in Arabic as a Second Language: Typological Features and Their Processing Implications. In: *Cross-linguistic Aspects of Processability Theory* (pp. 117 - 153), M. Pienemann ed. Amsterdam: John Benjamins.

Nation, I. S. 2001. *Learning Vocabulary in Another Language*. Cambridge: Cambridge University Press.

Nation, I. S. 2006. How Large a Vocabulary Is Needed for Reading and Listening?. *Canadian Modern Language Review/La revue canadienne des langues vivantes* 63 (1), 59 - 82.

Nation, P., & Beglar, D. 2007. A Vocabulary Size Test. *The Language Teacher* 31(7), 9 - 13.

Payne, T. E. 2011. *Understanding English Grammar*. Cambridge: Cambridge University Press.

Pienemann, M. 1998. *Language Processing and Second Language Development: Processability Theory*. Amsterdam: John Benjamins.

Pienemann, M., & Kessler, J. U. (Eds.). 2011. *Studying Processability Theory: An Introductory Textbook* (Vol. 1). John Benjamins Publishing.

Pienemann, M., Di Biase, B., & Kawaguchi, S. 2005. Extending Processability Theory. In: *Cross-linguistic Aspects of Processability Theory* (pp. 199 - 252), M. Pienemann ed. Amsterdam: John Benjamins.

Pienemann, M., & Håkansson, G. 1999. A Unified Approach Towards the Development of Swedish as L2: A Processability Account. *Studies in Second Language Acquisition* 21(3), 383 - 420.

Sakai, H. 2008. An Analysis of Japanese University Students' Oral Performance in English Using Processability Theory. *System* 36, 534 - 549.

Shirahata, T., Shigenori, W., & Muranoi, H. 2010. *Daini Gengo Shuutoku Kenkyuu: Riron kara Kenkyuu Hoohoo made (Second Language Acquisition Research: From Theories to Research Methods)*. Tokyo: Kenkyuusha.

Van Patten, B., & Houston, T. 1998. Contextual Effects in Processing L2 Input Sentences. *Spanish Applied Linguistics* 2(1), 53 – 70.

Van Patten, B., & Williams, J. 2007. *Theories in Second Language Acquisition: An Introduction.* New Jersey: Lawrence Erlbaum Associates.

Van Valin, R. D. 2005. *Exploring the Syntax-semantics Interface.* Cambridge University Press.

Van Valin, R. D., & LaPolla, R. J. 1997. *Syntax: Structure, Meaning, and Function.* Cambridge: Cambridge University Press.

Yamaguchi, Y. 2008. The Early Development in Child L2 Acquisition: What Happens After "Canonical Order"? In: *Processability Approaches to Second Language Development and Second Language Learning* (pp. 245 – 266), J.-U. Kessler ed. Newcastle upon Tyne, UK: Cambridge Scholars Publishing.

Yamaguchi, Y. 2009. The Development of Plural Marking and Plural Agreement in Child English L2 Acquisition. In: *Research in Second Language Acquisition: Empirical Evidence Across Languages* (pp. 9 – 39), J-U.

Kessler & D. Keatinge eds. Newcastle upon Tyne, UK: Cambridge Scholars Publishing.

Yamaguchi, Y. 2010. *The Acquisition of English as a Second Language by a Japanese Primary School Child: A Longitudinal Study from a Processability Viewpoint.* PhD Thesis, University of Western Sydney, Sydney, Australia.

Zhang, Y. 2005. Processing and Formal Instruction in the L2 Acquisition of Five Chinese Grammatical Morphemes. In: *Crosslinguistic Aspects of Processability Theory* (pp. 155 – 178), M. Pienemann ed. Amsterdam and Philadelphia: John Benjamins.

Notes on contributors

Satomi Kawaguchi, PhD, is senior lecturer at the University of Western Sydney and teaches second language acquisition, research methods (in TESOL) and Japanese language. Her research areas include acquisition of English L2 and Japanese L2 as well as technological invention in language teaching and learning.

可加工性理论、英语作为第二语言的问句和词汇学习

Satomi Kawaguchi

School of Humanities & Communication Arts, Bilingualism Research Lab,
MARCS Institute, University of Western Sydney, Australia

提 要：本文通过二语习得(SLA)一个横断面的调查研究介绍可加工性理论(PT)如何运用在二语习得的研究中。例如,英语作为第二语言(ESL)的问句结构(包括一般疑问句和特殊疑问句)和词汇学习的关系。本文首先介绍了 PT 的重要组成部分。其次介绍了 9 名在澳大利亚 L1 为日语 L2 为英语学习者的横断面研究。这 9 名受试者是从参加标准化词汇量测试的 22 名测试者中按照测试成绩高、中、低各抽取 3 名而来。此外,这 9 名受试者参加了交际口语表达任务,所产出的语料用于第二语言言语分析。每位受试者的言语产出按照 PT 对英语为第二语言的问句结构的句法阶段进行分析。研究结果表明,词汇和语法的发展是密切相关的。中低等词汇量 ESL 学习者在问句结构方面存在一定问题,如助动词的选择。另一方面,高词汇量的学习者能够应对本研究中所调查的整体范围的问句结构。问句结构被证实为 ESL 学习者语法发展的一个关键指标。

关键词：第二语言习得 可加工性理论 问句 英语作为第二语言

Translating Word Play: A Pragmatic Approach

Wu Guo

Abstract: This paper explores how a pragmatic approach, guided by Lewis's (1985) concept of "abusive translation" and attention to both the signified and the play of signifiers (Venuti 1995), facilitates translating word play in literary works, resulting in appropriate renditions that retain the prominent formal features as well as the pragmatic force of the word play in the source text. The examples used in this paper were produced in a joint translation project entitled "Introducing Australian Children's Literature to China" where five Australian children's books were translated from English into Chinese and the translations were published by the People's Literature Publishing House in Beijing in 2009.

Key words: word play, translation, pragmatic significance, key signifier, key feature

Introduction

Word play is one of the most difficult areas in translation, involving both pragmalinguistics and sociopragmatics (He 1995/2001). Linguistic and sociocultural disparity between the source language (SL) and the target language (TL) often makes translating word play a mission impossible, as admitted by great translators such as Yu Kwang-chung 余光中 (1983:156) and Liang Shih-ch'iu 梁实秋 (1974:13 – 14) as well as scholars of translation studies such as House (2009:41). In practice, word play is generally treated in three ways: (a) by providing footnotes; (b) by writing explanations into the word play; and (c) by resorting to invention to preserve the original flavour (Hwang Mei-shu 黄美序 1980). Huang (1995/2000:923), expanding on these alternatives, proposes that

translators should strive to approximate the stylistic features of the original to reproduce the connotative meaning, or the "inner spirit" of a literary work. With a focus on results, Huang (1995/2000) provides some excellent Chinese translations of English puns to exemplify his point without, understandably, detailed discussion of the process through which the results were reached.

With a different focus from Huang's, this paper, however, is process oriented. It explores how a pragmatic approach and a more positive and creative attitude on the part of the translator facilitates translating word play in literary works, resulting in appropriate renditions that retain the prominent formal features as well as the pragmatic force of the word play in the source text (ST). It is one of a series of papers (see also Author 2010) coming out of a translation project entitled "Introducing Australian Children's Literature to China", sponsored by the Australia China Council (ACC) and the University of Western Sydney (UWS), where five Australian children's books were translated from English into Chinese and the translations were published by the People's Literature Publishing House in Beijing in 2009. UWS Interpreting & Translation students participated in translating two of these books, under the supervision of the author of this paper. The examples used here were produced during the above translation project.

Translating word play

In order to preserve in the target text (TT) as much as possible both the original pragmatic force and the formal features of a piece of word play, we find Lewis's concept of "abusive translation" to be instrumental that "seeks to match the polyvalencies or plurivocities or expressive stresses of the original by producing its own" (Lewis 1985: 41). In light of this concept, the problem for translators is no longer "how to avoid the failures... that disparity among natural languages assures", but rather "how to compensate for losses and to justify... the differences—how to renew the energy and signifying behavior that a translation is likely to diffuse" (Lewis 1985: 42). This daring concept of fidelity requires the translator to take on a more positive role to supply what is inevitably lacking in translation due to differences between the SL and the TL, and allows more flexibility and creativity in the translation process. According to Lewis (1985: 45), translation has two complicated aims: "First to reproduce the use and abuse of the original in the translation and second to supply for what cannot in fact be reproduced with a remobilization of use and abuse that further qualifies the original as used and thus disabused." These two stages, especially the second one that requires more creativity, are immensely useful in dealing with word play, a form of abuse.

In order to "produce its own" in the TL, the translator conducts a pragmatic analysis of the elements involved in the word play and prioritises the pragmatic force of each element to identify the key, secondary and minor features. Then the task is to find a signifier (or signifiers) in the TL that can represent the key features, i.e., the semantic and formal features essential to the play, and, at the same time, accommodate the secondary (and minor) features. Once the key signifier is identified, a second signifier (or signifiers) can be selected accordingly to represent the secondary features, which are often important to the play more formally and stylistically than semantically. The minor features, dependent on the secondary ones and not directly involved in the play, may have to be adapted in some way as required around the secondary signifier (or signifiers). In this process, the identification of the key signifier roughly fulfils Lewis' (1985: 45) "reproduce" aim, and the selection of a second signifier and adaption of the minor features, Lewis' (1985:45) "re-mobilization" aim. The process is demonstrated by the three examples we came across in translating *Being Bee* (Catherine Bateson 2006), of which the double meaning of the same word involved in example 1 is not intended by the speaker, but by the writer, and example 2 is a malapropism, i.e., the misuse of a word for a word with a similar sound, resulting in a nonsensical utterance, whereas example 3 is a case of multi-level word play. Although the first two examples may not be typical word play as discussed in the literature, their translation, nevertheless, has involved the same process.

Toasting

(1) Jazzi: "We're having a toast," she said to him, "to Nick and me."

Harley: "Toast with what? Jam? I hope it's not strawberry. I can't eat strawberries..."

(Bateson 2006:93)

Students' translation:

"我们正在敬酒,敬给尼克和我,"洁斯对他说。

"吃什么吐司?果酱吗?我希望不是草莓的。我不吃草莓的······"

Back translation:

"We're having a toast, to Nick and me," she said to him.

"Toast with what? Jam? I hope it's not strawberry. I can't eat strawberries..."

"Toast" has two meanings: good wishes uttered before drinking to a person, and sliced bread heated and browned. However, the word is unambiguous when used in context since the former is countable, but the latter is not. The fact that Harley took "a toast" for "a piece of toast" was most likely due to his absentmindedness, i.e., he caught the word "toast" without the whole utterance in which the word occurred. The play on "toast" here is used by the author to reveal Harley's character and create an amusing situation. Students, however, with their attention to the signified, translated the first "toast" as *jingjiu* "proposing a toast" and the second as *tusi* "a piece of toast" without attempting to explain the double meaning of "toast" and Harley's inattention. This left the conversation breakdown in the text unaccounted for, and the original word play was lost.

To deal with this difficulty our options were to either add a note to explain the play on "a toast" and "a piece of toast" as a result of Harley's absentmindedness, or try to reproduce a parallel situation in the TL. With attention to both the signified and the play of signifiers (Venuti 1995), we took the latter option. We tried first to identify the key signifier. Obviously, the key features of the play are the identical sound of the two homophones of "toast" and the countable meaning of toast, which is indispensable for the dinner party in the story. On the other hand, the phonetic feature of the uncountable toast is far more important to the play than its semantic meaning, a misinterpretation. As a result, we had to start with Chinese signifiers with a lexical meaning of the countable toast to see whether any of them could possibly be misinterpreted, preferably as the Chinese equivalent of a piece of toast or as another common food. Two Chinese words match the countable meaning of toast: *zhujiu* (drink a toast) and *gan1bei*1 (bottoms up). Only the latter has a homophone (albeit with a different tone)—*gan1bei*4—meaning "dried scallops", as in the sea food. This homophone with a different tone would be perfect to reproduce the cause of the misinterpretation since there is no equivalent of the English article "a" in Chinese, and dropping the article from "a toast" in English due to inattentive listening is comparable to failing to catch the full tonal feature of a word in Chinese for the same reason. The remaining issue, however, is whether the semantic features of the potential second signifier would be appropriate for the context.

Culturally, this rather exotic Chinese dish is quite different from Western toast, a common everyday food, and did not at first appear to be a possible substitute for toast. However, two contextual factors made the substitution possible here. Firstly, early in the story Australia is referred to as a multicultural society where you can enjoy food from a different country every day of the week. Secondly, the immediate situation of the misunderstanding is a dinner party, where Italian and Japanese foods are also being served. Therefore, we used *gan1bei*1 (bottoms up) as the key signifier and *gan1bei*4 (dried scallops) as the second to reproduce the misinterpretation, and adapted some minor features

accordingly. Jam and strawberry (jam) to go with a piece of toast were transformed into sweet and sour sauce and plum (sauce) to go with the scallop dish, as shown in (2).

(2) "我们正要干杯呢，" 洁斯对他说，"为尼克和我。"

"干贝加什么？糖醋汁吗？我希望不是李子酱。我不能吃李子。……"

Back translation:

"We're having a toast," she said to him, "to Nick and me."

"Dried scallops with what? Sweet and sour sauce? I hope it's not plum sauce. I can't eat plums..."

Acoustic/Autistic

(3) (*"Look Beatrice, don't you have anyone in your class at school who is, you know, a bit different?"*)

"Rebecca J's little brother Nat is different. He's acoustic."

"Acoustic?" Jazzi repeated.

The word didn't sound right to me either.

"Acoustic means not electric," Jazzi said. "Do you mean autistic?"

"Probably," I said...

(Bateson 2006: 35)

In (3) Beatrice, a teenage girl, fails to retrieve the more specialised word "autistic", and comes up with the word "acoustic". The latter word usually occurs in the context of popular music (acoustic/electric guitar) and would therefore reasonably be more accessible than the former to a teenager. This is evidenced by Jazzi's follow-up repair: "Acoustic means not electric." This misuse of "acoustic" for "autistic" is a tip-of-the-tongue phenomenon intended as an amusing mistake, and the key to the word play is the two words' similarity in sound and drastic difference in meaning. The fact that "acoustic" makes no sense in the context has forced a repair from the hearer, Jazzi, who suggests the intended word "autistic". It would be almost impossible to reserve the effect by translating the misuse literally into a target language not even remotely related to English such as Chinese. Nor would it be possible to find a pair of words with similar sound and meaning in Chinese to replace them. Under such circumstances a translator has to create a parallel situation in the target language with an equivalent misuse.

Students' translation of (3) is shown in (4):

(4)"吉·瑞贝卡的弟弟纳特不一样，他有狐僻症。"

"狐僻症?"洁斯重复了一遍。

这个词我也听起来不太对。

"狐僻症的意思是指身体有狐臭的意思,"洁斯问道,"你是说孤僻?"

"可能是吧,"我说……

Back translation:

"Rebecca J's little brother Nat is different. He has hupi-illness."

"Hupi-illness?" Jazzi repeated.

The word didn't sound right to me.

"Hupi-illness means when you sweat you really smell," Jazzi said. "Do you mean autistic?"

"Probably," I said …

The students translated the semantic meaning of "autistic" as 孤僻 (gu1pi4), and rendered "acoustic" as 狐僻症 (hu2pi4zheng4), a word they coined, similar in pronunciation and character representation to 孤僻症 (gu1pi4zheng4), and intended for it. This coinage 狐僻症 (hu2pi4zheng4) is, however, explained as 狐臭 (hu2chou4, bromhidrosis) in Jazzi's subsequent turn: "Hupi-illness means when you sweat you really smell."

It is obvious that the misuse situation created in the students' version differs from that in the original in at least three ways. Firstly, while the original involves two English words similar in sound with one more accessible than the other for a teenager, the Chinese version involves the intended word 孤僻 (gu1pi4, autistic) and a nonword 狐僻症 (hu2pi4zheng4, fox-odd-illness, or hupi-illness), which could be the result of a misreading of the character of 狐 (hu1 fox) for 孤 (gu1 alone), and makes no sense other than suggesting a kind of illness. Secondly, Jazzi's explanation of "acoustic" in the context of popular music (acoustic guitar) is a straightforward one, but the nonsense word 狐僻症 (hu2pi4zheng4, fox-odd-illness, or hupi-illness), the intended Chinese equivalent of "acoustic", is somehow explained as having the meaning of bromhidrosis, probably because the student translators could not make sense of the original "Acoustic means not electric". And thirdly, what is more problematic is that the misused word, interpreted as 狐臭 (hu2chou4, bromhidrosis), actually fits the context as well since both autism and bromhidrosis are medical conditions that would make someone different from others. This would have pre-empted any effort to repair or to offer an alternative word by the hearer, and thus killed the amusingly confusing effect of the word play. In contrast, the misused word in the original is absolutely out of context, causing incomprehensibility and forcing a repair from the hearer.

In order to create a parallel situation in Chinese, the translator needs to reproduce in the TT a misuse of a similar nature, due to the similar cause and with the similar effect of the misuse in the ST. As mentioned above, the cause of the original misuse, a tip-of-tongue phenomenon, is, firstly, that the two words are in the peripheral areas of the girl's vocabulary since she mistook one for the other. Secondly, "autistic" is somehow more specialised and less accessible to a teenager than "acoustic", which occurs in popular music terms such as "acoustic guitar" and would therefore be relatively more familiar to a teenager. And the amusing effect lies in the incompatibility of the context with the semantic meaning of the misused word that has caused a conversation breakdown and the subsequent repair from the hearer. It is clear that key features of the situation are the semantic meaning of the intended word "autistic" and the phonetic similarity between the intended and misused words. While the former is crucial to the story content, the latter is the core of the amusing effect. On the other hand, the exact semantic meaning of

the misused word is less important as long as it does not make sense in the context of the intended word.

On the basis of this analysis the Chinese equivalent of "autistic" is identified as the key signifier, and the next step is to find the second signifier in Chinese that sounds similar to the key signifier, but means something entirely different, and is used in popular culture or less specialised areas, thus relatively more accessible to a teenager than the Chinese version of "autistic". There are two words in Chinese meaning "autistic": 孤僻 (gu1pi4) and 自闭 (zi4bi4), the latter of which is more specialised for the medical condition described, and would thus be less accessible to a teenager. As for the misused word, we could find only one word that sounds similar to 自闭 (zi4bi4), and meets the requirements set out above. The word is 自备 (zi4bei4, self-prepare: to provide for oneself), which is neither specialised, nor a common everyday word. With a bit of a classical flavour and mainly used in written texts, it could be in a teenager's peripheral area of vocabulary, but still more accessible than 自闭 (zi4bi4). What is more important is that the meanings of the two words differ immensely and would not fit into each other's context. As a result, this pair of words and the subsequent explanation of 自闭 (zi4bi4) "Self-prepare means to provide for oneself," would create a misuse situation in Chinese with the same cause and effect as in the original. The improved Chinese version is shown in (5):

（5）"吉·瑞贝卡的弟弟纳特不一样，他有些自备。"

"自备?"洁斯重复了一遍。

这个词我也听起来不太对。

"自备是自己准备的意思，"洁斯问道，"你是说自闭，有自闭症?"

"可能是吧，"我说……

Back translation：

"Rebecca J's little brother Nat is different. He's kind of self-prepare."

"Self-prepare?" Jazzi repeated.

The word didn't sound right to me either.

"Self-prepare means to provide for oneself," Jazzi said. "Do you mean autistic?"

"Probably," I said...

Being Bee

Being Bee is about a teenage girl called Bee at a time of major change in her life. How to translate her name, and hence the title, was more complicated than it first appeared as three homophones of her name are used in the story to address her: Bea, Bee and (To) Be. Her name is actually Beatrice, which is shortened to Bea, but she has been called Bee at home and at school ever since her father said that she was like a busy bee buzzing around him. She is used to being called Bee, and doesn't like to be called by her full name, Beatrice. She is also occasionally called Be or (To) Be by another character in the story, Harley, the brother of Bee's father's girlfriend. Harley is somewhat autistic, but very good at English and Art. When Harley first hears Bee's name, he rhymes it with "To be or

not to be" and calls her (To) Be. Then there are the inflections of the English verb "to be": "Being" in the title and "been" also used by Harley. When he hears Bee say something weird, he says "To Be is a Been", "She has been there", meaning she has been to the mad side and come back, as he has. It would have been impossible to retain all of these linguistic features of the name Bee in Chinese, a non-inflected language. We considered three ways of dealing with it, focusing on each of the homophones in turn：

Option 1：Transliterating her name, Bea, with a character pronounced *bi*.

This is the most common way of dealing with foreign names in Chinese and would have retained the phonetic feature of Bee and Bea, but it would have broken the link between the girl's name and "a buzzing bee" and the rhyming of her name with "to be" in the sense of "to exist". In Chinese neither the equivalent of "bee" nor "to exist" sounds anything like *bi*, and there is not even a word for a bee-like insect that is pronounced anything like *bi*. It would also have been impossible to retain the SL inflection "been" with this rendering. Therefore, Bee and "To be or not to be" and Be would have sounded irrelevant unless there were explanatory notes on the phonetic link between *bi*, Bee and Be.

Option 2：Using the Chinese equivalent of bee—*feng*.

This would have best conveyed the connotation in her name of a buzzing bee, but not the phonetic connection between *feng* (Bee) and her original name, Bea. Neither would it have retained the phonetic link between Bee and "To be and not to be", or (To) Be since no Chinese equivalent of "to be" sounds like or is close to *feng*. As a result, such plays on Bee's name would have been out of place, and notes would have to be provided to explain the link in the SL.

Option 3: Using a homophone of the Chinese verb *zai*—the equivalent of "to be" as in "To be or not to be" in the sense of "to exist".

This rendering would have ignored the phonetic correspondence between the Chinese name and the original, instead attempting to retain the phonetic link between the girl's name and the meaning of (To) Be. It was one way of resolving the "To be or not to be" and (To) Be issues and to some extent, with the addition of the Chinese aspect marker *guo*, the Been issue as well. However, the phonetic link with Bee would have been totally lost, and a note would have to be provided to explain it. Another major problem with this solution was that there are only a small number of characters pronounced *zai* available, and none of them is normally used as a name, let alone a girl's name.

The students adopted option 1 but were unaware of the significance and source of the Shakespearian quote "To be or not to be" in (6) and produced the Chinese version in (7).

(6) "My name's Bee."
...

"To be or not to be."... "The question, little Bee, are you or are not?"

"I am," I said, "or I wouldn't be here, would I?"

(Bateson 2006:38)

(7) "我的名字是碧。"……

"是碧还是不是碧?"……"你是小碧碧?还是不是呢?"

"我是。不然我不会在这儿的,对吧?"我说。

Back translation:

"My name's Bee."...

"Are (you) Bee or not Bee?" ... "Are you little Bee? Or are you not?"

"I am," I said, "or I wouldn't be here, would I?"

As can be seen, the original play on the girl's name is completely lost. Since none of above methods really resolved the problem, an analysis of the pragmatic significance of each element involved in this multiple word play was carried out after consultation with the author, Catherine Bateson. The pragmatic significance of the three links—Bea/Bee, Bea/(To) Be and Bea/been—were prioritised as follows:

• Key feature: Bea/Bee connection

○ Semantic-crucial to the development of the story;

○ Phonetic-crucial to the word play.

• Secondary: Bee/ "To be or not to be."/(To)Be connection

○ Phonetic/rhetorical-crucial to the word play;

○ Connotative/cultural/humorous effect-important to the word play;

○ Semantic-insignificant to the word

play, but of some importance to the subsequent text.

• Minor: Be/Been inflectional connection.

The Bea/Bee connection was the most important because the embroidered honey bee on Bee's skirt and the references to bees on the other objects in her bee box were crucial to the development of the story. And the phonetic link between Bea and Bee was what made the word play possible. As for "To be or not to be?" and (To) Be, these were simply Harley's plays on Bee's name. In such word play, of primary significance were the rhyming and the rhetorical structure of the Shakespearian quote; then came the humorous effect of the abuse or playful use of the famous line on a solemn theme in a casual conversation with a teenager. The semantic substance of the quote itself is insignificant, and could be dispensed with if necessary. The least important play on the word was the Be/Been inflectional connection, because this took place only inside Harley's head. This analysis gave us a clear idea of how to deal with the play on Bee's name, and to render them differently to retain the SL features as much as possible.

The importance of the Bea/Bee connection makes Option 2 the best option, i.e., rendering Bee as *Feng* 蜂, meaning "honey bee" in Chinese. This means we would be able to use a homophone of *feng*, e.g., 丰 (meaning "rich"), for Bea so as to retain the Bea/Bee connection. As for "To be or not to be", since the meaning of this was not as important as its rhyming with the girl's name, it could be replaced by an equally famous line on a solemn theme from a Chinese poem that rhymed with *feng*, and was well known to our prospective teenager readers. Ideally, we wanted this line to be an alternative structure that could lead to the subsequent question about existence: "Are you or are you not?" Unfortunately, such a line was not to be found. The best we could come up with was the first line of a poem on Lushan (Mount Lu) by the famous eleventh-century poet Su Shi 苏轼 (1037 - 1101):

(8)《题西林壁》
横看成岭侧成峰，
远近高低各不同。
不识庐山真面目，
只缘身在此山中。

Inscription Upon the Western Forest Wall

Looking from the side it forms a range, from the end it forms a peak;

From far away or nearby, up high or down below, it's never the same.

I do not know Mount Lu's true face and eyes,

And this is simply because I am in the very midst of the mountain itself.

(Hargett 2006: 13 - 14)

The philosophical point of this poem is that often you can't grasp the whole picture or understand a situation because you are too close to it, as in "You can't see the forest for the trees". The first line ends with *feng* 峰 (meaning "peak"), a homophone of *feng* (honey bee/Bee) whose radical designates "mountain" instead of "insect", as in the character 蜂 meaning "honey bee". Although the line itself is not an alternative structure, it does imply one by expressing the poet's confusion about the shape of the mountain, as in its profile. However, unlike its ST counterpart with double rhyming on "be"—"to be or not to be"—the Chinese line contains only a single rhyme on *feng*, which would need to be compensated for.

Therefore, in translation, while replacing the Shakespearian line with Su's, we added *feng*, a repetition of the girl's name, before the Chinese line to reproduce the double rhyming effect. And after "The question is", we added an alternative question "Are you a range or are you a peak?" which is both a play on the famous line, and an abuse in the TL because it is derived from a rather unconventional interpretation of the poem. Su's poem is about the true nature of something that appears in different guises rather than identifying its actual appearance. This addition made the translation stronger and more forceful by supplying the loss occasioned by the imperfect substitution of the original abused line of Shakespeare's with Su's, and linked up smoothly with the subsequent question in the ST about existence. As a result, the original in example (6), repeated below for convenience, was translated as (9):

(6) "My name's Bee."

...

"To be or not to be."... "The question, little Bee, are you or are not?"

"I am," I said, "or I wouldn't be here, would I?"

(Bateson 2006:38)

(9)"我的名字是蜂。"

"峰,横看成岭侧成峰。"……"问题是,你到底是岭,还是峰呢? 你存在,还是不存在呢?"

"我存在,不然我不会在这儿的,对吧?"

Back translation:

"My name's Bee."

"Peak, a range looked at from the side, a peak from the end." ... "The question is, are you a range or are you a peak? Do you exist or not?"

"I do, or I wouldn't be here, would I?"

From then on we used *Feng* 峰 (peak) when Harley referred to Bee as To Be or Be and simply translated the less important word play "Been" semantically in context.

This resolved the issue of the three homophones of Bee's name in the original: Bea(trice), Bee, and Be now corresponded to three homophones in Chinese represented by three characters: 丰(特丽丝), 蜂 and 峰. As a result, the word plays on Bee's name in the original were retained as much as possible at the expense of the phonetic features of Bee's name, which was of little significance. And, finally, the title of the book *Being Bee* was accordingly translated to "小蜂的故事"(*The Story of Little Feng*). These results are shown in the table 1 below:

195

Table1 *Being Bee*

Original	Beatrice/Bea	Bee	To Be/To be or not to be	Being Bee
Character	丰（特丽丝）	蜂	峰/是岭还是峰？	小蜂的故事
Sound	*feng*	*feng*	*feng/shi ling haishi feng?*	*Xiaofeng de gushi*
Meaning	rich/abundant	bee	peak/are you a range or a peak?	The Story of Little Feng

Concluding remarks

Our experience in translating word play as demonstrated above has shown that one useful way to reproduce the often humorous effect, or the "inner spirit" of word play in translation is to create a parallel situation in the TL on the basis of a thorough understanding of the nature of the word play in question. An analysis of various features involved at different levels of meaning, in terms of their pragmatic significance, helps the translator prioritise what are needed in building such a situation and rendering these features in different ways accordingly. At the productive stage the first step is to find a signifier (or signifiers) in the TL that best expresses the key features and, at the same time, accommodates secondary or minor features. And the second step is to identify a second signifier and adapt the minor features around it as required by the word play, and to compensate for the loss occasioned at the first stage by supplying what is missing to reinforce the signifying behaviour of the TT. The whole process requires some creativity, a more positive attitude towards translation, and a little bit of luck. Our experience has confirmed Lewis' view on the work of translation:

"... the integration that is achieved escapes, in a vital way, from reflection and emerges in an experimental order, an order of discovery, where success is a function not only of the immense paraphrastic and paronomastic capacities of language but also of trial and error, of chance. The translation will be essayistic, in the strong sense of the word." (1985:45)

References

Bateson, C. 2006. *Being Bee*. Brisbane: University of Queensland Press.

Hargett, J. 2006. Su Shi and Mount Lu. In: *Traditions of East Asian Travel* (pp.1 - 20), J. A. Fogel ed. Oxford and New York: Berghahn Books.

He, Ziran. 1995/2001. Pragmatics. In: *An Encyclopaedia of Translation* (pp. 835 - 845), S. W. Chan & D. E. Pollard eds. Hong Kong: The Chinese University Press.

House, J. 2009. *Translation*. Oxford: Oxford University Press.

Huang, I-min. 1995/2001. Puns. In: *An Encyclopaedia of Translation* (pp. 918 - 924), S. W. Chan & D. E. Pollard eds. Hong Kong: The Chinese University Press.

Hwang, M. S. 1980. Translating Puns for the Stage. *Renditions* 14, 73 - 78.

Lewis, P. E. 1985. The Measure of Translation Effects. In: *Difference in Translation* (pp.31 - 62), J. F. Graham ed. Ithaca: Cornell University Press.

Liang, S. C. 1974. On Translating Shakespeare. (S. C. Chau and D. Herforth, Trans.). *Renditions* 3, 13 - 14.

Venuti, L. 1995. *The Translator's Invisibility*. New York & London: Routledge.

Wu, G. 2010. Translating Differences—A Hybrid Model for Translation Training. *The International Journal for Translation and Interpreting Research* 1, 24 - 37.

Yu, K. C. (Trans) 1983. 不可儿戏（*The Importance of*

Being Earnest). Taipei: Great Earth Press.

Notes on contributors

Wu Guo(Email: g. wu @ uws. edu. au), PhD, Senior

Lecturer in the school of Humanities and Communication Arts, University of Western Sydney. His research interests are Chinese/English translation studies, Chinese linguistics, Chinese Pedagogy.

谐音词的翻译:注重语用意义的方式

Wu Guo

School of Humanities and Communication Arts, University of Western Sydney

提 要:本文探讨如何用一种注重语用意义的方式翻译文学作品中的同/近音词,提出本着 Lewis (1985)"滥译"的原则,兼顾语言符号的文本意义和语言符号之间的互动(Venuti 1995)有助于产生得体的译文,既保留原文中同/近义词活用的语用意义,又保留原文主要的语言形式特点。文中的译例取自一个名为"介绍澳大利亚儿童文学到中国"的合作翻译项目,在此项目中有五部著名的澳大利亚儿童文学作品被译成汉语,译本由人民文学出版社于 2009 年在北京出版。

关键词:同/近义词 翻译 语用重要性 关键符号 关键特征

Contrastive Genre Analysis in Translation Studies: Tourism Websites in China and Australia

Wang Wei

Abstract: This paper considers how contrastive genre analysis can be applicable in translation studies with a view to providing references and insights in translation practice. By taking genre as a descriptive and analytical tool rather than a prescriptive one, genre analysis should not only include descriptions of the characteristics of actual texts, especially organisational structures, but also needs to include a contextualised perspective on genre with focuses on exploring how the texts were produced and why the texts were produced as they are in the sociocultural contexts. Informed by genre analysis in the traditions of systemic functional linguistics and rhetorical genre studies, and, in particular, drawing on Critical Discourse Analysis, this paper proposes an analytical model of contrastive genre analysis with the aim of applying it in contrastive and translation studies. A sample cross-linguistic genre study on analysing tourism websites produced in China and Australia is used to illustrate the proposed analytical framework. The paper concludes with discussions of its applications in translation studies.

Key words: contrastive genre analysis, translation studies, critical discourse analysis, tourism website

The notion of genre in applied linguistics

Genre is a type of discourse that occurs in a particular setting. It is often regarded as a way in which people "get things done" through their use of spoken and written discourse. As a genre occurs in a particular setting, it is usually recognisable by members of social groups. For example, medical doctors may recognise conventional ways of providing medical consultations, scientific researchers may recognise conventional ways of reporting a research project, and tour guides may recognise conventional ways of introducing a scenic spot. Within each of these groups, we might find variants in relation to the socio-rhetorical context in which the genre occurs: medical consultations, research reports and tour introductions might vary greatly depending on factors like workplace contexts, target audience, academic disciplines or geographic regions.

As socially recognised forms of language use, genres play a crucial role in understanding language. Genres embody a social group's expectations not only for linguistic forms, but also for content involved, rhetorical strategies, procedural practices, and other dimensions which might intersect within a genre. Genre analysis, thus, aims to describe features of these socially recognisable forms and practices. The purposes of genre analysis are often set to "investigate instances of conventionalised or institutionalised textual artefacts in the context of specific institutional and disciplinary practices, procedures and cultures in order to understand how members of specific discourse communities construct, interpret and use these genres to achieve their community goals and why they write them the way they do" (Bhatia 2004, p. 6).

Theories of genre as a typified form of discourse have different disciplinary orientations. In applied linguistics, there are three academic schools which are most notable, namely, systemic function linguistics (SFL), English for Specific Purposes (ESP), and rhetorical genre studies (RGS). Martin (1984), from the Sydney genre school (SFL), describes genre as "a staged, goal-oriented, purposeful activity in which speakers engage as members of our culture" (p. 25). This view draws on Halliday's work and that of the anthropologist Malinowski and, in particular, the view that "contexts both of situation and of culture [are] important if we are to fully interpret the meaning of a text" (Martin 1984, p. 25). Examples of genres examined in this perspective include service encounters, research reports, academic essays, casual conversations, and micro-genres (Martin 1997). ESP genre studies are based largely on Swales' (1990, 2004) work on the discourse structure and linguistic features of texts. Swales uses the notion of moves to describe the discourse structure of texts. These studies have had a strong influence on the teaching of ESP, and

especially the teaching of academic writing to second language graduate students. Genre studies in composition studies, and in what is often called the rhetorical genre studies (RGS) (Schryer 2011), has been influenced in particular by a paper written by the speech communications specialist Carolyn Miller (1984) titled "Genre as social action" and has been discussed, in particular, in relation to undergraduate writing and professional communication in North American settings. In rhetorical genre studies, discussion is centred more on social and contextual aspects of genres, rather than the language or discourse structures of texts (see Berkenkotter 2009; Devitt 2004; Schryer 2011).

While distinctions between these three orientations remain in terms of theoretical perspectives and research approaches, they share several general characteristics of genre as a category of discourse. The characteristics of genre that they agree upon might include that genres are primarily a socially situated rhetorical category which are intertextual, not isolated, and genres reflect and enforce existing structures of power (Tardy 2011). As an approach or set of analytical methods for studying particular texts in their social contexts, genre has widely been employed as a framework in many areas of linguistic research, including intercultural rhetoric and translation studies.

Current developments in translation studies

In the past two decades, translation

studies have witnessed great transformations from a linguistic focused orientation to more culturally orientated and power-focused perspectives. Bassnett, Lefevere, Gentzler, Tymoczko and Venuti, among others, have played key roles as advocates in the so-called "Cultural Turn" (Bassnett & Lefevere 1990) or "Power Turn" (Álvarez & Vidal 1996; Venuti 1995) in translation studies. Since this "Cultural Turn", which has been inspired to a great extent by cultural studies, anthropology, poststructuralist, postmodern, and postcolonial theories (Bassnett & Lefevere 1990), modern translation research becomes less concerned with only examining whether a translation is a "faithful" reproduction of the source text. Instead, the focus shifts to social, cultural, and communicative practices of translation behaviour. This implies that translation is recognised as not only to do with language, but with languages and texts in culture, and that difference is not situated solely in the linguistic code, but in culture as well.

A subsequent development in translation studies in the same period has focused more on functions and processes of translating, rather than only on the end product of translation. This means not only the final text of translation, but the translating process and behaviour, and in particular how a translated text can achieve the same social function as the source text, have become research focuses today. In the same vein, current topics in translation studies include the cultural and ideological significance of translating and of translations, and the interactions between translation behaviours and sociocultural factors.

Culture-oriented translation studies include a number of different trends or approaches. These include descriptive translation studies (also polysystem theory and manipulationism), skopos theory and translational action, hermeneutics, deconstructionist-poststructuralist approaches, and postcolonial studies. These trends or approaches do not necessarily correspond to clearly differentiated and delimited tendencies in translation studies, but rather to a cluster of common features shared by representatives of each approach. These approaches are more concerned with social, political, or ideological issues than the linguistic equivalence-based relationship between a source language text (SLT) and a target language text (TLT). In other words, they are more function- and practice-oriented than product-oriented in translation.

In addition, when doing translation or translation studies, it is important to be aware of the fact that texts can be translated in different ways and the reason why a text is translated in one particular way can probably be found in how it is manipulated to achieve desired effects. As Lefevere (1992) argues, concerning the interaction between poetics, ideology and translation, "on every level of the translation process, it can be shown that, if linguistic considerations enter into conflicts with considerations of an ideological and/or poetological nature, the latter tend to win out" (Lefevere 1992: 39). That suggests that, in many communicative events, it is more important to fulfil the needs and expectations of the target audience living in the target culture rather than retaining the linguistic integrity of the texts in the source language.

However, when coming to the point of actual rendition of a text, translators would frequently be facing problems as to how to manipulate the text to fulfil the social functions or effects of the given texts in the target culture. In other words, translators are keen to find out any possible guidelines or reference points, which they can draw upon in the translating process with the purpose of enabling the translated version to fulfil the social expectations of the audience in the target culture. For example, in translating promotional genres such as advertisements and product introductions, translators might engage in heavy load of adaptation, manipulation, or even rewriting of the SLT. In doing so, it will be much desirable if any possible guidelines or reference points can be provided for their translating and manipulative practices.

On this ground, it would be highly desirable to establish an approach to develop understanding of how a genre is produced and practised across different languages and cultures. Such contrastive genre studies would provide insights or reference points for translators in transferring the given texts into the target language with a view to achieving the same or similar social effects in the target culture.

An integrated model of genre analysis

With an aim of constructing a functional contrastive genre study, it is essential to develop an analytical framework with a thorough understanding of its origin and relevant theories. Contrastive genre studies have its origin or close links with intercultural rhetoric(Connor 1996, 2004), which compares genres in different languages and cultures. Many studies in this area have focused on written genres. Intercultural rhetoric originated from the work of Kaplan (1966) who examined different patterns in the academic essays of students from a number of different languages and cultures. Kaplan has since revised his strong claim that differences in academic writing are the result of culturally different ways of thinking. Subsequently, many studies have also revealed that the differences in the ways in which texts are written in different languages and cultures may result from many other factors. For example, some studies indicate that Japanese and Chinese people tend to be more indirect than Americans in their writing (Kaplan 1966, 1987, 1988; Cai 1993); and Finnish and English speakers tend to have different coherence conventions (Jenkins and Hinds 1987; Mauranen 1993). The major focus of these studies is on textual or structural regularity in relation to different genres. Intercultural rhetoric research has found that rhetorical patterns are an essential component of language. These rhetorical patterns are arbitrary yet rule-governed, and they are also socially constructed and transmitted. Intercultural rhetoric research also shows that rhetorical structures differ between languages and cultures, and these differences are dynamic and change as the society changes (Ostler 2001). Intercultural rhetoric has, in more recent years, moved to emphasize the social situation of writing rather than just discourse patterns across cultures. Intercultural rhetoric (Connor 2004, 2011) is now examining writing in relation to the intellectual history and social structures of different cultures.

In recent translation studies, there is a rapid development in setting up contrastive studies, involving both parallel and comparable corpora. The term parallel corpora is typically used in linguistics to refer to texts that are translations of each other, while the term comparable corpora refers to texts in two languages that are similar in content and/or in the same genre, but are not translations of each other. The contrastive analysis approach has developed into "a coherent, composite and rich paradigm that addresses a variety of issues pertaining to theory, description, and the practice of translation" (Laviosa 1998), and it has been argued to be "central to the way that Translation Studies as a discipline will remain vital and move forward" (Tymoczko 1998).

The current study is particularly concerned with comparable corpora produced in Chinese and English languages. It is argued that to make the comparable corpora viable and applicable in translation studies and for translating practice, it is critical to establish a *tertiumcomparationis* (Connor & Moreno 2005), which is the quality that two things which are being compared have

in common. It is the point of comparison which prompted the author of the comparison in question to liken something to something else in the first place. To set up the comparable corpora for contrastive genre studies, the same genre produced in different languages and cultures should be used.

According to Miller (1984), genre in its broadest sense refers to social action. More specifically:

Genre refers to language use in a conventionalised communicative setting in order to give expression to a specific set of communicative goals of a disciplinary or social institution, which give rise to stable structural forms by imposing constraints on the use of lexico-grammatical as well as discoursal resources. (Bhatia 2004, p.23)

This view of genre attempts to capture how writers achieve their social purposes by using various structural forms, constructing different focuses and manipulating topics and readers by using various linguistic resources, all of which are aspects of the dynamic and "stabilised-for-now" (Schryer 1993, 2011) status of genres. In this sense, genre is a descriptive and analytical tool rather than a prescriptive one. Genre analysis should thus not only include descriptions of the characteristics of actual texts, especially organizational structures, but also needs to include a contextualised perspective on genre which includes consideration of how the texts were produced and consumed (Kress & Threadgold

1988; Devitt 2004; Connor 2011). This perspective on genre suggests that generic meanings are construed between and across texts in both reading and writing.

As for the conceptionalisation of genre inempirical contrastive genre studies, a crucial concern is how genre can be analysed and described by using various linguistic and non-linguistic techniques developed in different schools of genre analysis. Martin's demarcation of genre (or macro-genre) and elemental genre (micro-genre) (Martin 1994, 1995, 1997), for example, may be a relevant framework for contrastive genre studies. As a key figure in the "Sydney School" of genre studies (Hyon 1996), Martin proposes a definition of genre from the perspective of systemic functional linguistics (Halliday 1994; Halliday & Matthiessen 2004; Halliday & Hasan 1985; Martin 1984, 1992). While advocating that genre is a "social activity", Martin's study of genre focuses predominantly on the analysis of "staged and goal oriented" aspects of genre (see e.g. Martin 1994, 1997). However, Martin's idea of micro-genre can be used as an analytical tool in contrastive genre studies. Martin's micro-genre is in line with what Biber (1989) calls "text type". Micro-genres characterize texts in terms of rhetorical functions such as exposition, discussion and problem-solution. For further explications of the differences between genre, micro-genres and text type see Martin (1997), Lee (2001) and Paltridge (1996).

In discourse studies, a number of researchers such as Fairclough (2003, 2010), Wodak (2011; Wodak & Meyer 2009), van Dijk (2001) and van Leeuwen (2008) have considered the use of language from a particularly critical perspective; that is, how discourse is shaped by relations of power and ideology, and the effects discourse has upon social identities, relations, knowledge and beliefs. This perspective, critical discourse analysis (CDA), starts with the assumption that language use is always social and that discourse both reflects and constructs the social world. The analysis might commence with an analysis of the use of discourse and move from there to an explanation and interpretation of the discourse. From here, the analysis might proceed to deconstructing and challenging the texts, tracing ideologies and assumptions underlying the use of discourse, and relating these to different views of the world, experiences and beliefs. In CDA, the most influential approach arguably would be Fairclough's three layers model (1995, 2003, 2011). Fairclough's analysis is based on three components—description, interpretation and explanation. Linguistic properties of texts are described (textual analysis), the relationship between the productive and interpretative processes of discursive practice and the texts is interpreted, and the relationship between discursive practice and social practice is explained (Fairclough 1995). In doing this, Fairclough attempts to establish a systematic method for exploring the relationship between text and its social context.

To examine genres across languages and cultures, this article proposes an integrated research model which incorporates perspectives from CDA and genre studies in SFL and RGS. The following figure summarises the model.

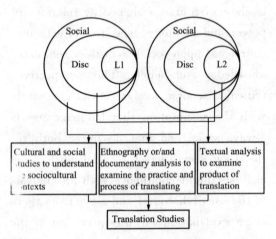

Figure 1 A genre-based analytical model for translation studies (adopted from Wang 2007, p. 60; Wang and Xia 2011, p. 65)

As a point of departure, this model draws on Fairclough's (1995, 2003, 2010) three layers model in CDA, which covers text, discourse practices and social context. This model regards "language as social practice" and considers the context of language use to be crucial (Fairclough 2010). It aims to explore the contextual factors which contribute to the production of the genre by drawing on cultural and social studies. This model represents a context-concerned approach to texts and writing practice. It attempts to describe the ways in which practices of writing embody the subject and the social world that the writers and readers inhabit. In other words, this view not only aims to describe the linguistic characteristics of the genre in question, but also attempts to reveal how the genre has been produced and consumed in relation to its socio-cultural context.

In this model, detailed text analysis, drawing on rich technical resources, such as those developed in genre and register analysis (e.g., Biber & Conrad 2009; Halliday & Matthiessen 2004; Martin 1992, 1997), is employed to examine the L1 and the L2 texts. At this level, the L1 texts and the L2 texts are compared and contrasted with a view to identifying similarities and differences. These findings could also be compared with previous intercultural rhetoric studies (e.g., Connor 1996, 2004; Scollon 1999, 2000; Scollon & Scollon 1997) and other relevant contrastive linguistic studies. At the second level of analysis, i.e., discourse practice, the genre production and consumption process will be examined; document analysis of existing literature and ethnographic research techniques such as interview, survey, observation may be utilised. At the third level of analysis, i.e., contextual level, social and cultural studies will be drawn on in an attempt to uncover the connections between the genre and the socio-cultural and socio-political contexts in which the genre occurs.

A sample study

This paper reports a contrastive genre analysis of tourism websites produced in China and in Australia. It examines the on-line travel publications for 10 renowned tourist attractions in each country with 20 relevant websites being examined. This contrastive genre study aims to provide detailed analysis of the same genre produced across different languages and cultures which could provide reference points in terms of linguistic forms, content covered, rhetorical strategies and procedural practices for translation in tourism. As argued by Dann (1996), the language of tourism, through pictures, brochures and other media, attempts to seduce the public into becoming tourists and subsequently to control their attitudes and behaviour. As tourism is a fast-growing sector on the web, many types or micro-genres of tourism websites are found online. According to Pierini (2007), there are three major types of tourism websites found active online, namely, informational, promotional or commercial. Promotional sites refer to websites of tourists' board or other tourism organisations, which do not mean to fulfil an immediate business obligation, rather to promote the destination areas in general. Commercial sites include sites of intermediaries, which put potential customers into contact with service providers (tour operators, travel agencies, etc.), and sites of service providers, which are individual firms providing services in the sectors of accommodation, catering, transportation and tours. The websites included in this study meant to be limited to promotional ones run by tourists' boards or other tourism organisations rather than service providers. With an aim of promoting relevant scenic spots, these websites employ various strategies to draw the attention of potential tourists, but not providing services such as accommodation and catering. However, due to the sociocultural differences in China and Australia, sometimes there is not a clear boundary between promotional and commercial types of web sites in China. This issue of categorisation of websites in terms of their features and functions will be further addressed in the following section of discursive analysis.

Following the analytical model illustrated above, this study examines the websites on three layers of analysis, i.e., textual, discursive, and contextual. Below is the list of the tourism websites for 20 well-known tourist attractions with 10 from each country.

Table 1   The travel introductory texts and the websites examined in this study

Chinese texts	Tourist attraction and the website
C1	黄山[Huangshan]http://www.51yala.com/html/2006117112448 - 1.html
C2	杭州[Hangzhou]http://destination.cthy.com/City3301/
C3	九寨沟[Jiuzhaigou]http://www.jiuzhai.com/index.php/overview/about-jiuzhaigou.html
C4	丽江[Lijiang]http://www.ljtour.com/ljfq/
C5	青海湖[Qinghai Lake]http://trip.elong.com/qinghaihu/jianjie/
C6	厦门鼓浪屿[Gulangyu, Xiamen]http://xiamen.lotour.com/gulangyu/jianjie
C7	长江三峡[Three Gorges, Yangtze River] http://www.lxexpress.net/html/threegorges/20121010/499.html

Continued

Chinese texts	Tourist attraction and the website
C8	黄河壶口瀑布［Hukou Falls，Yellow River］http://www.hkpb.cn/
C9	北京故宫［The Palace Museum］http://s.visitbeijing.com.cn/html/j－117873_gl.shtml
C10	长城［The Great Wall］http://www.mutianyugreatwall.com/index_jqjs.asp
Australian texts	Tourist attraction and the website
A1	Blue Mountains http://www.visitbluemountains.com.au/
A2	Barossa Valley，SA http://www.southaustralia.com/regions/barossa.aspx
A3	Western Australia http://www.australia.com/explore/states/wa.aspx
A4	Canberra，ACT http://issuu.com/acttourism/docs/canberra_visitors_guide_2013？e＝4323857/2253403
A5	Alice Springs http://www.tourism.thealice.com.au/
A6	Sydney Opera House http://www.sydney.com/destinations/sydney/sydney-city/city-centre/attractions/sydney-opera-house
A7	Bondi Beach，Sydney http://www.sydney-australia.biz/bondi/
A8	Gold Coast http://www.lonelyplanet.com/australia/queensland/gold-coast
A9	The Twelve Apostles，Victoria http://www.visitvictoria.com/Regions/Great-Ocean-Road/Activities-and-attractions/Nature-and-wildlife/Beaches-and-coastlines/12-Apostles.aspx
A10	Tasmania http://www.discovertasmania.com.au/

Textual analysis

The textual analysis of the study focuses on the introductory texts of each website with the aim of identifying special textual features of the genre in question. In examining linguistic features of texts, there would be different focuses and aspects that can be analysed. With regard to the genre in question, the following aspects can be analysed.

—Rhetorical organization (e. g., schematic structure of written texts)

—Grammatical features that specifically relate to linguistic complexity (e. g., relative clauses, adverbial clauses, depth of embedding)

—Lexical features (e. g., type/token ratio, average word length, use of idiomatic/erudite and general words, formulaic language, and word classes)

It is worth noting that almost all lexico-grammatical characteristics are useful indicators of text types and communicative task differences (Biber & Conrad 2009). The communicative tasks of the introductory texts on each website are to present a general guide to a city, a region, or a renowned scenic spot in China or Australia. These texts are written in the Chinese or English language respectively. They are relatively short and concise, offering a comprehensive overview of a particular tourist location to the general publics—the target audience. The textual analysis reveals distinctive differences between the Chinese and Australian texts in terms of rhetorical organisations, grammatical, and lexical features.

(1) *Rhetorical organization*

The Chinese set of texts demonstrates distinctive rhetorical organizations, with emphases on aspects such as historical, political, or economic positions of the tourist locations. These features are rarely seen in their Australian counterparts. For example

Excerpt 1: C2

杭州位于中国东南沿海北部,是浙江省省会,副省级城市,也是长三角第二大经济城市,南翼经济、金融、物流、文化中心。浙江省政治、经济、文化中心,中国东南重要交通枢纽。杭州是浙江省省会,长江三角洲南翼中心城市,"东南第一州"。也是中国最著名的风景旅游城市之一,"上有天堂、下有苏杭",表达了古往今来的人们对于这座美丽城市的由衷赞美。元朝时曾被意大利著名旅行家马可•波罗赞为"世界上最美丽华贵之城"。[Hangzhou, being located in the northern part of China's southeast coast, is the capital of Zhejiang province. As a deputy provincial city, it is the second largest economy in the Yangtze River Delta. As the political, economic and cultural hub of Zhejiang Province, it is also an important transportation centre in southeast China. Hangzhou is the capital of Zhejiang province, a central city at the south wing of Yangtze River Delta, the "first city in the Southeast". It is also one of the China's most famous tourist cities, "a paradise on Earth", which expresses the heartfelt praise of this beautiful city throughout the ages. In Yuan dynasty, the renowned Italian traveller Marco Polo praised it as "the most beautiful and luxurious city in the world."]

This text highlights the geographical, economic, and cultural importance of Hangzhou, the capital city of Zhejiang province, as well as a well-known tourists' attraction in China. It describes the characteristics of this city by using an overwhelming amount of factual or absolute statements. Absolute statements here refers to assertions or declarations whose contents are recognised as true, valid and non-negotiable, such as most of the sentences in the above excerpt.

Another important feature in the Chinese introductory texts is that of describing scenic spots with rich histories, such as Huangshan, Three Gorges and Hangzhou, with an inundation of well-known praises and remarks by renowned figures who have visited that place in the past. For instance, in the text above, Hangzhou has been praised as "a paradise on Earth" and "the most beautiful and luxurious city in the world". Also, these texts might be packed with lines from ancient poems and erudite phrases and expressions. For example

Excerpt 2: C1

方圆 154 平方公里的黄山风景区无处不景,无景不奇,以奇松、怪石、云海、温泉"四绝"著称于世,徐霞客称赞:"薄海内外无如徽之黄山,登黄山而后天下无山,观止矣"。后人传颂为"五岳归来不看山,黄山归来不看岳。"[Within an area of 154 square kilometres, Huangshan Nature Reserve is full of astonishing scenic spots with strange pines, outlandish rocks, massive clouds, and hot springs, which are the "four wonders" known to the world. Xu Xiake praised it: "Across the land, there is no rivalry for Huangshan. There will be no other mountain (that you will like to go) after you have been to Huangshan." Later people eulogized that "Trips to China's five great mountains render trips to other mountains unnecessary, and a trip to Huangshan renders trips to the five great mountains unnecessary."] (*Note*: *Xu Xiake* (*1586 - 1641*), *a Chinese travel writer and geographer of the Ming Dynasty*, *known best for his famous geographical treatise.*)

In sum, the focuses in the Chinese texts tend to highlight what the place is and how important and wonderful it would be to visit. The texts are apt to be writer-centred with writer's presentation about the uniqueness and attractions of the given place. With the absolute statements, the texts might have left little space for the readers to negotiate or think about what to do at those places knowing these facts.

However, while most introductory texts in the Australian set are also constructed around information on general facts, special attention is paid to the audience's interests in information of not only what the place is, but also what to see (sightseeing, monuments, and natural environment), what to do (events, sports, cultural activities, gastronomy…) and where to find more information, with little mention of the historical, economic, and even cultural importance of these places. For example

Excerpt 3: A5

What's so great about "The Alice"? Well we reckon it's the 5 C's: the Climate, the Colours, the Culture, the Characters and the Closest proximity to every beach in Australia. So don't forget to check out the Tide Times around the country.

So whether you fly, drive or take the train, you might want to set aside 7 - 10 days to take in everything there is to see and do in Alice Springs as well as the stunning scenery of the Western and Eastern (Macs) MacDonnell Ranges.

If you think "The Alice" is hot, flat and dusty then you had better think again, because there are stunning ranges, spectacular gum trees, refreshing waterholes, beautiful palm trees, awesome colours, more waterholes, amazing wildlife, a lush green golf course, and did we mention the waterholes, so check out the photo's in the Gallery of Our Backyard.

This text starts from identification of

special features of "the Alice" by summarising them with the 5 C's. This paragraph features Australian humour, indicating that the Alice is within "the Closest proximity to every beach in Australia. So don't forget to check out the Tide Times around the country". As most people know, Alice Springs is at the centre of Australia, far away from any beach. However, the purpose of the humour here might be threefold. One, is to keep the consistency of the "5C's", the other is to add a bright and amusing tone to the text, and the third might be to potentially encourage tourists to travel afar across Australia. The text then proceeds with suggestions of "what to see and do" in Alice Springs. The last paragraph aims to change the stereotypical attitude towards "the Alice" as being "hot, flat and dusty". The whole text is created in a light and engaging manner with the audience's view and interest in "the Alice" set as the priority. Such features of "closeness to readers" and humorous tones are not commonly found in the Chinese texts.

(2) *Grammatical features*

In terms of grammatical features, the Chinese set of texts indicate that, first and foremost, the factual or absolute statements demonstrate the importance of the destination in terms of its social, political, economic, historical and cultural context. In particular, these statements aim to emphasise how important/wonderful the destination is and most sentences in the sample texts are of this nature. Examples can be found in excerpts 1 and 2 above. Second-

ly, no questions are found in the sample texts. This suggests that the writers of these texts do not intend to introduce preparatory conditions for potential interactions with the audience. The information flow under such circumstance is unidirectional, that is, only from the authors to the readers, while the readers have been taken as the pure receivers of the information. Third, some exclamation sentences are found in the sample texts, such as(C4) "好客的丽江人民欢迎您的光临!" [Hospitable people in Lijiang will welcome you!], (C10) "慕田峪旅游区以其秀丽的景色、优质的服务、雄伟的长城,欢迎您的光临!" [Mutianyu Tourist Area known for its beautiful scenery, excellent service, the majestic Great Wall, welcomes you!]. These exclamations are used to directly welcome the audience to the tourist location.

In the Australian set of data, the key grammatical features include, firstly, features of colloquialism, including the use of questions, imperatives and deixis (i.e., words and phrases that cannot be fully understood without additional contextual information). These features create the impression of interpersonal communication and communicative immediacy. For instance, in Excerpt 3, the text starts with the question "What's so great about 'The Alice'?", which immediately draws the readers' attention to the key attractions of the Alice. Secondly, a light style of writing is employed with a tendency to use short and simple sentences. Thirdly, the informative and descriptive sentences in the texts possess a persuasive force with the purpose of enticing the receivers. That is, through reading the website, the receivers might be persuaded to change their beliefs and/or behaviours. They do this because they have come to believe that is the right or the best thing to do. Thus, they would do it willingly, even gladly, not grudgingly. For instance, (A7) "At Bondi, you can find some great restaurants, plenty of eateries, pubs and clubs nightlife", (A10) "With so many amazing and recognised world-class experiences throughout our island to choose from, it is little wonder Tassie is on most people's 'must visit' holiday list." These sentences are all informative or descriptive in nature, but they have a strong persuasive force that attracts the audience to take actions to visit the place.

(3) *Lexical features*

In comparing the Chinese and Australian sets of texts, many Chinese texts appear to use more descriptive adjectives and figures of speech such as metaphors and similes, which might be closely related to a poetic register. For instance

Excerpt 4: C3

　　九寨沟是大自然鬼斧神工之杰作。这里四周雪峰高耸，湖水清澈艳丽，飞瀑多姿多彩，急流汹涌澎湃，林木青葱婆娑。蓝蓝的天空，明媚的阳光，清新的空气和点缀其间的古老村寨、栈桥、磨坊，组成了一幅内涵丰富、和谐统一的优美画卷，历来被当地藏族同胞视为"神山圣水"。九寨沟景区开放后，东方人称之为"人间仙境"，西方人则将之誉为"童话世界"。[Jiuzhaigou is a masterpiece of nature gods. Here enclosed by snowy peaks, the clear lakes are gorgeous, surrounded by colourful waterfalls, surging rapids, and whirling green trees. The blue sky, bright sunshine, and fresh air are dotted with ancient villages, bridges, mills, composing of a content-rich, beautiful picture of harmony and unity. The local Tibetans have traditionally regarded Jiuzhaigou as "holy water". Jiuzhaigou scenic spot, after the open-up to the public, has been hailed as "paradise on earth" by the Orientals, and the "fantasy world" by the Westerners.]

Here the author purposely employs many descriptive adjectives such as those underlined in the excerpt above to illustrate the beauty of Jiuzhaigou. Then, a series of similes are used to indicate how the local, Oriental, and Western people have regarded Jiuzhaigou. These similes are highlighted by quotation marks in the excerpt above.

Another lexical feature found in the Chinese set of texts is the lack of first or second personal pronouns used in the texts. The most commonly used nouns are those proper nouns referring to the names of the exact places or well-renowned people related to that place. It might suggest that the writers of the Chinese texts tend not to engage the audience at a personal level, and they are apt to present the places in an authoritative manner, by which the information they provided expects to be recognised or accepted as true and reliable.

In the Australian texts, the lexical features include a preference for first and second person pronouns (we, you) and possessive adjectives (our, your). The message is often formulated in the first person plural (we), and is addressed directly to the receiver (you-addressing) in the present tense and/or the imperative. For instances, (A1) "Challenge yourself, the elements and the clock as you ride through the stunning Capertee Valley...", (A2) "You wouldn't expect to find traditional Vietnamese food in the Barossa but you'll be glad you did. Find the magic, and unexpected flavours, in the Barossa." Another lexical feature in the Australian texts is the common use of action verbs, for instances, "ride", "book", "get to", "walk", "feed", "kayak", "soak up", etc. These verbs urge the potential tourists to take part in particular activities while visiting the place. Both lexical features aim to reduce the distance between the writers and the readers in an attempt to attract potential visitors.

Discursive practices

Tourism websites under examination are a multi-semiotic entity that results from interplays of various resources, including written language, and sometimes spoken language, pictorial (images, video clips, and icons), graphic (layout, typographic features) and acoustic elements (sounds and music). In such circumstances, meaning is generated in its totality of verbal and nonverbal means. In other words, language (both written and oral) plays a crucial, yet partial role in this meaning making process.

Taking these websites as a genre would suggest that production and consumption of tourism websites (i.e., the discursive practices of websites) be profiled as a class of communicative events characterised by the interaction of verbal and non-verbal features. These communicative events should fulfil a set of communicative purposes (e.g., informing, promoting, and influencing the receivers' behaviours). The differences in the communicative purposes would very much influence the choices of language and other semiotic resources. So the categorisation of genre would be pivotal in further examining the discursive features and functions of the websites. It might also potentially influence the applicability of the research findings in translation studies and practices.

As summarised by Butt et al. (2001, p. 5), an English brochure in Australia should reflect the main functions of language explained by:

—Talking about what is happening, what will happen and what has happened. A travel introductory text generally expresses what the visitors can do during their visit.

—Interacting and/or expressing a point of view. The authors of tourism texts wish to draw the attention to their region and through the texts change the viewpoints or attitude of the readers and demonstrate to the readers why people should visit their tourist destination.

—Turning the output of the previous two functions into a coherent whole. The way the authors write by describing the attractions of their region and how they present them in a convincing introduction should bring coherence to the text.

In the Australian context, a noteworthy feature or function of tourism discourse or promotional genres in general is the transactional dimension. This means that the message may have consequences in the real world, and the receivers may purchase the promoted product or service and become a customer. This promotional purpose may have influenced many of the linguistic features, multi-semiotic choices, and discursive practices of the tourism discourse. It has been clearly demonstrated in the previous textual analysis that the writers of the Australian websites tend to address the audience directly by drawing on various linguistic resources.

However, in the Chinese context, in which the tourism web pages are produced and consumed, promotional discourse is still a developing genre (see Ji and Wang, forthcoming), which is under a further commodification process. Commodification is a term proposed by Fairclough, to describe "the process whereby social domains and institutions whose concern is not producing commodities in the narrower economic sense of goods for sale, come nevertheless to be organized and conceptualized in terms of commodity production, distribution and consumption"(Fairclough 1992, p.207). In other words, Fairclough views commodification as a process in which discourse types associated with commodity production permeate the discursive practices of institutions not originally in the economic domain (Fairclough 1992, 1993). The textual analysis of the Chinese set of data indicates that the purposes of the Chinese tourism websites are much aligned with being informative rather than promotional or commercial. This sample study originally aimed to collect data of promotional websites prepared by tourists' boards, or bureaus in the Chinese context, in introducing the tourist attractions rather than by commercial organisations. However, the study failed in fulfilling the task, highly due to the fact that the roles of tourism institutions in China are more complex than and not as clear-cut as they are in the Australian context. The role of the institutions running the tourism websites in China will be further discussed in the contextual analysis section.

Contextual analysis

In the Australian context, there is a clear social system that regulates and administers the tourism industry. At the Federal Government level, "Tourism Australia" is the Australian Government agency responsible for international and domestic tourism marketing. Tourism Australia's role is to:

—Influence people to travel to and throughout Australia;

—Increase the economic benefits to Australia from tourism;

—Help foster a sustainable tourism industry in Australia.

At the State or local Governments level, each state and territory in Australia has its own government tourism agency that works with the tourism industry. The role of the state tourism organisations (STOs) is to "support the development and marketing of sustainable tourism destinations and experiences within their state, to increase awareness and attract visitors". (See more details on the website http://www.tourism.australia.com)

So the Australian websites included in this study are mostly from the governmental tourism agencies and the local tourists' boards, which are not selling the tourism products such as flights, accommodations and tour packages, but rather promoting the tourism industry in general. This communicative purpose has been clearly evidenced in the textual and discursive practices analysed above.

The Chinese contexts in which the data were collected are much more diverse and complex than the Australian ones. As previously mentioned, the original plan of collecting data from websites run by tourism bureaus was not successful due to the fact that it appears that the websites run by the governmental agencies are very much informative or administrative in nature rather than promotional. A quick look at the website such as the one by China National Tourism Administration (http://www.cnta.gov.cn) will show that its function is mainly for governmental administration purposes rather than to "influence people to travel to and through China". It appears that this website provides information about this government agency and the government policies pertaining to tourism. This website also provides administrative support for its subordinate organisations.

Given the differences between the Chinese and Australian websites, the question of how to establish a *tertiumcomparationis* that is a shared platform for contrastive analysis (Connor& Moreno 2005) remains. In the present study, all efforts have been made to collect data in the Chinese contexts, which could be regarded as promotional rather than purely informative and commercial. These efforts have led to a diversity of ownership of the Chinese websites, which includes local tourists organisations such as C3 (http://www.jiuzhai.com) and C1 (http://www.51yala.com), and the commercial websites which tend to link the potential customers to service providers such as C5 (http://trip.elong.com), C6 (http://xiamen.lotour.com), and C9 (http://s.visitbeijing.com.cn). It might be argued that these commercial websites are both promotional and profit-seeking.

However, the purpose of the context analysis here is not to challenge the validity and reliability of the data collection and analysis, but to show the complexity and difficulty in establishing the shared platform in which every effort should be made to ensure that contrastive studies are worthwhile and applicable in potential translation practices.

Discussion and conclusion

This genre analysis model for translation studies provides an analytical and theoretical model that highlights textual features, discursive practices and contextual issues of a genre produced in different languages and cultures. The findings in the sample study provide rich insights which could be drawn upon in the process of translating or localisation of the genre.

While localisation refers to making a product/service linguistically and culturally appropriate to the target locale (country/region and language) where it will be used and sold (Esselink 2000). Within the localisation theory, translation is viewed as

> The process of converting written text or spoken words to another language. It requires that the full meaning of the source material be accurately rendered into the target language, with special attention paid to cultural nuance and style.(Esselink 2000, p.4)

Pym (2004) provides a lengthy discussion regarding the relationship between localisation and translation. Although localisation and translation are distinct areas, it would be more fruitful to consider commonalities between them two (Munday 2007), especially in relation to contrastive studies, e.g., common concepts, common problems, and common solutions. In doing so, the analysis presented above would provide very valuable input in the processes of translation or localisation.

This study has revealed that translations will need to take into account the impact of contextual, generic, sociocultural, historical and ideological factors that influence linguistic features and functions of the genre under question. In the sample study, the Australian readers are taken as more practical and personal. The Australian web-

sites are more directed to the readers' hearts: "What would you like to do there?" However, in the Chinese texts the historical, cultural, and social factors and poetic features highlighted are just as important to the readers as they want to see the benefit from a journey to these regions.

With regard to the applicability of the sample study in translation practice, this paper may have indicated how subtle the principle of "faithfulness" to the source language might be, for it might produce something that would potentially fail to fulfil the sociocultural function of the original text in the target culture. Demonstrated in the translated excerpts above, remaining "faithful" to the source text will surely fail to fulfil the social function of attracting tourists in the target culture. For this reason, translators should conduct a thorough contrastive analysis of the same genre produced and consumed across different languages and cultures with a view of developing a "thick picture" of the genre and text which will be translated or localised into the target culture and language.

Surely, as a result of the limited corpus size and research focus in the sample study, the research findings should be interpreted in close relation to their specific settings.It is therefore not appropriate to use the findings in generalising all tourism websites between these two languages and sociocultural contexts. By comparing a larger corpus of tourism websites, a more credible consensus could be obtained for Chinese and Australian tourism websites. Future studies in this area may include multimodal analysis on interactions between multi-semiotic (pictorial, graphic and acoustic) elements of the websites. They could also be diachronic studies to examine the shifts of website styles over time.

References

Álvarez, R., &Vidal, M. C. (Eds.).1996. *Translation, Power, Subversion*. Clevedon: Multilingual Matters.

Bassnett, S., &Lefevere, A. (Eds.). 1990. *Translation, History and Culture*. London/New York: Routledge.

Bassnett, S., &Lefevere, A. (Eds.). 1998. *Constructing Cultures: Essays on Literary Translation*. Clevedon: Multilingual Matters.

Berkenkotter, C. 2009. A Case for Historical "Wide-angle" Genre Analysis: A Personal Retrospective. *Ibérica: Journal of the European Association of Language for Specific Purposes* 18, 9 - 21.

Bhatia, V. K. 2004. *Worlds of Written Discourse: A Genre-based View*. London: Continuum.

Biber, D. 1988. *Variation Across Speech and Writing*. New York: Cambridge University Press.

Biber, D. 1989. A Typology of English Texts. *Linguistics* 27(1), 3 - 43.

Biber D., & Conrad, S. 2009. *Register, Genre, and Style*. Cambridge: Cambridge University Press.

Butt et al. 2001. *Using Functional Grammar: An Explorer's Guide*. Macquarie: NCELTR.

Cai, G.1993. *Beyond Bad Writing: Teaching English Composition to Chinese ESL Students*. Paper presented at the college composition and communication conference, San Diego, CA.

Connor, U. 1996. *Contrastive Rhetoric: Cross-cultural Aspects of Second Language Writing*. Cambridge: Cambridge University Press.

Connor, U. 2004. Intercultural Rhetoric Research: Beyond Texts. *Journal of English for Academic Purposes* 3, 291 - 304.

Connor, U. 2011. *Intercultural Rhetoric in the Writing Classroom*. Ann Arbor: University of Michigan Press.

Connor, U., & Moreno, A. 2005. Tertiumcomparationis: A Vital Component in Contrastive Rhetoric Research. In: *Directions in Applied Linguistics: Essays in Honor of Robert B. Kaplan*, P. Bruthiaux, D. Atkinson, W. Grabe & V. Ramanathan eds. Clevedon, England: Multilingual Matters.

Dann, G. M. S. 1996. *The Language of Tourism: A Sociolinguistic Perspective*. Wallingford: CAB International.

Devitt, A. J. 2004. *Writing Genre*. Carbondale: Southern Illinois University Press.

Fairclough, N. 1992. *Language and Social Change*. Cambridge: Polity Press.

Fairclough, N. 1993. Critical Discourse Analysis and the Marketization of Public Discourse: The Universities. *Discourse and Society* 4(2), 133 - 169.

Fairclough, N. 2003. *Analyzing Discourse: Textual Analysis for Social Research*. London: Routledge.

Fairclough, N. 2010. *Critical Discourse Analysis: The Critical Study of Language*. Second edition. London: Longman.

Halliday, M. A. K. 1994. *An Introduction to Functional Grammar*. Second edition. London: Edward Arnold.

Halliday, M.A.K., & Hasan, R. 1985. *Language, Context, and Text: Aspects of Language in a Social-Semiotic Perspective*. Geelong, Victoria: Deakin University Press.

Halliday, M. A. K., &Matthiessen, C. 2004. *An Introduction to Functional Grammar*. Third edition. London: Edward Arnold.

Hyon, S. 1996. Genre in Three Traditions: Implications for ESL. *TESOL Quarterly* 30(4), 693 - 728.

Jenkins, S., & Hinds, J. 1987. Business Letter Writing: English, French, and Japanese. *TESOL Quarterly* 21, 327 - 354.

Jenkins, S., & Hinds, J. 1987. Business Letter Writing: English, French, and Japanese. *TESOL Quarterly* 21, 327 - 354.

Ji, Weining, & Wang, Wei. (Forthcoming). 45 Years' Evolution of a Genre: Commodification of the University Textbook Prefaces in China. *Critical Approaches to Discourse Analysis Across Disciplines (CADAAD) Journal*.

Kaplan, R. B. 1966. Cultural Thought Patterns in Intercultural Education. *Language Learning* 16, 1 - 20.

Kress, G., & Threadgold, T. 1988. Towards a Social Theory of Genre. *Southern Review* 21(3), 215 - 243.

Laviosa, S. 1998. The Corpus-based Approach: A New

215

Paradigm in Translation Studies. In: *Special Issue of Meta: Journal des Traducteurs*, Sara Laviosa ed., 43 (4), 474 – 479.

Lee, D. Y. W. 2001. Genres, Registers, Text Types, Domains, and Styles: Clarifying the Concepts and Navigating a Path Through the BNC Jungle. *Language, Learning and Technology* 5(3), 37 – 71.

Lefevere, A. 1992. *Translating Literature—Practice and Theory in a Comparative Literature Context*. New York: The Modern Language Association of America.

Martin, J. R. 1984. Language, Register and Genre. In: *Children Writing: A Reader* (pp.21 – 30), F.Christie ed. Geelong, Vic: Deakin University Press.

Martin, J. R. 1992. *English Text: System and Structure*. Philadelphia: John Benjamins Publishing Company.

Martin, J. R. 1994. Macro-genre: The Ecology of the Page. *Network* 21.

Martin, J. R. 1995. Interpersonal Meaning, Persuasion and Public Discourse: Packing Semiotic Punch. *Australian Journal of Linguistics* 15, 33 – 67.

Martin, J. R. 1997. Analysing Genre: Functional Parameters. In: *Genre and Institutions: Social Processes in the Workplace and School* (pp.3 – 39), F. Christie & J. R. Martin eds. London and New York: Continuum.

Mauranen, A. 1993. *Cultural Differences in Academic Rhetoric*. Frankfurt and Main: Peter Lang.

Miller, C. R. 1984/1994. Genre as Social Action. In: *Genre and the New Rhetoric* (pp.23 – 42), A. Freedman & P. Medway eds. London: Taylor & Francis.

Munday, J. 2007. *Translation as Intervention* (edited volume). London: Continuum and IATIS.

Ostler, S. E. 2001. Contrastive Rhetoric: An Expanding Paradigm. In: *Academic Discourse*, J. Flowerdew ed. London: Longman.

Paltridge, B.1996. Genre, Text Type, and the Language Classroom. *ELT Journal* 50(3), 237 – 243.

Pierini, P. 2007. Quality in Web Translation: An Investigation into UK and Italian Tourism Web Sites. *The Journal of Specialised Translation* 8, 85 – 103, available at http://www.jostrans.org/issue08/art_pierini.pdf.

Pym, A. 2004. *The Moving Text. Localization, Translation, and Distribution*. Amsterdam and Philadelphia: Benjamins.

Schryer, C. F. 1993. Records as Genre. *Written Communication* 10(2), 200 – 234.

Schryer, C. 2011. Investigating Texts in Their Social Contexts: The Promise and Peril of Rhetorical Genre Studies. In: *Writing in Knowledge Societies. Perspectives on Writing* (pp.31 – 52), D. Starke-Meyerring, A. Paré, N. Artemeva, M. Horne & L. Yousoubova eds. Fort Collins, CO: The WAC Clearinghouse and Parlor Press. Available at http://wac. colostate. edu/books/winks/.

Scollon, R. 1999. Mediated Discourse and Social Interaction. *Research on Language and Social Interaction* 32(1 & 2),149 – 154.

Scollon, R. 2000. Generic Variability in News Stories in Chinese and English: A Contrastive Discourse Study of Five Days' Newspapers. *Journal of Pragmatics* 32(6), 761 – 791.

Scollon, R., & Scollon, S. W. 1997. Point of View and Citation: Fourteen Chinese and English Version of the "Same" News Story. *Text* 17(1),83 – 125.

Swales, J. M. 1990.*Genre Analysis: English in Academic and Research Settings*. Cambridge: Cambridge University Press.

Swales, J. M. 2004.*Research Genres: Explorations and Applications*. Cambridge: Cambridge University Press.

Tardy, C. M. 2011. Genre Analysis. In: *The Continuum Companion to Discourse Analysis*, Ken Hyland & Brian Paltridge eds. London: Continuum.

Tymoczko, M. 1998. Computerized Corpora and the Future of Translation Studies.In: *Special Issue of Meta: Journal des Traducteurs*, Sara Laviosa ed., 43(4), 652 – 659.

van Dijk, T. 2001. Critical Discourse Analysis. In: *The Handbook of Discourse Analysis*, D. Schiffrin, D. Tannen & H. Hamilton eds. Oxford: Blackwell.

van Leeuwen, T. 2008. *Discourse and Practice: New Tools for Critical Discourse Analysis*. Oxford: Oxford University Press.

Venuti, L. 1995. *The Translator's Invisibility: A History of Translation*. London/New York: Routledge.

Venuti, L. 1998. *The Scandals of Translation: Towards an Ethics of the Difference*. London/New York: Routledge.

Venuti, L. (ed.) 2000. *The Translation Studies Reader*. London/New York: Routledge.

Wang, W. 2007.*Genre Across Languages and Cultures: Newspaper Commentaries in China and Australia*.

Saarbruecken，Germany：VDM Verlag.

Wang，W. ，& Xia，L. 2011. Researching the Translation of Political Discourse in China. *Translation and Interpretation Review* Ⅰ(1)，59 - 86.

Wodak，R. 2011. Critical Discourse Analysis. In：*Continuum Companion to Discourse Analysis*(pp. 38 - 53)，K. Hyland & B. Paltridge eds. London：Continuum.

Wodak，R.，& Meyer，M. (Eds).2009.*Methods of Critical Discourse Analysis*. Second edition. London：Sage.

Notes on contributors

Wang Wei(Email：wei. wang@ sydney. edu. au)，PhD，Senior Lecturer in the Department of Chinese Studies，School of Languages and Cultures，the University of Sydney. His research interests are Chinese/English translation studies，discourse studies and genre analysis，Chinese language education，intercultural communication，second language acquisition.

对比文体分析在翻译研究中的应用：
中国和澳大利亚旅游网站

Wang Wei

Department of Chinese Studies，School of Languages and Cultures，
University of Sydney

　提　要：本文探讨如何将对比文类分析运用于翻译研究，同时探索文类分析结果如何为翻译实践提供参考和借鉴。在本文中，文类不仅是一个规范性概念，而且被当作一种话语分析的研究工具。据此，文类分析不仅包含对实际文本及其结构特点的分析和描述，同时也研究在特定的社会文化背景下，构建文类和消费文类的过程。本文借助批评话语分析的相关理论以及系统功能语言学和修辞文类研究中相关的文类研究方法，建构新的对比文类分析模型。同时，本文也运用该分析模型对中国和澳大利亚旅游网站进行了对比文类研究。最后，本文讨论了该分析模型在翻译研究及实践中的应用。

　关键词：对比文类分析　翻译研究　批评话语分析　旅游网站

第十二届城市语言调查国际学术研讨会
在内蒙古大学成功举办

2014 年 9 月 2 日至 4 日,由南京大学中国语言战略研究中心和内蒙古大学蒙古学学院联合主办的第十二届城市语言调查国际学术研讨会在内蒙古呼和浩特成功举办。本届会议主题为"语言多样性和多语社区",来自国内 17 所高校以及日本、美国、英国、新西兰、德国等国的多位学者出席会议。会上发表的 30 篇论文内容涉及言语社区、语言景观、新媒体语言、语言规划、语言经济、少数民族语言信息处理等多个话题。其中,内蒙古大学确精扎布的"关于蒙古文编码的思考"、日本国立国语研究所井上史雄的"进行中语言变化的城乡差异"、复旦大学游汝杰的"当代中国大城市的语言生态"、内蒙古大学巴达玛敖德斯尔的"蒙古语言文字的社会应用"、日本一桥大学田中克彦的"都市语言与游牧语言"、华东师范大学俞玮奇的"城市化进程中新城区的语言状况变化研究"等大会主题报告引起热烈反响。

首届城市语言调查学术研讨会于 2003 年在南京大学召开;之后的历届会议在中国、德国、荷兰、日本等国的 10 个不同城市先后召开,近 20 所高校及科研单位主办或联合主办了各届会议,总计来自 21 个国家和地区的 600 余名学者参加了历届会议。第十三届城市语言调查国际学术研讨会将于 2015 年在陕西师范大学召开。

2014 年度第五届中国语言经济学
论坛在扬州大学成功举办

2014 年 10 月 31 日至 11 月 1 日,第五届中国语言经济学论坛在扬州大学成功举办。本届论坛由江苏省哲学社会科学联合会、扬州大学、山东大学经济研究院联合主办,扬州大学文学院承办,南京大学中国语言战略研究中心协办。来自南京大学、山东大学、武汉大学、北京语言大学、澳门大学、日本国立国语研究所等国内外 40 余所高校和科研机构的 50 多位语言学界及经济学界专家学者参加了本届论坛。

本届论坛分为主题报告、大会报告和分组报告等不同形式。北京语言大学李宇明教授、德国日本研究所 Coulmas 教授和山东大学经济研究院黄少安教授分别从语言服务的概念和类型、语言的经济学特征及语言与经济的关系、交易成本节约与民族语言多样化之间的矛盾及其化解等方面做了论坛主题报告。南京大学中国语言战略研究中心徐大明教授、武汉大学中国语情与社会发展研究中心赵世举教授、日本国立国语研究所井上史雄教授、扬州大学文学院李现乐博士、山东大学语言经济研究中心张卫国副教授、首都师范大学北京语言产业研究中心陈鹏教授分别从语言交换理论、语言制度对经济的影响、汉语和日语的经济地位、语言服务的价值形态、影响第二语言习得的社会因素以及语言能力、语言技术和语言产业的关联等方面做了大会报告。论坛的分组报告包括语言经济和语言服务两个小组。语言经济小组集中讨论了有关外语教育与经济发展、母语经济、语言经济与语言政策、语言距离等理论与实践问题。语言服务小组讨论了有关外语服务、汉语国际推广、语言规范、语言环境、行业语言服务、语言舆情与语言服务等理论与实践问题。

中国语言经济学论坛2009年由山东大学经济研究院、南京大学中国语言战略研究中心、北京航空航天大学外国语学院等院校共同发起创办。该论坛旨在提升国内语言经济与语言服务研究水平，推动语言经济学学科发展。截至目前，该论坛共举办了五届，本届语言经济学论坛的规模在参会人员数量、高校分布以及议题等诸多方面都是历届之最。

（李现乐）

国家语委"语言文字国际高端专家来华交流项目"圆满完成

2014年10月31日至11月6日，国家语委"语言文字国际高端专家来华交流项目"在南京、扬州开展。围绕"语言经济与语言规划"的学术主题，南京大学中国语言战略研究中心邀请了德国日本研究所所长、国际知名社会语言学家Florian Coulmas教授来华交流。

在为期一周的交流活动中，承办方先后举办了包括主题报告、学术沙龙在内的多种形式的交流活动。在题为"Languages as Collective Goods and Public Choice"的主题报告中，Coulmas教授从经济学视角分析了语言的经济学特征以及语言与经济的关系。在主题为"语言多样性的经济学思考：民族语言文字政策讨论"的学术沙龙上，来自德国、日本，中国内地、澳门地区等地的10余位专家学者就民族语言保护与经济发展、社会和谐等问题进行了深入的交流。在主题为"我们应该采取什么样的语言经济政策"的学术沙龙上，Coulmas教授与来自南京大学、澳门大学、北京语言大学、扬州大学等高校的10余名学者就语言经济政策与语言政策、外语教育政策及其与社会经济发展之间关系进行了深入广泛的讨论。在题为"The New Economics of Literacy"的学术报告中，Coulmas教授指出，评估一种语言的价值，需要综合考虑把该语言作为第一语言和第二语言的使用者数量、使用该语言的国家数量以及主要国家的经济实力等因素。

在华交流期间，Coulmas教授还与与会学者就语言经济学研究的理论和方法进行了深入的交流，与中国语言战略研究中心讨论了有关期刊的办刊和合作组稿等问题，达成了初步的合作意向。本次活动先后在扬州、南京组织学术报告、学术沙龙等活动 6 场,来自国内 40 余所高校的师生 200 余人次参与了其中的学术交流。

国家语委从 2013 年起实施"语言文字国际高端专家来华交流项目",计划不定期邀请一批国际上从事语言文字应用研究的高端专家来华开展交流活动,以借鉴国外语言文字工作的研究成果,加强国家语委相关科研机构和专家队伍建设,提升我国语言文字工作的国际合作与交流水平。本次活动邀请的 Coulmas 教授为国家语委第二批(总序第六位)受邀国际高端专家。

(李现乐)

Contents

图书在版编目(CIP)数据

中国语言战略.2015.1 / 徐大明,王铁琨主编.——
南京:南京大学出版社,2015.5
ISBN 978 - 7 - 305 - 15242 - 9

Ⅰ.①中… Ⅱ.①徐… ②王… Ⅲ.①语言规划—研
究 Ⅳ.①H002

中国版本图书馆 CIP 数据核字(2015)第 126181 号

出版发行 南京大学出版社
社　　址 南京市汉口路 22 号　　　　　邮　编 210093
出 版 人 金鑫荣
书　　名 中国语言战略(2015.1)
主　　编 徐大明　王铁琨
责任编辑 荣卫红　张　静　　　　编辑热线　025 - 83593963
照　　排 南京紫藤制版印务中心
印　　刷 南京大众新科技印刷有限公司
开　　本 787×1092　1/16　印张 14.5　字数 326 千
版　　次 2015 年 5 月第 1 版　2015 年 5 月第 1 次印刷
ISBN 978 - 7 - 305 - 15242 - 9
定　　价 36.00 元

网址:http://www.njupco.com
官方微博:http://weibo.com/njupco
官方微信号:njupress
销售咨询热线:(025)83594756

Appendix

Seven color figures in "The Economic Status of Chinese and Japanese" (Fumio Inoue, p.p.10 – 22) are collected in this appendix.

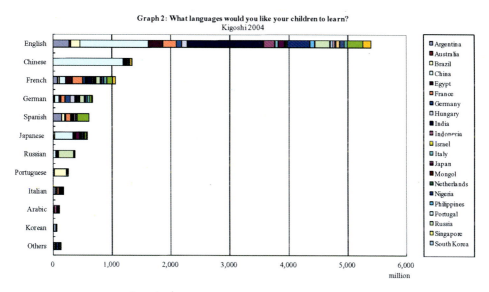

Figure 4   What language would you like your children to learn?

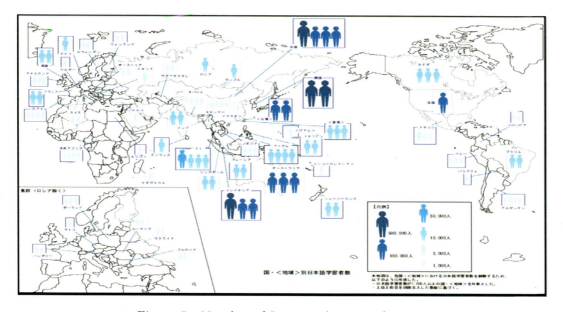

Figure 7   Number of Japanese language learners

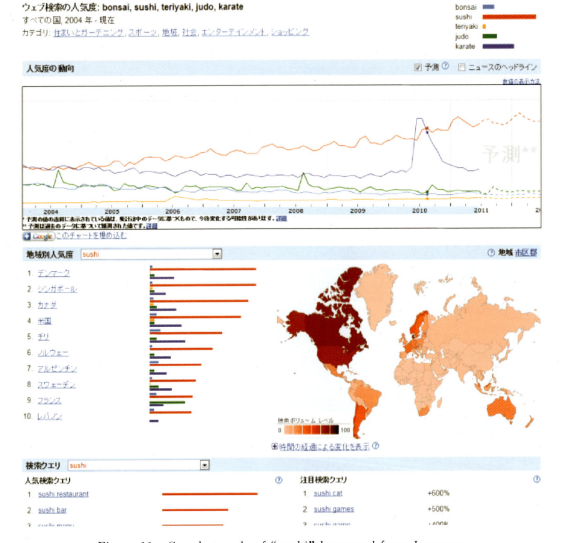

Figure 11　Google trends of "sushi" borrowed from Japanese

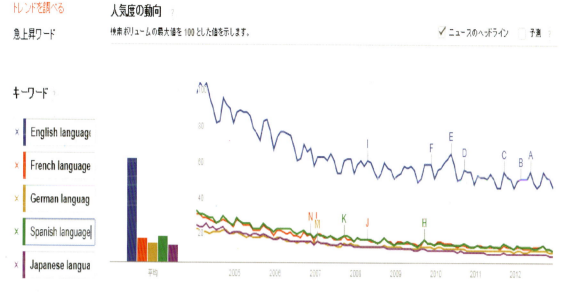

Figure 14　Google trends of Japanese and European languages

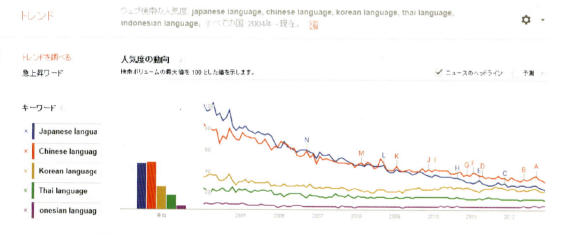

Figure 15　Google trends of Japanese and Asian languages

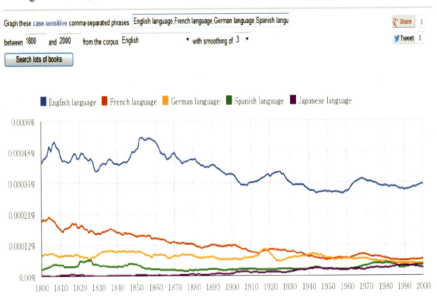

Figure 17　Google Ngram viewer of Japanese and European languages

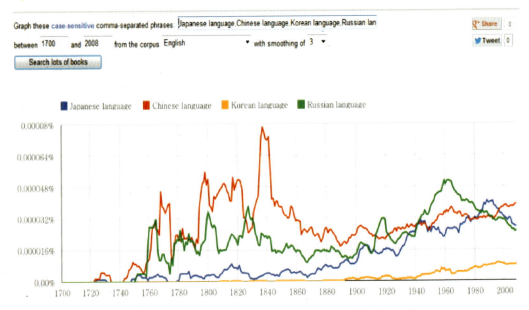

Figure 18　Google Ngram viewer of Japanese and Asian languages